About the Author

John J. Collins received his A.B. from the University of Buffalo and his Ph.D. from the State University of New York at Buffalo. Dr. Collins has completed anthropological fieldwork in Mexico and New Mexico and is a member of the American Anthropological Association. A prolific contributor to scholarly journals in anthropology, religion, and sociology, he is also the author of *Anthropology: Culture, Society, and Evolution* (1975) and the editor of *Readings in Social and Cultural Anthropology* (1969). He is listed in *Who's Who in the East, Outstanding Educators in America,* and the *Dictionary of International Biography.* Dr. Collins is Professor of Anthropology at Jamestown Community College in Jamestown, New York, and has also been a member of the faculties of Hobart & William Smith Colleges, the State University of New York at Buffalo, and Southern Methodist University.

DEDICATION

To my family—Molly, Becky, and Chris—
who always supplied moral support and privacy
while I prepared the manuscript for this book.

primitive religion

john j. collins

rowman and littlefield

Published 1978 by
Rowman and Littlefield

Copyright © 1978 Littlefield, Adams & Co.

Library of Congress Cataloging in Publication Data

Collins, John J   , 1938–
   Primitive religion.

   Bibliography: p.
   Includes index.
   1. Religion. 2. Religion, Primitive. I. Title.
BL48.C565 1978b   291'.042   78–7052
ISBN 0–8476–6076–1

Printed in the United States of America

CONTENTS

Part III   Related Issues

Introduction

This volume is an introduction to religion approached from the anthropological point of view. It builds on the vast realm of data accumulated by fieldworkers as they have studied so-called primitive societies around the world. The initial two chapters briefly survey some of the theoretical problems and viewpoints taken with respect to the topic of religion. They survey a small portion of the history of such speculations on religion. The last chapter deals with explanations—why religion exists and how it might have begun. Chapters 3 through 8 deal with expressions, types of rituals, and related topics. Selectivity is necessary on such an immense variety of material, and the present "state of the art" in religion studies is such that major dimensions have not been defined or agreed upon.

Though the approach taken is anthropological, material from related perspectives on religion is included, since in many cases it is suggestive of dimensions largely neglected by anthropologists. Likewise, although most of the descriptive examples are taken from primitive societies, some data are also extracted from ancient civilizations. Such an approach will undoubtedly become more common as scientists work toward a unified science of religion.

In sum, then, this text includes what one particular writer believes will be useful to the general, introductory anthropological student of religion—and to the general reader. It is intended as a first view only. A list of some standard introductory texts on religion that I have found valuable is included following this introduction for readers who wish wider exposure or other points of view. At the end of the text, there is a similar list of volumes dealing with surveys of religion. Hopefully, the reader will be sufficiently aroused either by interest, disagreement, or discomfort to read more deeply about this unique human behavior.

SELECTED GENERAL RELIGION TEXTS

Banton, Michael, ed.
  1966. *Anthropological Approaches to the Study of Religion.* New York: Praeger.
Clark, Walter Houston.
  1958. *The Psychology of Religion.*
  New York: Macmillan.
DeVries, Jan.
  1967. *The Study of Religion.*
  New York: Harcourt, Brace & World.
DeWaal, Malefijt.
  1968. *Religion and Culture.*
  New York: Macmillan.
Fallding, Harold.
  1974. *The Sociology of Religion.*
  Toronto: McGraw–Hill Ryerson Ltd.
Goode, William J.
  1964. *Religion Among the Primitives.*
  Glencoe: Free Press.
Goodenough, Erwin.
  1965. *The Psychology of Religious Experience.*
  New York: Basic Books.
Howells, William.
  1948. *The Heathens.*
  Garden City: Doubleday.
Johnson, Paul E.
  1959. *Psychology of Religion.*
  Nashville: Abingdon Press.
King, Winston L.
  1968. *Introduction to Religion.*
  New York: Harper & Row.
Norbeck, Edward.
  1961. *Religion in Primitive Society.*
  New York: Harper & Brothers.
O'Dea, Thomas F.
  1966. *The Sociology of Religion.*
  Englewood Cliffs, N.J.: Prentice–Hall.

Schneider, Louis.
      1970. *Sociological Approach to Religion.*
      New York: Wiley & Sons.
Streng, Frederick J.
      1969. *Understanding Religious Man.*
      Belmont, Calif.: Dickenson.
Swanson, Guy E.
      1960. *The Birth of the Gods.*
      Ann Arbor: University of Michigan Press.
Van Der Leeuw, G.
      1963. *Religion in Essence and Manifestation.*
      New York: Harper & Row.
Vernon, Glenn M.
      1962. *Sociology of Religion.*
      New York: McGraw–Hill.
Wach, Joachim.
      1962. *Sociology of Religion.*
      Chicago: University of Chicago Press.
Wallace, Anthony F. C.
      1966. *Religion: An Anthropological View.*
      New York: Random House.
Yinger, J. Milton.
      1970. *The Scientific Study of Religion.*
      New York: Macmillan.

PART I

BACKGROUND

CHAPTER 1

Definitions and Approaches

Religion is one of the greatest of human institutions. Anthropologists have yet to encounter any existing human society that lacks at least some such expressions. At the dawn of recorded history, the first written records (c. 3500 B.C.) of the Sumerians demonstrate religion as occupying a very important place in the lives of people, if not actually providing the focal point of existence. Comparable data exist for other early civilizations. How far back in time religious belief and behavior may be said to go is a matter of some speculation. Certainly "hard" archaeological evidence exists for the neolithic period (c. 10,000 B.C.), when food production was invented; and in the earlier paleolithic period, when humans pursued a hunting-and-gathering way of life, there are also traces of religious practice. Evidence exists of a cave bear cult and of the burial and ritual treatment of human dead going back perhaps 100,000 years. Before this point in prehistory there is no real evidence that the religious experience was part of the repertoire of human behavior. Nevertheless, such nonfossilizing behaviors as singing and dancing may well have characterized even earlier human predecessors. Today, of course, despite the rise of other interpretations and world views, religion continues to play a vital role for the human species, reflecting a profound dependency on the religious view of the realities of human existence.

In fact, religion may be the most distinct product of the "human experiment." Other animals share with us our need to adapt and adjust to the environment and to other group members in order to survive. Certainly environmental and social interaction for humans differs substantially from that of other creatures, due to our heavy reliance upon cultural ways of satisfying such needs; but fundamentally we have the same basic spheres of such interaction. Until proven differently, however, we may assume that the human species is unique in also interacting with a world beyond that of the physical and social environments: the realm of unseen beings, powers, and events. That humans should infuse their behavior with such interaction based upon such an assumption and that they derive adaptive benefit in the process not only makes the human world a unique evolutionary event or direction but makes the study of religion a most useful perspective from which to understand ourselves.

APPROACHES TO THE STUDY OF RELIGION

How does one approach the study of religion? Certainly one's personal background and fields of interest will in some way determine the approaches taken and the answers obtained. "Religion brings to mind various images for different people. . . . In a large measure, the importance, and the way of studying the religious life of man depend on an individual's experience with what he labels religion" (Streng, 1969: 1). This author, along logical lines, distinguishes three general approaches. First is what he labels the "sectarian approach." This is the view taken by the proponents of some specific creed, accepting their own beliefs and behaviors as religion. This limiting view—holding one's own experience as authoritative and genuine—is, of course, not productive of an understanding of the totality of the religious experience for the whole human species even if it is psychologically satisfying. Second is the view of "disinterest." This rejects the truth of the beliefs of religion and reduces this realm of human behavior more to philosophical speculation. This approach ignores the fact that religion is an aspect of human existence, adaptive and valuable, regardless of the truth or falsehood of its doctrines. In assuming what has yet to be proven, it is as narrow and as limiting as the first approach. The most advantageous approach, that of the serious scholar, is of "neutrality." Here one approaches religious belief and practice without a specific dogmatic perspective or a concern with the necessary truth of specific manifestations. It is the examination of this dimension of being human simply as a part of human behavior—a dimension we wish to understand and to which we apply the same scientific tools of analysis as we apply to the rest of human behavior.

In a more specific sense, how does one pursue such a neutral approach? Here there are limiting factors determined by the fields of traditional scholarship. Though the open-minded approach may be the same, the questions and thus the results may differ considerably. We can too simply suggest that each field of interest pursue its own concerns. The historian of religion, for example, has interests in the developments and changes in religious beliefs and practices and in how these fit into the cultural milieu of the times. The theologian appears to have even narrower pursuits, dealing with doctrinal justifications for behavioral expressions, morality, the good life, and related concerns. The psychologist usually deals with how religion affects the individual in terms of the learning process, meeting basic human needs, conversion phenomena, and similar experience in religious awareness, worship, and belief. The sociologist deals with religion more from a group perspective, giving data on its institutionalization and types of religious organizations, on how belief and behavior integrate with other sociocultural behaviors and contexts, and on social functions and conflicts. This brings us to the position of anthropology and of the present text.

Anthropology takes a comparative approach to all of human behavior, examining the exhibition of a given behavior such as religion in all human societies. This is in the attempt to grasp the full variety of such manifestations. Anthropology is also holistic, attempting to integrate findings from many other more specialized fields to accomplish the task of generalization. The result is a rather comprehensive treatment of human behavior, one that gives a sense of over-all understanding rather than in-depth attention or analysis. This is the approach taken in this and the following chapters with respect to the understanding of religion. It should be stated, however, that this anthropological approach also has its limi-

tations; it is not a substitute for a truly integrated study of
the phenomenon of religion.

DEFINITIONS OF RELIGION

If there are general and specific problems in understanding
religious belief and behavior, a most limiting factor—but a
methodological necessity—is that of arriving at a satisfactory
definition of the totality of the behavior to be studied. The
problem of supplying a definition for religion (as for many
concepts in the behavioral sciences) is that of exclusiveness
and inclusiveness. In the first case the definer wishes the scope
of the coverage of the defined concept to be sufficiently narrow so as to clearly delimit the scope of study. With respect
to religion, then, such behaviors would stand out as distinct
from other cultural behaviors. In the second case, the attempt
is to broaden the definitional perspective to cover a wider
scope of study, for religion specifically to include a great deal
of material that does not immediately strike one as "religious."
The rationale often given for this broader approach is that it
allows the student to perceive commonalities in human behavior obscured by a more convenient and hence exclusive approach. This is to a large extent true. Narrow conceptualizations lead to overlooking valuable data and possibly to limited
understanding. However, to "open wide the gates" for one's
subject matter may make it difficult to ever set parameters
for the study of a topic such as religion. "This insistence on . . .
[inclusiveness] . . . in the interests of comparative social
science is . . . an obstacle to the comparative method for it
leads to continuous changes in definition and, ultimately, to
definitions which, because of their vagueness or abstractness,
are all but worthless" (Spiro, 1966: 86). So, do we narrow our
study to a neatly circumscribed topic, losing valuable data;
or do we expand our topic to wider coverage and chance
making the data too vast to deal with efficiently? With notable exceptions, most students of religion fall somewhere in
between these obvious extremes. We can give definitions here,
discuss them briefly, and then press on to other related conceptual problems.

We can begin by offering the definition of the author cited
above as an example of the more exclusive approach. He

writes, "I shall define religion as an institution consisting of culturally patterned interaction with culturally postulated superhuman beings" (Spiro, 1966: 96). In effect, this limits religion to shared beliefs and behaviors exhibited by humans as they conceive of the desires and attributes of superhuman beings and attempt to influence them or to gain their aid in human concerns. The superhuman beings are those entities having greater powers than do humans themselves—for example, gods and spirits. Such a definition does indeed limit the field of religious study. It is of some interest to note that Spiro is fairly typical of anthropologists in taking such a narrow approach. Is this because anthropologists, with a greater range of data to make sense from, have had to circumscribe such attempts more carefully? Robin Horton, another anthropologist, takes a highly similar approach—dealing with religion as a special sort of interaction but one based upon that between humans themselves.

. . . In every situation commonly labelled religious we are dealing with action directed towards objects which are believed to respond in terms of certain categories . . . which are also the distinctive categories for the description of human action. . . . In short, religion can be looked upon as an extension of the field of people's social relationships beyond the confines of purely human society . . . one in which human beings involved see themselves in a dependent position vis-à-vis their non-human alters . . . (Horton, 1960: 211).

Here again, although the theoretical aspects and emphasis are slightly different from Spiro, we find a similar, narrow approach.

These and many other anthropological formulations (but also see Geertz, 1966, and Goody, 1961) may be seen to focus on certain types of belief and behavior with respect to certain types of entities, carefully circumscribed. Other writers, however, have insisted that what is to be studied and understood is not so much religion as the religious attitude—a way of thinking or feeling rather than specific behavior or the objects of that behavior. This approach considerably broadens the focal points of religious study and is often found in the writings of sociologists, psychologists, and scholars in departments of religion. One well thought out approach along these lines is that of J. Paul Williams, who writes:

Religiousness is a mental quality which modifies certain aspects of the life of individuals [and through individuals of groups]; this quality must have each of the following characteristics in some degree:

A belief-attitude that the Ultimate for man exists . . . and that certain aspects of life derive from the Ultimate; a belief-attitude that the derivation (from the Ultimate) of these aspects of life is beyond empirical demonstration; a belief-attitude that these aspects of life are of supreme importance . . . for the concern of the individual . . . (Williams, 1962: 8).

By the concept *ultimate,* this writer means the "final reality" that affects or determines human life, the basic source of life —even though its precise definition will differ from society to society. It may be far removed from humans or be manifest everywhere (impersonal or personal), and in fact it may be left undefined. All that matters to the religious person is that some final reality exists! The ultimate, therefore, rests upon faith; it is beyond empirical demonstration, although theologians and/or philosophers in many societies have made attempts at "proving" its existence. Finally there is the notion that such belief-attitudes deriving from the ultimate deal with issues of major importance in human existence. What is considered fundamental may vary from society to society, although issues such as morality and death may universally receive such attention.

An approach such as that of Williams obviously opens up a much more vast array of cognitive and behavioral phenomena for the attention of the student of religion. Many other writers would shorten his view to simply defining religion as a concern with ultimate questions and answers. Any such inclusive attempts at definition soon lead to the consideration of many things not commonly recognized as being of the same character as "conventional" religion. Communism, for example, has often been cited as displaying much of the general character of what has been discussed above as well as overlapping with some specific religious behavior. Some elements would include: ultimate answers to fundamental questions, a moral code, nonempirical forces (historic dialectic), rituals such as May Day, prophets and martyrs, and so on. So also does psychoanalysis in a broad sense partake of religion! One begins to perceive here the difficulty of inclusive definitional approaches as well as the loss of insight when one sets more specific limits on the definition of religion.

Ward Goodenough, one of perhaps a growing number of anthropologists who opt for a more inclusive type of view on religion, also defines religion in terms of certain problems of human existence. Speaking specifically of the problem of salvation, he makes clear the difficulty of setting up arbitrary definitional limits.

Among people whose cosmology includes . . . anthropomorphic beings endowed with superhuman powers, intellectually and emotionally acceptable definitions may have to take account of such beings. For people whose cosmology allows for the existence of nothing that is unconfirmed by or inconsistent with empirical observation, intellectually and emotionally acceptable definitions of salvation and means to salvation must exclude any reference to such . . . beings. If concern with salvation is a religious concern, then I cannot dismiss Marxist definitions of it from the domain of religion because they eschew reference to spirits. In other respects, I often find it hard to distinguish behaviorally between those . . . who are ardent Marxists and those who are ardent Fundamentalists (Goodenough, 1974: 168).

In spite of the truth of the above statement, the viewpoint taken in the present text is primarily that of a more exclusive approach. This is partly due to the fact that religious materials from primitive societies have traditionally been couched in such terms. And, it partly is due to the belief that for practical purposes the best entry point for understanding the religious dimension of human experience is that of the human–supernatural relationship. This does not preclude awareness of a more inclusive view, ascribing attributes, behaviors, and functions to religion operating without supernatural referents; nor does it preclude the possibility that other areas of human behavior may reveal similar concerns. It does, however, indicate a lack of data with respect to these for most societies with which anthropologists have had experience. Even so, at least for the present, we give no actual definition for religion. The remainder of this introductory chapter accomplishes three things. It gives the perspectives on religion of two scholars generally neglected by anthropologists; it relates religion in the narrow sense of supernaturalism to magic, and it suggests some possible differences between primitive religious systems and more modern religious expressions.

THE SACRED WORLD PERSPECTIVE

Two nonanthropological writers have made general theoretical contributions to the resolution of the nature of the religious experience. Both assume a more inclusive viewpoint than this text. Both have been criticized by anthropologists, but both are suggestive so they are very briefly noted here.

The first of these approaches is that of Mircea Eliade, whose considerable number of books and articles offer a well-documented perspective on religion. Two books in particular (*Cosmos and History* and *The Sacred and the Profane*) reflect his theory in application to primitive societies. It is Eliade's contention that the major category for religious study is the world of the sacred, which he suggests is qualitatively different from the world of the profane. "The sacred is equivalent to a power, and, in the last analysis, to reality. The sacred is saturated with being. Sacred power means reality and at the same time enduringness and efficacity" (Eliade, 1961: 12). The profane world is correspondingly thought to be unreal. In the mind of "premoderns," he suggests, activities and objects become valuable and real as they participate in the world of the sacred, in this reality that transcends them. "The object appears as the receptacle of an exterior force that differentiates it from its milieu and gives it meaning and value" (Eliade, 1959: 4). Activities and objects display the sacred if they are given an exemplary model or archetype; those of the profane world lack such substantiation. In modern societies much of life has lost such extrahuman archetypes and hence is profane; for example, dancing and trees have been for the most part desanctified and participate in no higher reality. In primitive societies, however, it is suggested that almost every act and object has a sacred basis.

Eliade extends this sacred–profane reality distinction into the realm of time. Rituals, essentially, are devices that repeat the mythic acts that substantiate them. Religious activities repeat what ordinarily took place in creation. And by such repetition one participates, over and over again, in reality and being.

. . . an object or act becomes real only insofar as it imitates or repeats an archetype. Thus reality is acquired solely through repetition or participation; everything which lacks an exemplary model . . . lacks reality. . . . the man of a traditional culture sees himself as real only to the extent he ceases to be himself . . . and is satisfied with imitating and repeating the gestures of another.

Further,

. . . insofar as an act (or an object) acquires a certain reality through . . . repetition . . . and acquires it through that alone, there is an implicit abolition of profane time, of duration, of "history", and he who reproduces the exemplary gesture thus finds himself transported into the mythical epoch in which its relevation took place (Eliade, 1959: 34, 35).

This process occurs during rituals and in effect abolishes the past by restoring or recreating the original state of affairs and sacredness. Since time is resumed again from the beginning in this endless manner, time itself is a cyclical conception—primitives live in the "eternal present." The profane view (history) holds time to be an irreversible process. Eliade examines rituals and related religious phenomena with a regard to seeing how symbolically and behaviorally they accomplish such a task. In sum then, Eliade sees "religion" as a concern with the sacred, the world of ultimate reality and being that in a timeless fashion is recaptured through ritual and other activities. Things are real as they can be substantiated by the sacred, and religion is thus a search for meaning and the attempt to avoid losing contact with reality.

The second theoretical contribution is that of the sociologist Peter Berger, who was influenced by the work of Eliade. Berger begins with the assumption that human culture is not only a product of human activities but that (in a dialectical fashion) humans are also products of their creations; for example, we invent language and are then influenced by its rules. This world of culture is above everything else an ordering of experience. It is imposed upon individuals as a Nomos, a meaningful order that because of socialization we share with other individuals in a society. Since it provides meaning, the Nomos is a "shield against terror," against the lack of meaning in life.

When the Nomos is taken for granted, its meanings merge
with what are assumed to be the meanings inherent in the
universe itself; the Nomos and the Cosmos are merged.
". . . when the Nomos is taken for granted as appertaining to
the 'nature of things', . . . it is endowed with a stability deriving from more powerful sources than the historical efforts of
human beings" (Berger, 1969: 25).

Religion is seen here as a device of legitimization. Religion
considers the Cosmos itself as sacred (as an alternative to the
scientifically considered profane or secularized Cosmos).
Sacredness for Berger consists of mysterious and awesome
power beyond the purely human, extraordinary and different
from the normal routines of life. Since Nomos and sacred
Cosmos are coextensive, human culture is grounded in and
legitimized by a higher order of reality.

The Cosmos posited by religion both transcends and includes man.
The Sacred Cosmos is confronted by man as an immensely powerful reality other than himself. Yet this reality addresses itself to
him and locates his life in an ultimately meaningful order. . . .
It can thus be said that religion has played a strategic part in the
human enterprise of world-building. Religion implies the farthest
reach of man's self-externalization, of his infusion of reality with
his own meanings. Religion implies that human order is projected
into the totality of being. Put differently, religion is the audacious
attempt to conceive of the entire universe as being humanly
significant (Berger, 1969: 26, 27, 28).

So religion is the attempt to locate cultural institutions not
only in a cosmic, but also in a sacred, frame of reference,
providing ultimate meaning and legitimacy for them. For
"modern" societies, sectors of the Nomos are removed from
such contexts, and hence (as for Eliade) we are left with a
profane world lacking in meaning. Like the contributions of
Eliade, Berger's general theory of religion merits wider attention by anthropological students of religion. We can return now to the more specific considerations of religion espoused by the present text.

RELIGION AND MAGIC

The exclusive approach to religion previously outlined emphasized religion as a belief in supernatural beings and the

practices relating to them. Certain fairly well-defined characteristics follow this supposition. If gods have power, then there is a dependency relation between them and human beings. Such supernaturals are in the "driver's seat," so to speak; and if a person wishes to accomplish something via supernatural means (success in hunting, relief from sickness), he must somehow motivate the gods to accomplish it on his behalf. Or, in a negative sense, one must motivate the gods not to do any harm to human beings.

From this characteristic, a number of more specific features are derived (as summarized in a classic statement by William J. Goode, 1964). Although religious practice may have specific goals, quite often it is motivated more toward general welfare, the next life, and so on. "Why did you come to church today?" "Because I feel better, just having gone." Such goals are often termed *otherworldly*. In fact, religion is often characterized as being engaged in as an end in itself rather than purely as a means to some end. Since the gods have the special powers, religion tends to be propitiatory and supplicative in its approach to them. "Get down on your knees and pray for salvation." It is most often an asking rather than a telling approach. In the event of failure, some kind of rationalization usually occurs. There is either acceptance of the will of the gods, or the desired result is postponed and failure not really considered. The gods work in mysterious ways. Perhaps in the effort to avoid not reaching goals, along with the previously mentioned attitude of supplication, religion often displays a great degree of emotionalism, manifest in feelings of awe, fear, inadequacy, and hope as one relates to power-laden, supernatural beings.

Religious practices seem heavily to be group-oriented phenomena; gods are usually connected to "churches." This may be true both in group participation in its rituals as well as in the feeling of group benefit. Moreover, as a consequence, much of religious behavior is also public and open. Religious rituals, at least those of a group-public nature, are generally fixed and obligatory; they occur as scheduled or repetitive activities. They must be carried out; and—one suspects—innovation is fairly unusual, since they tend to follow traditional patterns. In religion, the relation between leader and follower is designated by Goode as the Shepherd–flock or Prophet–follower relation. Such leaders counsel, direct, and lead their followers along ways felt to be pleasing to the gods. Finally as a character of religion is the notion that "Religious rituals are not thought of as even potentially directed against the society . . ." (Goode, 1964: 53). This would not preclude using one's gods against the members of another society, but the suggestion is that there is no attempt at misuse (or it doesn't work) within one's own group. These are, of course, idealized statements, and there are exceptions to each. However, they do provide a kind of a base line for analyzing religious behaviors.

Another base line is provided by the concept of magic, which has a long history, if at times one of controversy, as a theoretical tool for anthropologists. Magic, unlike religion, assumes the existence of supernatural power that humans themselves can obtain and use for their own ends. It allows for an independent rather than a dependent relationship to the supernatural world. Before comparing and contrasting magic and religion in terms of attributes previously discussed for the latter, we can very briefly discuss magic in general.

In the rituals of magic there are found three essential components. First, there are special objects or things that are used. Sometimes these materials are unique kinds of things, for example an unusual piece of wood or quartz crystals. Perhaps more often the materials of magic are simply ordinary things that are put together in "unnatural" ways—eye of lizard and wing of bat, for example. The things used, however, are not sufficient to make proper magic. One must also employ the right words—the verbal component. This is usually referred to as the *spell* or *incantation* and may range from a simple saying to an involved formula. Flim, flam, biff, bam, may teacher die before the exam! Materials and words are combined with/by various manipulations, the things done that comprise the third element of magic. One takes special water from a special container and pours it on the ground, bangs special stones together like thunder, and says the words for rain magic.

Years ago a classic statement on the various aspects of magic was made by Sir James Frazer in his twelve-volume work, *The Golden Bough* (1911–1915). Although much of his work has been subsequently regarded with suspicion, his analysis of the mental principles of magic thought is of perhaps more than historical interest. It is given very briefly here to help give some of the "flavor" of magic. Frazer held that there were two basic principles of magic: the *law of similarity* and the *law of contact*. The first operates on the notion that like produces like; it works by imitation. For example, destroying an image of someone one wishes to harm or pretending to successfully hunt some animal. He also called this *homeopathic magic*. The second principle assumes that things once in contact continue to be connected and hence can subsequently affect one another. Here the magician can work on the part to affect the whole. For example, one can harm a person by harming his nail clippings. Frazer termed this mental principle *contagious magic*. Of course, both principles can be combined in practice; so Frazer, recognizing that they assumed a "secret sympathy" between things, called them both *sympathetic magic*.

Whatever its mental operations, magic manipulates objects and words in its rituals. It must be understood, however, that these components are not all equally weighted in various human societies. Though magic may be a complex, the stress on the components varies. An excellent illustration of this is supplied by Evans–Pritchard (1929) in his comparison of two primitive societies. Among Trobriand Islanders, the materials are rather inconsequential; but the spells are complex, unalterable formulas that must not deviate at all from tradition, lest their effects be nullified. Among the Zande, on the other hand, the spell is not very complex, and its words can be varied to suit the individual practitioner. The strange roots and woods that make up Zande magic are correspondingly of greater emphasis. These differences, like many of the variations in magic and religion, are closely linked to other cultural variables.

As a final, general perspective on the concept of magic, we can mention that it is often classified on the basis of the specific goals desired for such practices. Probably most magic is protective or productive. This is to say that its intent is to prevent or rectify misfortune or to gain some kind of benefit —rain, success in hunting and war, and so on. It may involve ritual or simply the wearing of a good luck charm. Less common is destructive magic (black magic), the intent of which is to harm one's fellow humans and that—unlike the first two types—is usually not a socially approved endeavor. We can now examine (along lines suggested by Goode) the more specific attributes of magic that seem to differentiate it from religion.

Because of the independent relation of magic, that humans can "plug into" supernatural powers themselves, the attitude is one of manipulation—of putting the components of magic together in a proper, efficacious manner. Because of this mechanistic nature, the emotionalism associated with religion is generally lacking in magic practice. What is found is usually a detached, impersonal feeling. There is less fear and awe if one can oneself perform in a superhuman fashion. It should be added that if one is the target of destructive magic, there is emotionalism—especially fear. In contrast to the sometimes general goals of religion, magic appears to be oriented only toward very specific goals. It does not seem to be engaged in for its own sake; it is only a means to an end—not an end in itself. From this it follows that it is not generally a scheduled type of supernatural activity, not fixed and obligatory. Rather, magic ritual occurs when and if there is a need for its benefits. This is generally decided by the magical leader, whose relationship to followers Goode designates as the professional–client relationship. Perhaps everyone knows some magic, but those who because of special attributes are magical leaders are like doctors and lawyers in other societies—skilled professionals who function on behalf of persons needing aid who become their clients.

Since this professional–client relation exists in magic, the quality of the behaviors involved is said to be both individual in benefit and participation and private in nature. Only a few individuals are involved, as opposed to the more group-oriented, public nature of religion. There are cases of public magic, however; it is inappropriate to state that magic never has a church! As previously discussed, magic can at least potentially be bad. One can harm others in one's own group; the magician can be guilty of malpractice. Finally, magic differs from religion according to Goode, in that failure is recognized and the attempt is made to deal with it. "With regard to the process of achieving the goal, in case of magical failure, there is more likely to be a substitution or introduction of other techniques. Stronger magic will be used, or magic to offset the countermagic of enemies, or even a different magician" (Goode, 1964: 53).

In this connection, we might briefly deal with a highly related topic. If religion is not really seen to fail, perhaps because the gods aren't listening, would magic not be suspect as a belief-technique if it failed repeatedly? It could not be rationalized in the same manner as religion. Even discounting the fact that sometimes it would work because of trickery, pure accident, or some unintended virtue in what is being done, there would still be a considerable number of occasions when it would fail. One suspects its efficacy is not questioned, however, simply rationalized in ways different from religion. Countermagic may be thought to nullify it, the practitioner may have made some error in the ritual itself (especially if it is long and complicated) or may have used the wrong technique or may have been the wrong type of professional for the task required. Finally, the professional or his or her client may not have observed the proper purification or taboos required to make even a correct ritual work. In other words, with such rationalizations for failure, magic as a belief-technique is probably not called into question any more than the reality of religion.

CRITIQUE OF MAGIC AND RELIGION CONCEPTS

Once again it must be stated that these attributes of magic and religion are idealized statements. Probably no ritual displays all the attributes of one or the other. So Goode's scheme is primarily an analytical device. He himself demonstrates that great similarities in thought and behavior link magic and religion together—ritual systems, concern with nonempirical entities, and pervasive symbolism, for example. Nonetheless, there has been considerable dissatisfaction with this dichotomy. Very simply, two approaches have emerged as attempts to resolve such conceptual difficulties—discarding the concept or reworking it.

Rosalie and Murray Wax have justifiably pointed out that anthropologists have continued to employ the terms *magic* and *religion* in their discussions of the supernatural realm of human experience, even though they are unhappy in their ability to precisely separate them in observation and description. So, for example, ". . . in actual application these distinctions become awkward and less than useful, since it is often difficult to distinguish whether the person observed is being manipulative or supplicative toward the supernatural in his concern over a good harvest or a successful hunt" (Wax, 1962: 179). They present the notion that such concepts are of little value in the definition and understanding of supernatural activity; and they believe that attempts to lump such behaviors into a single category such as "magico-religious" are also wide of the mark.

In their attempt to present a new solution, the Waxes point out that the crucial factor to be taken into account is the concept of "power" and that this is the central organization point of what they term the "magical world view." Though this view sounds somewhat like that of Berger and Eliade, in fact it is different. Briefly summarized, their arguments in such a direction can be expressed as follows: The definition of the term *magic* as part of a magical world view based on the conception of power will allow new freedom of use for the term—one not impeded by its past connotations. The magical world view is the observation–interpretation of the world on the part of non-Western societies as peopled with beings—some human and some nonhuman; whereas we of the Western world perceive lifeless objects. In the former view, things occur because of these beings—things that we ourselves would attribute to natural events. The prime mover of this magical world is power, regarded by a person in the "magical world" as awesome and wonderful. When people who hold this view translate it into action, we have magical activity, and since these activities deal with power, they may take any one of a number of forms depending on their relationship to that power—manipulative, supplicative, emotional, impersonal, and so forth.

Considering these relations in this sense allows us to see them as particles of the same thing—the expression of the magical world view—and not one approach or another as the Goode scheme forces us to do. In sum, then, ". . . magic derives its meaning from within a process of cross-cultural interaction and really designates forms of conceptualizing the world that are utterly different from those which are characteristic of Judaeo-Christianity and the 'rational' West" (Wax, 1963: 503). This does represent one way to solve our unhappiness with the magic–religion dichotomy; but what seems to have happened is that our dichotomy has been recreated on a higher level: rational versus nonrational or Western versus non-Western. And does the Judaeo-Christian tradition have no similar concept of power? It might also be pointed out that the Waxes' scheme does not allow for any analysis of differences within such a power system.

An approach to this problem that does leave room for the analysis of differences is that of Mischa Titiev. In his formulation, he has attempted to introduce into the literature a new pair of terms free from past connotations. In his words,

As a fresh start towards a workable dichotomy, it may be well to distinguish two kinds of activities on a new basis, one that rests on a criterion that is precise, but has not been traditionally utilized by former analysts. In all primitive societies one set of practices involving the supernatural always takes place recurrently, and may, accordingly, be termed Calendrical; while the other set, which is celebrated only intermittently, and then only when an emergency or crisis seems to have arisen, may be called Critical (Titiev, 1960: 293).

These types would indeed seem to reflect differences, and they are largely discrete patterns of behavior. If we extend their meanings, we discover that the calendrical activities are usually found in the hands of shepherd types of practitioners and are generally for group benefit. Likewise the practitioners involved in critical activities tend to be professional types with a more individualistic orientation. Considered in such a manner, it is perhaps appropriate to feel that these general terms are at least partially identifiable as the "poles" of magic and religion as presented in the Goode summary. That is to say that calendrical activities more nearly approximate what we have been accustomed in the past to calling the religious approach and that the critical practices seem identifiable with some of the emphasis of magic. Despite the fact that the new terms do not by themselves suggest manipulation or supplication, the total effect appears simply to be a substitution of a new set of terms for older ones. Titiev's approach does, however, seem to be the more fruitful of the two.

NATURALISM AND SUPERNATURALISM

By this point, the student should be reeling with theoretical distinctions: magic, religion, power, the sacred, the profane, and ultimate questions. Religion is narrow in definitions; it applies to many wider activities! As previously mentioned, this text takes a more exclusive approach. As an area of study, religion is still in its infancy. As a recent scholar has put it, "It could be said that the scientific study of religion is today in a more primitive state than was biology two centuries ago. We have not yet had our Darwin; we have hardly had our Linnaeus to sharpen our basic descriptive terms and their classifications . . ." (Burhoe, 1974: 15). As such, despite an overlap with other areas of life that also deal with similar concerns, our position is that the specific subject matter to investigate is that area of life in which humans relate in any way to superhuman beings and powers—an area to which the terms *magic* and *religion* may be supplied in the ideal sense. In general terms, this is the special realm of the sacred.

Further, as Edward Norbeck has suggested, we can use the general term *supernaturalism* for the kinds of behaviors we are going to describe. By this term he means ". . . to include all that is not natural, that which is regarded as extraordinary, not of the ordinary world, mysterious, and unexplained or unexplainable in ordinary terms" (Norbeck, 1961: 11). Supernatural means more than natural, and this is not the same thing as superstitious! Naturalism, on the other hand, is the view that things happen because of the operation of perfectly ordinary, nonmysterious causes and circumstances. This is the world of science rather than of magic and religion. This is generally the sacred–profane distinction of Eliade and Berger. Further is the idea in supernaturalism that its special world transcends the purely natural one; it is more real than that which is normally perceived and dealt with in purely scientific terms. The view is often held that human existence can only realize its potential in proportion to our acceptance of and reliance upon the world of the supernatural. We are real, in other words, as Homo religious, not as Homo scientificus. Man in this view cannot be self-made. "It is he who has made us and not we ourselves." In any event, human beings usually merge these two views in some way.

. . . man interprets his universe in two principal and different ways, and on the basis of these interpretations he is afforded patterns of behavior with relation to that universe so that he may know how to act. One of the kinds of interpretation we may call naturalistic, the other supernaturalistic. Naturalism and supernaturalism are both ways of adjusting to the universe. Man's behavior has been based upon both of the principal lines of interpretation, separately, alternately, and in combination; and they have affected his life in ways of which he has not always been aware (Norbeck, 1961: 12).

This is the approach taken in the present text, based on the expedient that we should thoroughly understand a specific and limited area of behavior before pursuing more inclusive materials.

PRIMITIVE AND MODERN RELIGION

We conclude this first chapter with a consideration of the possible differences between "primitive" and "modern" supernaturalism, a distinction that will probably turn out to be more apparent than real as we come to understand more of primitive practices. Some years ago, William Howells (1948) listed a series of what he felt were specific differences between the two. First, he said that modern religions were world religions; that is, they have spread from their points of origination either by the migration of followers or missionary travels. For example, Buddhism began in India, but it spread to Tibet, China, Japan, into Southeast Asia, and ultimately to almost all areas of the world. The history of Christianity and other modern faiths displays comparable developments. In contrast, his assumption is that most primitive faiths remain limited to the people who originated them. Are there Pygmy churches beyond their location in Africa? As a relative phenomenon, this distinction is probably justified, although nativistic movements certainly show rapid spread beyond the areas of first formulation.

Second is the notion that these world faiths have a sense of history, tracing back to some historical founder(s)—Buddha, Christ, Mohammed. In contrast, primitive systems either do not remember a founder or have their sense of origin in myth. They assume less a sense of human origin. This distinction is harder to support, since some primitive systems postulate originating "culture heroes" and some modern faiths such as Hinduism list no special human founders.

Another distinction drawn by Howells for modern systems is that of exclusivism, ". . . a jealousy of their own doctrines and an intolerance of others, which they relentlessly seek to blot out" (Howells, 1948: 5). They believe that they are either

the one true faith (there is no god but Allah) or that they are
the most correct, the best vehicle for salvation. Primitive systems, on the other hand, are said to be more open to suggestion and tolerant of the faiths of other people. Though
primitive faiths have not been well studied under natural conditions of contact, one could question this distinction on logical grounds, based on what we know of human ethnocentrism
in other areas of life. They may be tolerant only to the
extent that they do not actively propagandize!

A fourth distinction is the assumption of a moral/ethical
flavor in modern-world systems of supernaturalism as contained in sets of principles to guide human behavior: the Ten
Commandments or the Holy Eightfold Path in Buddhism, for
example. It is possible that primitive faiths lack explicit behavioral statements, but there are certainly moral/ethical considerations to dealing with gods and powers—don't break
taboos or misuse magic. So this may not be a really valid
distinction unless it is only one of emphasis.

Finally, there is the notion that world faiths have what
might be called a "tidy theology." Perhaps as a consequence
of trying to convert other peoples, the first principles and
theological ideas are worked out in a logical and systematic
fashion. In contrast, the theologies of primitives, Howells feels,
are much less organized and consistent. ". . . the wide-eyed
native cults, . . . are open to any suggestion and will accept
any idea that seems appealing or useful, sometimes even if
it opposes a prevailing one" (Howells, 1948: 5). It is extremely
hard to agree with this distinction. So-called modern faiths
have many contradictions that escape the notice of their followers but that are argued over endlessly by their theologians;
and part of the lack of primitive theology is the lack of understanding on the part of those anthropologists who have
studied them! By way of apology here, it must be said that
most primitive faiths are not associated with the writing systems that would make their systemization and study much
easier. In sum, though one may suppose that there are differences between primitive and modern supernatural systems (as
in other areas of society and culture), full documentation and
comprehension of primitive systems may reveal our present
comprehension of differences to be largely a product of misunderstanding. We now turn to a series of related theoretical

issues—types of belief and practice and the various specific components of supernaturalism.

REFERENCES

Berger, Peter L.
      1969. *The Sacred Canopy.*
      New York: Doubleday and Company.
Burhoe, Ralph Wendell.
      1974. *The Phenomenon of Religion Seen Scientifically.*
      In *Changing Perspectives in the Scientific Study of Religion,* ed. A. W. Eister, pp. 15–39.
      New York: John Wiley and Sons.
Eliade, Mircea.
      1961. *The Sacred and the Profane.*
      New York: Harper and Row.
————. 1959. *Cosmos and History.*
      New York: Harper and Row.
Evans–Pritchard, E. E.
      1929. The Morphology and Function of Magic: A Comparative Study of Trobriand and Zande Rituals and Spells.
      American Anthropologist 31: 619–641.
Geertz, Clifford.
      1966. Religion as a Cultural System. In *Anthropological Approaches to the Study of Religion,* ed. M. Banton.
      New York: Praeger.
Goode, William J.
      1951. *Religion Among the Primitives.*
      Glencoe: Free Press.
Goodenough, Ward E.
      1974. Towards An Anthropologically Useful Definition of Religion. In *Changing Perspectives in the Scientific Study of Religion,* ed. A. W. Eister.
      New York: John Wiley and Sons.
Goody, Jack.
      1961. Religion and Ritual: The Definition Problem.
      British Journal of Sociology 12: 143–164.
Horton, Robin.
      1960. A Definition of Religion and Its Uses.
      Journal of the Royal Anthropological Institute of Great Britain & Ireland 90: 201–226.

Howells, William.
        1948.   *The Heathens.*
                Garden City: Doubleday and Company.
Norbeck, Edward.
        1961.   *Religion in Primitive Society.*
                New York: Harper and Brothers.
Spiro, Melford E.
        1966.   Religion: Problems of Definition and Explanation.
                In *Anthropological Approaches to the Study of Religion,* ed. M. Banton.
                New York: Praeger.
Streng, Frederick J.
        1969.   *Understanding Religious Man.*
                Belmont, California: Dickenson Publishing Company.
Titiev, Mischa.
        1960.   A Fresh Approach to the Problem of Magic and Religion.
                Southwestern Journal of Anthropology 16: 292–298.
Wax, Rosalie and Murray.
        1963.   The Notion of Magic.
                Current Anthropology 4: 495–503.
———. 1962.   The Magical World View.
                Journal for the Scientific Study of Religion 1: 179–188.
Williams, J. Paul.
        1962.   The Nature of Religion.
                Journal for the Scientific Study of Religion 2: 3–14.

CHAPTER 2

Aspects of Supernaturalism

In the last chapter we discussed some of the definitions of and approaches to supernatural belief and practice. Before turning to descriptive accounts of such behavior, we must first deal with some other aspects of this topic. We must also deal with the forms of such expressions and the various elements that comprise this area of human behavior.

PERSPECTIVES OF SPACE, TIME, AND UNDERSTANDING

When a student of supernaturalism attempts to study a specific system of belief and practice or supernaturalism in general, he or she must be aware of at least three factors that will greatly influence comprehension. These are the factors of space, time, and understanding, which we can briefly discuss in reverse order. The problem of understanding involves two different types of difficulties. First, there is the obvious problem of ethnocentrism. Even if the researcher takes the view of neutrality, one is at least unconsciously habituated to a particular pattern of thinking and perception—that of one's own culture and society. Hence it is extremely difficult not to impress one's own categories onto the data one elicits about another supernatural system, to formulate their behavior patterns in the mold of your own and not to understand it in its own terms. This can occur on a number of levels. Thus, for example, the notion that a particular society may have relative to a sun god or animal sacrifice may be quite different than I (coming from a system lacking these) interpret it.

When they worship the sun is it as a physical deity or as a symbolic representation of superhuman phenomena? If two different societies have sun gods, are their notions comparable? Fieldworkers are apt to interpret phenomena such as this in terms of their own preconceived notions of what sun gods are!

On a deeper level is the idea that "gods" themselves and their varieties are also a preconceived notion based on Western experience. True, one must have categories to make possible data collection and study, but one must remain aware of the fact that they are just that—categories—not the reality under investigation. Does, for example, the concept of *god* really exist for the people in question? For many years anthropologists have argued over the meaning of the concept of mana, a phenomenon supposedly widespread among Pacific peoples and usually designated as a kind of impersonal supernatural power or influence. Our attempts to understand this notion linguistically, conceptually, and behaviorally have pretty much ended in frustration (see, for example, Firth, 1967). Likewise the idea of totemism has been discussed in many different ways (Levi–Strauss, 1963) and may in fact mostly be an illusory concept of anthropological construction. Could it be that we experience difficulties with such constructs because our categorization precludes proper perception and understanding? In short, we must be careful of our own preconceptions and attempt to understand other supernatural systems in their own terms. We must ensure that our models do not become substitutes for reality.

The second level of difficulty in understanding is more in the nature of an accident. When fieldworkers begin to learn about someone else's supernatural beliefs and practices, they often (in the attempt to maximize effort) derive information from the specialists involved—the priests, medicine men, theologians, and so on who can offer the most comprehensive account of it. In so doing we have often gained a rather biased view of these behavioral complexes. "In the religious sphere, the gap between the theology of the higher philosophers . . . and the religious principles that guide the behavior of an ordinary churchgoer may be very wide indeed. In studies of comparative religion a failure to take into account this distinction between philosophical religion and practical religion has often led to grave misunderstanding" (Leach, 1968: 1). The gods may mean different things to the leader than to the follower, who may have to deal with more mundane aspects of life; the Brahman and the Untouchable certainly approached the Hindu gods differently. We must make sure that our study of supernaturalism is balanced and not simply an "elite" study.

Similar problems result from the study of supernatural systems in time. It is easy enough, perhaps, to give a detailed description of supernatural beliefs and practices as they exist at the time of study. To understand these, however, may require insight into the previous developmental stages of that system. Students of the history of religion have observed this injunction fairly regularly, but many anthropologists have failed to do so—except perhaps with respect to cult movements and related phenomena. As a result we have often been confused, for example, over why certain myths and rituals may not be mutually reinforcing, why the functions and attributes of gods overlap, and why some rites seem not to fit well with other cultural practices. It is probable that the proper solution to these difficulties could be supplied if the time dimension for expression of supernaturalism would or could be taken into account. Part of this problem, of course, is the historic nature of some primitive systems, but a good portion of it represents anthropological oversight in methodology. So, to take a specific case, it would be most difficult to understand classic Greek religion from a "frozen time" perspective. Greek religion expressed itself in two ways (see Guthrie, 1955, and Nilsson, 1964). These were in the cult of the Olympic deities such as Zeus and Apollo and in cults such as the mysteries—a form of involvement with the supernatural forces much deeper than the "bargaining" with high gods. This dualism is explicable with reference to the earlier Mother Goddess with its personal contact by song and dance roots found in Minoan religion, which later merged with a male-oriented, sky-god religion brought by invaders into the area. The resulting synthesis and its accommodations in behavior is not fully understandable without knowledge of the time dimension. So also one cannot even begin to understand the beliefs and practices of classical Hinduism unless one gains knowledge of the Vedic religion (some also would say the even earlier Indus religion), the rise of Buddhism and Jainism, and later philosophic reformulations designed to make Hinduism more attractive to the masses.

There is a second and related aspect of the time dimension that creates problems for the analyst or student of supernaturalism. This is the idea of using practices exhibited by living peoples in the attempt to reconstruct comparable practices in the past. This would involve, for example, using the religious or magical behaviors of some contemporary hunting-and-gathering society as a model for those who existed in the archaeological past. Morton Levine has attempted this to a limited degree by analyzing the sacred art of Australian Aborigines and other hunting peoples, discovering its supernatural meaning and function, and comparing this to the cave art tradition of the late Old Stone Age. "The material remains of past civilizations sometimes include art. Where this is so, as in the spectacular case of Upper Paleolithic art in Western Europe, we may be able to add an ideological dimension to our understanding of the ancient people" (Levine, 1957: 949). His work resulted in several trial interpretations of this art, but he is careful to point out that the explanations one can arrive at by using the present as a model for the past are at best limited to plausibility. There have been, however, less carefully reasoned attempts, and there is no guarantee that reconstructions such as these are even remotely valid.

Finally, there is the problem of the space dimension. Supernatural systems exist not only in time but also in space. If anthropologists have generally ignored the influence of time in their attempts at understanding, so also have they all too often not considered the proximity of other supernatural systems. Even for rather isolated primitive societies, the process of diffusion (spread of culture traits) can be demonstrated. If we inquire as to how supernatural beliefs and practices have evolved over time, it is also appropriate to ask if influences from outside have changed them. Such diffusionary experiences may also be invoked to explain a multiplicity of gods or some ritual type. In the American Southwest there are some major commonalities in ritual practice among the various Pueblo groups and the Pimans, Navaho, and Apache. What have the mutual influences been, and how does this alter our specific understandings of them? Can we understand a supernatural complex without reference to its spatial configuration?

In sum, then, there are major perspectives on supernaturalism that go beyond definitions and approaches. These are the problems of observer's bias and sampling error and the failure to take into account in our interpretations both the developmental nature of supernatural phenomena and the possible influences from other societies. Such failures place constraints both on the level of understanding gained in some particular study as well as on its usefulness in the wider understanding of supernatural experience.

THE EXPRESSIONS OF SUPERNATURAL EXPERIENCE

Before we investigate some of the major types of supernaturalism (elements, groups, ritual forms), it is necessary to deal with the general kinds of supernatural experience. In theoretical terms this is a topic on which anthropologists have generally been silent except as a by-product of their descriptions. We can make a logical distinction here between theoretical and practical expressions—between belief and practice. People have beliefs, and so they express them in practices; they have practices that they justify by beliefs. Do either occur by themselves? Which is the primary expression of supernaturalism? This is a topic of some anthropological interest for which no satisfactory answer has been forthcoming. In general, however, we can now say that most writers have abandoned the search for at least the ultimate primacy of either belief or practice. So, for example, "What are the respective relations between myth and ritual, doctrine and cult, theology and worship? The most plausible interpretation would seem to be that which considers the theoretical and practical as being inextricably intertwined and would depreciate any attempt to impute primacy to either one or the other" (Wach, 1962: 19). This writer would also, on logical grounds, add a third dimension to the theoretical and the practical—that of the sociological. This he bases on the idea that social relations are created and sustained by supernatural beliefs and practices. People come together in "flocks" or they seek professionals. They share beliefs and practices in common.

Although it is true that people and their beliefs and practices are the expressive vehicles for supernaturalism, many writers have discussed the dimension of experience from different and more specific points of view. These contributions seem seldom applied to the data we draw from primitive societies. We may look very briefly at three of these schemes that we can then think about as we examine the descriptive data that comprise most of the rest of this volume. We first examine the scheme of Frederick Streng (1969). He feels there are four ways of expression based upon how a person becomes "religious" and what such a person does. One way is to *personally apprehend the holy*. This is becoming aware of some greater reality/power than oneself. Streng generally defines this as God. As he puts it:

When a personal apprehension of the Holy is regarded as the prime way to be religious, there is a great emphasis on (1) the internal life of the individual and, (2) the intensity of his involvement in the transcendent reality. The unique quality of religious experience is emphasized; and such experience resists any attempt to communicate it in everyday language. Such total commitment sometimes involves the devotee in activities and interpretations of life . . . that are unintelligible or irrelevant to those who are not compelled by a similar apprehension of the Holy (Streng, 1969: 53).

In such expressions it is the individual and his or her personal experience of the supernatural that is emphasized. Many supernatural practitioners display such an expression, as do followers in many cults and religious movements.

A second expression according to Streng is in what he calls *myth and ritual,* which in this case have become all-important. Along the lines suggested by Eliade, these expressions become the symbol for the sacred reality itself; they become its manifestation. This is a much less personal expression, and the sociological element places an emphasis on ritualists and leadership, sacred places, and congregations. A third expression is called *harmony with cosmic law.* Here everyday behavior becomes the vehicle for expressing the conceptions of a higher supernatural reality. Ordinary activity itself becomes sacred, since it is "matching" the way things "really are." The emphasis is upon good works. Though all systems of supernaturalism pay at least lip service to how to live the good life, some—especially Eastern systems—make this a central focus. So, for example, in classic Hinduism performing one's caste duties and obligations and observing proper behavior was the way to gain sufficient karma so as to be reborn on a higher level of existence, to gain salvation. So also is this expressive emphasis found in Confucianism (which may not be a religion in the narrow sense). "In the Confucian focus on propriety [li], for example, the concern with human action itself dominates the character of religiousness. Confucius and his followers . . . directed their attention to the Tao [way] of men and provided little metaphysical speculation on the nature of man or the cosmos. Their concern was with rules of morality as the means and power whereby the truly noble and wise man was perfected" (Streng, 1969: 66).

The last of these four expressions of supernaturalism is *freedom through spiritual insight* or what is generally called the *mystical experience*. As in the first case, this tends to be individualistic, although there are sociological dimensions. In the mystical experience, one comes to grasp, via discipline and knowledge, the true nature of reality, however defined, and gains freedom from the ordinary world of human limitations. In some cases, one even becomes united with the higher reality. Probably all supernatural systems have some room for persons to exhibit such traits. Certainly the medicine man in primitive societies may be a person apart from others in his or her experience of the supernatural. Some systems, of course, emphasize such transcendencies more than others as the behavioral goal.

A second perspective along different lines is supplied by Stark and Glock (1968) who emphasize five dimensions of religiosity.

If we examine the religions of the world, it is evident that the details of religious expression are extremely varied; different religions expect quite different things of their adherents. . . . Beyond the differences in specific beliefs and practices, there seems to be considerable consensus among all religions on the general ways in which religiousness ought to be manifested. We propose that these general ways provide a set of core dimensions of religiousness (Stark and Glock, 1968: 14).

These they feel can fairly accurately be measured, and they comprise the following. First, there is the *ideological* dimension, the expression of belief. This can be formalized in some official creed or intellectualized in a more informal fashion. Such beliefs may contain descriptions of the nature of reality, of human beings and their obligations, and so on. This is the cosmology that is espoused by systems of supernaturalism. Closely related to it is the expression of knowledge, the *intellectual* dimension. This refers to the information held by a person regarding his or her religious organization, theology, sacred writing, history, and related matters. What do they know about their own beliefs and practices?

A third dimension is the *emotional,* the expression of feeling. This comprises the emotional responses of a person toward those things defined as supernatural—for example, pride, enjoyment, or fear. As in the above cases, this dimension can be measured from person to person as well as across societal lines. There is also the *ritualistic* dimension. This is the expression of actual practices and devotion—the activities of a person that are specifically defined or labeled as *religious* or *supernatural.* Not only can individuals differ with respect to this dimension (in involvement and frequency), but we may characterize societies as broader or narrower in such terms. Clearly primitive peoples infuse more of life with sacredness than do moderns, who tend to segregate such concerns to separate and limited behavioral realms.

Finally are the effects—the *consequential* dimension—the results of all the other dimensions in everyday life. For example, does one seek converts, use sacred ethics in interpersonal relations, and gain personal insight? As in the case of the expressions proposed by Streng, the dimensions of Stark and Glock have great potential for cross-cultural comparisons. In the United States, for example, it is felt that the emotional —the expression of feeling—is most important, with practice important but decreasingly so. Correspondingly, such dimensions as knowledge, at least for most people, are underdeveloped and not considered important. How many people know the history and theology of their own denomination? How would a primitive society rate in terms of these dimensions? Which would be most important? This is an area of urgent theoretical application for anthropologists.

The last scheme (of literally dozens) takes a somewhat different orientation. This is an approach taken by Rodney Stark (1965). "As we define the term, all religious experiences, from the dimmest to the most frenzied, constitute occasions defined by those experiencing them as an encounter between themselves and some supernatural consciousness" (Stark, 1965: 99). It is suggested that four varieties of such experiences exist. The first is the *confirming experience,* an experience in which one gains an intuition or feeling that one's beliefs are true. Here one senses, somehow, the presence of the supernatural. This may be in a general sense of "reverence, awe, or solemnity" that one may experience on a ritual occasion, or it may comprise a more specific sense of awareness of the supernatural, a feeling that it is present near you. For example, the feeling that God is with you in some beautiful place in nature. Stark points out that some people go no further than this in their experience of the supernatural.

The second expression is the *responsive experience,* which goes beyond the feeling of awareness of the supernatural to the idea that somehow the supernatural has also taken notice or account of the individual. The awareness is dual. Stark feels there are three ways by which the divine (supernatural) is thought to take such notice. These include salvational, in which the divine chooses in some way to protect or save the individual; miraculous, in which the divine intervenes on one's behalf in a specific situation; and sanctioning, in which the divine interferes in some way to punish or redirect an individual.

The third type of possibility is the *ecstatic experience.* This builds upon the first two experiences of confirmation and response by adding the dimensions of personal relationships; supernaturals and humans develop intimacy and affective contact. In some ways this is close to the mystical experience of Streng and is common in faith healing and in many cult activities. It is also quite common in primitive societies.

Finally, there is the *revelational experience.* "Here the divine has not only taken the person to his bosom, but into his confidence. The recipient is given a message concerning divine wishes or intentions" (Stark, 1965: 107). This may involve such phenomena as visions and/or voices—quite common at least for some types of people in primitive societies and in cult movements (see Chapter 6). Such experiences vary widely. They may be meant just for the individual or have wider application; they may agree with traditional notions or depart significantly from them; or they may be simply knowledge or special instructions that require action.

In examining briefly these four experiences, or the dimensions of Stark and Glock, or the scheme of Streng, one sees a great deal of theory potentially applicable to the societies traditionally studied by anthropologists. The vision quest of Plains Indians, for example, (discussed later) is certainly a revelational experience as well as fitting into categories in other classifications. Certainly what is needed is a scheme that blends these and other approaches into a more comprehensive and multidimensional taxonomy of supernatural experiences. This requires an urgent focusing of anthropological attention. We return to this topic in Chapter 7.

RITUAL ELEMENTS

Having discussed some perspectives on the various types of supernatural experiences, we can now examine from a theoretical vantage point what elements of behavior go into making up these experiences. What are the component parts of supernatural activities? How can we compare one supernatural system of practices with another? Here again anthropological theory has lagged behind description.

Charles O. Frake (1964) suggested a structural approach in terms of certain categories of behavior as he presented data on a Philippine society. "The first step in describing Subanun religious behavior is to describe the performance of offerings themselves in terms of discovered categories of constituent locales, objects, performers, and acts" (Frake, 1964: 115). Though applied only to a specific type of activity—offerings— this does constitute an element approach. The categories he used were *settings*—where the ritual takes place; *provisions*—the feast foods employed in the offerings; *paraphernalia*—the various other physical objects manipulated or employed in performance of the offering (especially altars); and *participants*—both human and supernatural. Those of a human nature he subcategorized into the audience, beneficiary, functionary (professional and nonprofessional), and assistant. Those of a supernatural sort he divided into four types: souls, spirits, demons, and gods. We discuss such subdivisions in appropriate later chapters. The point is that here are elements; some things that go into making up a supernatural activity and that, presumably, vary from occasion to occasion as well as cross-culturally. There is a place where people participate and interact with supernaturals by employing certain kinds of physical things. "To complete a description of the constituent structure of offerings there should be an analysis of the actions or routines followed in the performance" (Frake, 1964: 122). He then goes on to discuss the various types of activities or actions that make up such a routine—which are unique and which are repetitive and how one can predict such formats.

RITUAL SPECIFICS

This limited approach of Frake is highly suggestive. We need to define categories or elements of supernatural behavior both for comparative purposes and for data gathering, provided they do not impede our objectivity. It does seem, however, as though they ought to be of broader conceptualization and hence of application. It also seems logical to keep the actual elements separate from the "routines" or patterns of their application. Along these lines, the present text divides supernatural behavior into two main categories of description and analysis (following my own field research, Collins, 1968). We can first deal with *ritual specifics*. Under such a heading are listed and described all the various component parts of elements of a supernatural activity. These are the building blocks or paraphernalia used in the actual activity itself, as in Frake's provisions. How many such elements exist? The answer depends upon how broadly these categories or elements are conceived. Anthony F. C. Wallace feels there are thirteen minimal categories of such behavior which ". . . are always found in association with one another and which are the substance of religion itself" (Wallace, 1966: 52). Some of these categories are not entirely exclusive. We can list and very briefly paraphrase these categories as conceived by Wallace so that the student may gain a sense of the range of such phenomena and look for them in the descriptive accounts beginning in the next chapter.

1. *Prayer* is communication with the supernatural—giving thanks, requesting aid, or perhaps even keeping "on the good side" of the gods. Such an element is greatly variable by occasion and context, and may even include requests to spirits to refrain from possessing humans, i.e., exorcism.

2. *Music* is expanded by Wallace to include not only the

playing of instruments, but also song and dance. Such elements may also, of course, act as a means of addressing the supernatural and take an immense variety of forms from calm to frenzied.

3. *Physiological exercise* has to do with attempts at the production of states of euphoria and dissociation by affecting human physiology and psychology. This is accomplished by drugs, deprivation of the senses, mortification of the flesh, and deprivation of basic needs such as food and water. The effect in many rituals is to produce an ecstatic experience.

4. *Exhortation* involves communication with other human beings, generally via a leader–follower relation and comprising such phenomena as preaching, threatening, advising, and so forth, depending upon the ritual context in question. Such exhortors usually occupy some special relation to the supernatural itself.

5. *Reciting the code* refers particularly to the sacred literature and other aspects of the belief system—myth, cosmology, ethics, and related elements such as ideas and notions about the supernatural beings. Such is often discussed or recited in ritual contexts.

6. *Simulation* involves imitating things in ritual activities. This is not only along magiclike lines—pretending to kill animals—but may involve humans impersonating gods. All this ". . . supposedly produces an effect that would have been impossible to attain by applying energy directly to the object itself, since the object may be distant in space or time, inaccessible in a supernatural realm, or otherwise invulnerable to natural manipulation" (Wallace, 1966: 60).

7. *Mana* refers to the idea of gaining power from some sacred thing by the avenue of contact with that thing—by touching it. Such power may offer general benefit or bestow some specific capacity on the receiver. The power may come from the gods or other supernaturals or may be of the more impersonal, magical variety.

8. *Taboo* refers to the idea of not touching or coming into contact with certain things in the effort to prevent injury to human beings. This is the negative side of mana; if one can gain power, one can also be injured by such power. Taboo takes the form of prohibitions against not only touching but certain other behaviors displeasing to the supernatural as well.

9. *Feasts* involves the consumption of food items (eating

and drinking) in a supernatural context, or in a narrower sense, such behaviors as the blessing of ordinary food. Since consumption is often a part of supernatural activity, one often wonders if food and the realm of the sacred do not have some practical connection in early human experience.

10. *Sacrifice* is also a common supernatural theme, referring to giving things of value to supernatural beings in return for actual or expected favors. These, of course, vary from complete destruction of the offering to reuse by humans and from items of little value to those involving a real sense of loss to the worshipers.

11. *Congregation* reflects the sociological dimension of supernaturalism previously mentioned—the coming together of the adherents of a system into groups to engage in the acts discussed above. This does not discount any purely individual concerns and activities.

12. *Inspiration* is related to the experience of revelation as a dimension of supernaturalism and involves possession, ecstasy, and other supposed forms of interaction with supernatural beings or with the sacred. It is an alteration of mental and physical states of a more spontaneous sort than physiological exercise.

13. *Symbolism* involves the construction and use of special objects that are associated with gods, come to have power, or are reflections of the world of the sacred. The variety of such things is, of course, almost endless.

These categories give an indication of the range of elements that may be employed or appear in some ritual activity. Most of Wallace's components are of an "action" nature—meeting, sacrificing, praying, eating, touching, and so forth. It seems to the present writer that these might be simplified somewhat in number and at the same time might include other elements such as beings and powers that he appears to omit or take for granted. Then, too, symbolism in a wider sense can be associated with things other than those of an object nature. In my own research I distinguish only five general types of ritual specifics (components). *Material paraphernalia* are the basic material objects of any nature that are related to, manipulated, or used in any fashion in the activity. This includes the meeting place, altars, masks, magic stones, clothing, foodstuffs, and the like. *Ideological paraphernalia* are the nonmaterial components of such activity—the things said or done and the rules for behavior that relate to the component parts. Examples of this category include prayers, dancing, possession, and rules for passing objects. Although these are not material things in the same sense as the first category, they are distributed in a similar fashion throughout a ritual. *Human paraphernalia* refers to the participation of individuals and groups in the activity—leaders, congregation or clients, and onlookers. It is also concerned with such elements as the age and sex of participants and the number of participants. *Supernatural paraphernalia* refers to the presence (or absence?) of supernatural beings of any sort that are invoked, are made the objects of sacrifice, or are related to in the activity. It also includes more impersonal supernatural powers. The fifth category of specifics is *mythologic paraphernalia*. This includes the mythic underpinnings of the ritual in question, if such occur, or supporting myths for any of the other component parts. Also included under this heading are rationalizations of a nonmythic sort made by the participants, for example, what they feel they gain from their participation or what the ritual means to them.

Certainly there are many subcategories under each of these headings, but in the most general sense (and until research on supernaturalism explores each in a more systematic fashion) they do represent a minimal categorization—people, physical and nonphysical things, beliefs and ideas, and supernatural beings or powers. They are the ritual specifics (elements) that go together in making up the supernatural activity.

RITUAL STRUCTURE

The second main category of description and analysis is that of ritual structure. This incorporates the various component parts from the beginning to the end of the supernatural activity. It is the process of putting the various specifics into their proper contexts. As Wallace has put it with respect to his elements, "The program of a ritual may be regarded as a succession of discrete events belonging to one or more of the thirteen categories . . ." (Wallace, 1966: 68). These are the *routines* discussed by Frake. On this topic there has been some degree of anthropological work, although it has not yet altered many of our attempts at description.

Years ago, in a classic study of transition rituals—rites of passage—Arnold Van Gennep (English edition, 1960) pointed out that such activities (for example, initiation at puberty) could be subdivided into specific rites of separation, transition, and incorporation. These separate an individual from his or her old status, adjust the individual between statuses, and restore the individual by placing him or her into the new status. For example—boy, initiate, man.

These three subcategories are not developed to the same extent by all peoples or in every ceremonial pattern. Rites of separation are prominent in funeral ceremonies, rites of incorporation at marriages. Transition rites may play an important part . . . or may be reduced to a minimum . . . Thus, although a complete scheme of rites of passage theoretically includes preliminal rites (rites of separation) liminal rites (rites of transition), and postliminal rites (rites of incorporation), in specific instances these three types are not always equally important or equally elaborated (Van Gennep, 1960: 11).

These notions of subtypes or "phases" of ritual are meant to apply to a particular ritual situation, but other, later scholars suggest comparable phases may be of wider application. Edmund R. Leach (1961), for example, has pointed out the fact that supernatural activities, especially those involving sacrifices, are also mechanisms for changing the status of an individual from profane to sacred, or from sacred to profane. During the sacred status or condition (as Eliade would agree) there is a timeless element involved.

Viewed in this . . . way, the total sequence embraces four distinct phases or "states of the moral person".

Phase A. The rite of sacrilization or separation. The moral person is transferred from the Secular-Profane world to the Sacred world; he "dies".

Phase B. The marginal state. The moral person is in a sacred condition, a kind of suspended animation. Ordinary time has stopped.

Phase C. The rite of desacrilization, or aggregation. The moral person is brought back from the Sacred to the Profane world; he is "reborn", secular time starts anew.

Phase D. This is the phase of normal secular life, the interval between successive festivals (Leach, 1961: 34).

Although these phases correspond to conceptions of time and sacred–profane being, they can readily be employed for the description and analysis of many ritual activities. Because it may be both a change in secular status (boy to man) and ritual status (profane to sacred) that are involved in a ritual or simply in getting ready to perform it, my own feeling is that simplification of ritual phases—structure—is as important as it was for specifics. To this end we might simplify the three-phase structures of Van Gennep and Leach in the following manner. *Preparations* include all of the preliminary activities concerned with the performance of a ritual. This may include sacrilization; it may separate a person from his or her old status; it may simply involve getting the appropriate materials together. The *major activity* is the main event. It corresponds to the procedures performed in pursuit of the goal intended by the ritual—curing, hunting, giving thanks, and so forth. It reflects the high point of all the supernatural actions performed and may even be marked off as such by the performers involved. *Terminations* correspond to those activities that occur after the major portion of the ritual has been concluded. These may desacrilize participants, incorporate them into some new status, or simply be a leave-taking activity.

In sum, then, there appear to be three ritual phases in structure recognized in supernatural activities. Though these are called different things by different theorists and are said to have different functions, the fact that each of the three seems roughly comparable may be an indication of the usefulness of recognizing such a division.

Van Gennep	Separation (Preliminal)	Transition (Liminal)	Incorporation (Postliminal)
Leach	Sacrilization	Marginal State	Desacrilization
Collins	Preparations	Major activity	Terminations

Some authors have commented on other aspects of these ritual phases, especially that of the *major activity*. For example, Victor Turner (1964) has specifically dealt with the liminal (transition) phase of passage rites, demonstrating how the exhibitions, actions, and teachings involved at this time help the initiates to understand their cultural milieu in abstract terms and gives them ultimate standards of reference for their new status. Again, Collins (1969) has discussed the possibility that within the major activity itself there may be a heightened phase of sacrilization and one of desacrilization, even though the effect of the previous and subsequent phases (preparation and termination) is specifically to accomplish these tasks. At any rate, *ritual elements* have been viewed as comprising two general categories of phenomena: *specifics,* which comprise the constituent elements making up (or potentially so) a ritual activity, and *structure,* the actual program of events that occur. Each of these has been shown to be separable into a number of general divisions. We can now examine the last general topic dealing with aspects of supernaturalism, that of its general organization.

INSTITUTIONAL TYPES

When one deals with the organization of supernatural experience, there are many ways in which one can appreciate this dimension. Wach (1962) discussed family cults, kinship cults, local, racial, and national cults, as well as those based upon sex and age. For the most part, this approach is too specific. Some details of supernatural organization are supplied in Chapter 7. What we are interested in at this point, primarily, is some kind of overall general organization at an institutional level. Sociologists for many years have employed a general, if "ideal," typology that distinguishes between ecclesia, denomination, sect, and cult organizations, and we can briefly discuss each of these.

The *ecclesia* is ". . . extensive in its sphere of influence. The major characteristic of the Ecclesia is that it encompasses a broad territory, either national or international in scope. All children of members born within the territory are automatically, by virtue of birth, defined as members of the Ecclesia" (Vernon, 1962: 176). Because of its universality over an area, this supernatural institution often attempts to control the world in its own organizational interests, cooperating with or dominating the more profane aspects of society, including government. In fact, such societies may themselves be theocratic in orientation. The authority in this supernatural organization is highly centralized—ultimate power and doctrinal interpretation are concentrated in a few hands—and hierarchical. The emphasis is generally on formality and traditionalism, so such organizations are slow to change. The Roman Catholic Church of the Middle Ages is generally cited by sociologists as an historic example of an ecclesia. One may assume that many (most?) truly primitive societies fall under the ecclesia classification as well. What were the alternatives for an Eskimo or an Aborigine? In their attempts to extract data under often difficult conditions, anthropologists have generally not examined multiple possibilities of organization except in peasant or plural society situations, so this may be more apparent than real. Perhaps primitive supernaturalism may turn out not to be so "monolithic" in character.

The *denomination* is also a relatively stabilized group and ". . . a large group, well established and widely accepted by society" (Vernon, 1962: 172). It too recruits members primarily by birthright, although some members may be gained by the method of conversion. It is typically one of a number of supernatural organizations found in a given territory. It is fairly traditional and formal in its organization, with hierarchy and centralization in authority. However authority tends to be more varied than in the ecclesia. Generally speaking, the denomination, though it has less control over the profane aspects of life than the ecclesia, still cooperates with it, providing support for the ways of the secular world. It is suggested that a denomination is either a former ecclesia or some smaller supernatural group that has developed a high degree of stabilization.

The nature of the *sect* is quite different as an organizational phenomenon.

The sect, in contrast, is typically a small, exclusive group whose members join voluntarily, usually as adults. Authority is exercised by virtue of personal charisma rather than hierarchical sanction, yet nevertheless religious discipline is rigorous, and is commonly enforced by the mutual scrutiny of the group members. Sects are characterized by religious and ethical fervor. . . . Sectarian beliefs and practices sharpen the distinction between the small, closely knit group of sect members and the outside world (Nottingham, 1954: 63).

Behavior in sect situations often stresses spontaneity and emotionalism rather than the formality and traditionalism of the other groups, and the patterns of authority as indicated above are more personal. Sects reject rather than cooperate with the secular/profane world; and as a result they either withdraw from the world and create their own alternatives (Amish), or they may remain a part of the world and attempt to initiate changes more in keeping with their own doctrinal assumptions—becoming militant sects (Jehovah's Witnesses).

Finally, the *cult* is also a small membership group. Leadership, authority, and behavior are not formally structured, and acceptance of its beliefs is the only qualification for membership, which generally fluctuates widely. Such members may also belong to more traditional supernatural organizations, and the stimulus for membership, typically, is in response to feelings of frustration. Of the four organizational types, the cult is the least organized and the most transitory. Sect and cult phenomena are discussed in detail in Chapter 6.

Although sociologists have heavily utilized the above organizational scheme, anthropologists generally have not referred to it; nor have they dealt with this topic in a general theoretical manner. Such attention is obviously a matter of urgent necessity. Wallace (1966) again has made tentative statements in this direction and has suggested the use of a simpler model. He distinguishes four types of "cult institutions" (using cult in a different sense than above). These are *individualistic*, in which the leader–follower relation is not well defined (each person is his or her own magician–priest); *shamanic*, where a magician-type leader functions on behalf of clients; *communal*, where ritualists perform on behalf of groups but in which the layman is still important; and *ecclesiastical*, with a more formally organized priesthood who performs and centralizes responsiblity. Here the layman loses all but passive involvement. Wallace is to be applauded for his willingness to create such categories and suggest how they integrate in types of religions or systems of supernaturalism. A vast amount of research, however, will be required to arrive at a set of categories that adequately reflect the reality of the primitive situation. His categories have an uncomfortable overlap, and it is to be wondered just how much individual ritual really occurs.

RITUAL TYPES

If there are difficulties in defining major types of supernatural organization for primitive societies, so, too, are there difficulties in developing a typology for the ritual activities themselves. Again, somewhat unaccountably, anthropologists have made few theoretical ventures in this direction. For years we have made do with a simplistic twofold division of rituals into *rites of passage* and *rites of intensification*. The former are associated with transition situations for individuals or groups: birth, puberty, marriage, death, war, peace, and so on. All of the occasions mark changes in behavior. They are rather nonperiodic or critical in their distribution. Rites of intensification are of a more fixed or cyclical–calendrical variety and are generally of importance for all group members. They may correlate with changes in nature (spring, fall) or with the technological round of activities (harvest, movements of herd animals) or with astronomical events (phases of the sun or moon). They may mark changes in behavior but are more important in maintaining the solidarity and social equilibrium of the group.

As in the case of magic and religion, a dual division here does not really seem adequate to handle this topic; yet most leading texts devote less than one page to discussion of the variety of rituals. The exception, as one might guess, is Anthony Wallace (1966), who has made a valuable contribution along these lines. Once again we can briefly paraphrase his ritual scheme and then in succeeding chapters apply it to descriptive accounts. He discusses five major categories of rituals.

A. Technological Rituals

These ". . . are rituals intended to control various aspects of nature, other than man himself, for the purpose of human exploitation" (Wallace, 1966: 107). They are a supernatural means of manipulating environmentally related things for human benefit. Wallace feels there are three subtypes here:

1. *Divination* rites, which involve gaining information about the environment by discovering hidden knowledge and predicting the future.
2. *Intensification* rites, which involve controlling and obtaining the food necessary for life in hunting, gathering, herding, and agriculture.

3. *Protective* rites, which are undertaken to deal with the dangers and uncertainties found in nature—insects in the crops, bad weather for fishing, or perhaps just bad luck. All of these help to make nature amenable to those humans who dwell within it and exploit it.

B. Therapy and Antitherapy Rituals

The aim of these activities is to maximize human health or to interfere with or affect it in some manner. Here there are two subtypes, both seen as attempts to control human beings.

1. *Therapy* or curing rites that are performed to restore a sick person to health.
2. *Antitherapy* rites that are undertaken to harm people, witchcraft and sorcery being the most common varieties.

C. Ideology Rituals

These are ". . . intended to control, in a conservative way, the behavior, the mood, the sentiments and values of groups for the sake of the community as a whole" (Wallace, 1966: 126). There are various ways to accomplish this, and hence, a number of subtypes of rituals.

1. *Passage* rites, which deal both with changes in status of people and with geographical movements, i.e., marriage, trading.
2. *Social intensification* rites, like a Sunday morning service, which remind people of the nature of the sacred and of their obligations to it and to each other.
3. *Arbitrary ceremonial obligation* rites, like taboos, which also regulate human behavior or are symbolic of human concerns.
4. *Rebellion* rites, which instead of compelling or instructing people to perform the correct behavior, allow or require at least certain people to act in ways normally not permitted. Wallace feels this to be a "ritualized catharsis" that deals with such problems as frustration.

D. Salvation Rituals

These are designed to enable individuals to deal with their own personal problems of identity, self-esteem, and related difficulties. There are four subtypes:

1. *Possession* rites in which gods, demons, and so on take up temporary residence in human beings, permitting a person to alter his identity.
2. *Shamanic* rites in which a person (by means discussed in Chapter 7) comes to gain a new identity altogether (to substitute one for another), rather like permanent possession!
3. *Mystic* rites where, in essence, by merging with nature or the sacred, one loses identity altogether.
4. *Expiation* rites, which are attempts of a less drastic nature than those above to rebuild the old identity. This is usually accomplished by some kind of penance or engaging in good works. Confession and self-punishment are common forms.

E. Revitalization Rituals

These are rites designed to "cure" an identity crisis on the group or societal level, where more individualized salvation techniques are no longer effective. The result is often the development of a supernatural movement. The thinking of Wallace and other scholars on this ritual type and its varieties is examined in Chapter 6.

In sum, then, there is a classificatory scheme of five major ritual types with a number of subdivisional possibilities. This is far more complex and useful than the dual division previously mentioned. This does not mean it is a perfect rendition of the actual state of ritual affairs existing in some society or even the right approach. I personally feel that a classification based on structure rather than on function might be useful. However, it is the first attempt of any real degree of complexity, and anthropology is in Wallace's debt. In the next five chapters we deal with these ritual types in a general way. We take up technological rituals in Chapter 3, ideological (social) rituals in Chapter 4, those relating to human health in Chapter 5, and revitalization in Chapter 6. Since I believe that shamans and possession may be different types of phenomena, this ritual category is not discussed per se; but the shaman is dealt with in Chapter 7 under the heading of supernatural practitioners. Most of the emphasis in these chapters is descriptive, but where applicable or developed, theory is also included.

REFERENCES

Collins, John J.
> 1969. Transformations of the Self and the Duplication of Ceremonial Structure.
> *International Journal of Comparative Sociology* 10: 302–307.
———. 1968. A Descriptive Introduction to the Taos Peyote Ceremony.
> *Ethnology* 8: 427–449.

Firth, Raymond.
> 1967. *Tikipia Ritual and Belief.*
> Boston: Beacon Press.

Frake, Charles O.
> 1964. A Structural Description of Subanun "Religious Behavior." In *Explorations in Cultural Anthropology,* ed. Ward Goodenough, pp. 111–129.
> New York: McGraw–Hill.

Guthrie, W. K. C.
> 1955. *The Greeks and Their Gods.*
> Boston: Beacon Press.

Leach, Edmund R.
> 1968. *Dialectic in Practical Religion.*
> Cambridge: Cambridge University Press.
———. 1961. *Rethinking Anthropology.*
> London: The Atholone Press.

Levi–Strauss, Claude.
> 1963. *Totemism.*
> Boston: Beacon Press.

Levine, Morton H.
> 1957. Prehistoric Art and Ideology.
> *American Anthropologist* 59: 949–962.

Nilsson, Martin P.
> 1964. *A History of Greek Religion.*
> New York: Warton.

Nottingham, Elizabeth K.
    1954. *Religion and Society.*
        New York: Random House.
Stark, Rodney.
    1965. A Taxonomy of Religious Experience.
        Journal for the Scientific Study of Religion 5: 97–116.
Stark, Rodney, and Glock, Charles Y.
    1968. *American Piety: The Nature of Religious Commitment.*
        Berkeley: University of California Press.
Streng, Frederick J.
    1969. *Understanding Religious Man.*
        Belmont, California: Dickenson Publishing Company.
Turner, Victor W.
    1964. Betwixt and Between: The Liminal Period in *Rites De Passage.* In *Symposium on New Approaches to the Study of Religion,* ed. June Helm, pp. 4–20.
        Seattle: University of Washington Press.
Van Gennep, Arnold.
    1960. *The Rites of Passage.*
        Chicago: University of Chicago Press.
Vernon, Glenn M.
    1962. *Sociology of Religion.*
        New York: McGraw–Hill.
Wach, Joachim.
    1962. *Sociology of Religion.*
        Chicago: University of Chicago Press.
Wallace, Anthony F. C.
    1966. *Religion: An Anthropological View.*
        New York: Random House.

PART II

EXPRESSIONS

CHAPTER 3

Technological Rituals

Technological rituals are those employed by humans in the attempt to control nature or aspects of it. They manipulate the environment for human benefit. It will be remembered that in Wallace's scheme he designated three basic varieties: divination, intensification, and protection. It is most conceivable that other classifiers in the future may wish to add to the number of such types. The present chapter simply deals with some possibilities from a thematic approach, dealing with the major concerns involved. No attempt is made even to survey all of the generally agreed-upon types. Only some forms are given to supply the reader with the flavor of this general supernatural type.

DIVINATION RITUALS

One variety of technological ritual that has been reported on in depth for many groups is that of divination. Divination is the attempt to gather knowledge about things hidden from normal human perception either because these things are part of the future or because they are removed in space; for example, whether it will rain next week or the present whereabouts of the enemy. It also works to uncover information otherwise unobtainable; for example, the identity of a thief or adulterer. It should be pointed out that the application of the term *divination* is wider than just the environmental concerns suggested by Wallace. Since it overlaps with other concerns, it reminds us of the unreality of classification schemes.

Here we treat knowledge of other humans as part of environmental concerns.

Although the root of the term is *divine*, suggesting a relation to gods, divination techniques fall into both the categories of *magic* and *religion*. In fact most classifications of such techniques at least tacitly take such possibilities into account. In the desire to obtain needed information, literally no possibility seems to have been overlooked; and the level of scientific techniques for eliciting answers is no necessary indication of the presence or absence of appeals to divination. In our own society the popularity of astrology, tarot cards, and simple flipping of coins is testimony to the powerful urges gratified by divination.

How many specific techniques of divination exist? Few scholars have attempted to enumerate their totality except with reference to some particular society. H. J. Rose, in the *Hastings Encyclopedia of Religion and Ethics*, made a landmark general attempt by listing ten basic varieties. We may briefly paraphrase these, attempt some simplification, and then turn to specific descriptive cases. Rose indicated the existence of two main types, those that worked *automatically* without involving any supernatural being per se and *divination proper*, which did invoke the intervention of gods or spirits. Noting, however, the overlap in many cases, he simply listed his basic varieties in terms of the means employed by the diviner.

Dreams are one of the most common and widespread varieties, holding that knowledge is derived from the dream experiences of sleepers. The interpretations of such experiences vary—from the gods sending the message to the travels of the soul of the dreamer to visiting the spirit world or traveling in time or space. Of course, the information itself is variously assessed; it may be literal or the dream may require some further interpretation.

Presentiments are generally a lower level, personal type of divination. They work essentially by a person getting a feeling or hunch about something; for example, that one ought ought not to take a trip or hunt in some area. It should be emphasized that this is a before-the-fact kind of thing. The "I know I shouldn't have done it" feeling is not divination in this sense.

Body action may also be used to discover hidden knowledge or predict the future. By body action, Rose means various involuntary movements such as sneezing, stumbling, or dropping something. These actions are usually interpreted in preformulated terms as meaning good or bad luck, visitors coming, and so forth, rather than requiring on-the-spot interpretation.

Ordeals are fairly common in world distribution (especially Old World) and are usually connected to specific attempts to ascertain guilt or innocence and truth or falsehood. They are generally an adjunct to "legal" situations. Is a person a thief or a witch? The ordeal involves a suspect individual being forced to submit to some activity fraught with harm and danger. This experience may be a literal one—having to swallow poison or being tossed bound into water—or it may be that the danger is entirely supernatural. The taking, for example, of an oath of innocence may mean that a spirit will kill a liar. Again, the process may work out so that a person may be punished via the ordeal whether guilty or not or if guilty, be punished later. The belief may be that if a person is innocent the waters into which he is tossed will receive him; if not, he will remain on the surface—to be punished later by human agency. In the first case, if not promptly removed from the water, the innocent also suffers.

Possession. "Not only do spirits visit sleepers, but they often possess a diviner or priest, rousing him to a prophetic frenzy" (Rose: 777). This is a type of divination usually associated with a shaman or other professional worker in the supernatural and involves the conscious control of gods or spirits (see Chapter 7). Somewhat related to this is what Rose calls necromancy.

Necromancy is the practice of consulting the specific spirits of the dead, ghosts, or observing a corpse for hints of hidden knowledge; for example, the direction the hands point.

Animal types of divination also appear to have a near universal distribution. They, like the above two types, also are frequently in the hands of specialists. Rose distinguishes between those that bring results through observing the actions of living animals (augury) from those that involve killing the animal and inspecting its internal organs or gaining knowledge from the death itself (haurispicy). Great varieties in techniques of interpretation occur here.

Mechanical types, as a category, are perhaps the most variable and numerous variety, the specific types being almost countless. It involves people manipulating physical objects in some manner so as to produce an answer—one usually defined in traditional terms (heads means yes, tails means no in coin flipping). As do most anthropologists, Rose distinguishes between those that work purely by chance—like casting lots—and those that are subject to some manipulation, if only by unconscious muscular action—for example, a ouija board.

Nature types also exist, gaining knowledge or answers to questions from nature itself. Here also there are two main varieties: astrology, resulting in lucky and unlucky days and the like; and other natural phenomena, such as thunder and lightning, being given special meanings.

Miscellaneous divination is a category in which Rose catalogues types that may be fairly common but that do not easily fit into his other varieties; for example, the notion that a small misfortune may be a forerunner of one of greater severity.

Although the above listing is a useful classification attempt, most anthropologists seem to have opted for simpler schemes, or they merely list specific behaviors. For example,

There are two general types of divination, inspirational and noninspirational. In the former, answers are revealed through a change in the psychology or emotional state of the individual. . . . Noninspirational divination may be either fortuitous, such as finding meanings in black cats, hairpins, sneezing, and countless other omens, or deliberate, by means of astrology . . . ordeals, and the like (Lessa and Vogt, 1965: 299).

Since the second category contains an internal division, it seems reasonable to apply the same distinction to that of the inspirational variety. This results in four general divination types that cover fairly adequately the ground suggested by Rose.

	External (Noninspiration)	Internal (Inspiration)
By Chance	1	3
By Manipulation	2	4

In the first type the answer is gained from outside the individual in a purely fortuitous manner—for example, knowing what direction to take in hunting by observing a flight of birds. In the second type, the diviner is also seeking answers external to himself but is in some deliberate manner manipulating objects so as to produce knowledge "on demand" without having to wait for some chance event. An example here would be fortune-telling cards. In the third type, the answer comes from within the diviner via some psychophysical change, but it comes in a fairly nondeliberate fashion—as in dreams or in unsought cases of possession or in presentiments or body actions. The fourth type also seeks answers from within the individual but accomplishes this end by deliberately seeking an "inspirational" experience; for example, by deliberately communing with gods or spirits. In this category, we can also place ordeals, since these involve individual changes at least in the physiological sense. Based on these fairly obvious types we can now examine in detail some specific examples.

EXAMPLES OF DIVINATION

We can begin by discussing manipulative external types of divination, since these assume the greatest variety in primitive societies and appear as a general type to be the most common. An excellent account of the range of these techniques for a given society is given by Barrie Reynolds for the Barotse of Africa. Perhaps their most typical sort of techniques of this nature depend upon the use of a pattern of objects being manipulated. "By pattern divination is meant the use of a number of material symbols which, being shaken together and cast on the ground, provide answers by the positions they take up relative not only to each other but also to some outside factor or factors" (Reynolds, 1963: 100). Generally in the hands of professionals is the use of the *divining basket*. This is a shallow winnowing basket containing about one hundred symbols that represent aspects of the world—life, death, guilt, luck, and so on. When an answer is required, the diviner tosses the basket up and down a number of times, rearranging the contents until a pattern is established that can be interpreted. For example, should I take a boat trip? If the canoe symbol is upside down and near the symbol for death, a trip is not advisable! A more popular technique of pattern divination is the use of *divining bones*. These are also carved symbols of bone, wood, ivory, and horn with pre-established meanings. They are held in the hand or in a container and then cast on the ground or flat surface for subsequent interpretation. Such devices generally do not require a professional.

Another variety of manipulative Barotse external divination is of a simpler nature, yielding only yes–no sorts of answers. It involves the use of pointing devices. One such object is a *tortoise shell* filled with "medicine" and into one opening of which a bird feather has been inserted. The diviner places his fingers on the tip of the feather, and the shell moves along the ground toward either a symbol or a person, providing an answer by pointing. This technique is used in semidarkness to provide the illusion of supernatural forces directing the movement. Another pointing variety is the use of a *horn* or *stick*. This is held by two men, neither of which is the diviner, and is used to determine matters of guilt or innocence. When the men approach a guilty party their hands are made to gyrate violently or point the object to that individual. Another object so employed is a *gourd*, also filled with medicine and balanced on the hand. The diviner lets it fall, and the direction taken provides the answer. Finally, there is also the use of a small *mat*, which is folded in half and held by the fold so that the loose ends can swing free. An affirmative answer to some question—should I go hunting?—causes the mat to go rigid and straight rather than for the ends to go swinging back and forth.

Still another external manipulative type of divination among these people bases itself on revolving objects. Here also there are a number of discrete possibilities, all of which revolve on an axis with direction and speed of movement providing the answer rather than pointing. One example consists of the use of a *horn*. "A medicine filled duiker horn is attached, at one side of its mouth, to a short string which in turn is tied to the end of a small twig, fishing rod fashion. The diviner holds the twig so that the point of the horn just touches the ground and takes the weight of the horn. Answers are given by the direction clockwise or anti-clockwise . . . and by the speed at which it so circles" (Reynolds, 1963: 114). A final "mechanical" variety is that which employs the friction of one object upon another—a quite common technique in many African societies. Among the Barotse an *axe* is taken and laid on its side on the ground or on a grinding stone. The diviner holds it near its head and gently slides it back and forth along the surface. A question is posed and when the head no longer moves the answer is provided. Am I being harmed by . . . (a particular spirit) . . . ? The axe stops moving, so the answer is yes. Another variety here is the use of two wooden boards that are rubbed together. The Barotse manipulate a variety of objects in a deliberate fashion to obtain desired information: by pattern formation, by pointing or revolving, and by friction or sticking.

In other societies still other techniques of divination occur along comparable lines. Among the Bunyoro, another African society, John Beattie (1964) has reported the following. One way is to squeeze the juicy leaves of a special plant in the diviner's hands and examine the amount and disposition of the drips to determine the answer. Another possibility is to cut off the stem of a young banana plant and put a millet grain on the exposed surface. If the juice that comes from the stem removes the grain, the answer or outlook is unfavorable; if it remains on, it is favorable. Finally, there is the use of five small twigs with their bark peeled off; they are spit upon by the diviner and dropped into a water-filled basin. Their resultant pattern is then interpreted to provide the answer.

Still another manipulative means of divination occurred in an American Indian society, the Naskapi. Among these people aid in knowing where to hunt was considered all-important. Animal bones were constantly used in divination procedures (Moore, 1957), especially the shoulder blade of the caribou. Such a cleaned and dried bone was fitted with a handle and held over the hot coals of a fire for a brief period. As a result of the heat, cracks and burnt spots would form, and their pattern was interpreted by considering them in reference to the actual physical aspects of the environment— for example, cracks were equated with rivers. They then acted, based on the "road map" this technique provided.

As final examples of this general type of divination we can illustrate several uses of animals. Among the previously mentioned Bunyoro, a number of these devices for gaining knowledge occur. One example involves the use of a small forked stick (or grass stem), which is placed in the ground in a standing position. Since this is employed in prognosticating the outcome of illness, some saliva from the patient is placed upon the fork. The diviner places a beetle on the stem and observes its upward movements. If it moves toward the saliva, recovery is assured; if away from it, recovery is less certain. The veracity of such answers is often confirmed by appeal to other, more powerful forms of divination. Other forms of animal divination also occur in this society, especially the killing of chickens and the inspection of their internal organs. A classic example of chicken divining has been reported for another society in Africa, the Azande; and we can give some detail on this practice.

Among the Azande many answers about the future or hidden knowledge are gained by administering poison to chickens and observing the consequence of such action. "No important venture is undertaken without authorization of the poison oracle. In important collective undertakings, in all crises of life, in all serious legal disputes, in all matters strongly affecting individual welfare, in short, on all occasions regarded by the Azande as dangerous or socially important, the activity is preceded by consultation of the poison oracle" (Evans–Pritchard, 1937: 261). Some individuals are more prone to turn to divination for trivial matters than others.

A typical consultation situation would run about as follows. A man suspects he is being adultered and wishes to know the identity of the guilty party. He explains his anxiety to a diviner, and they set a time to meet in some private location to which the man himself must bring some chickens. Appropriate taboos must be observed beforehand to assure the efficacy and truth of the oracle. At the appointed time the diviner clears a space in the grass. Those concerned gather around, and the poison—in paste form—is forced into the beak of the chicken, which is then compelled to swallow it. The question is now put to the oracle (the poison inside the chicken), and often a second dose is administered. The questioner continues his questioning, often phrasing it in different ways, until some kind of result occurs. In some cases the chicken lives, in others it dies. The life or death supplies the answer, since the question is couched in such terms—if such and such is true, may the chicken die. In most cases attempts are then made to ascertain the correctness of the results.

There are two tests . . . If a fowl dies in the first test then another fowl must survive the second test, and if a fowl survives the first test another fowl must die in the second test for the judgment to be accepted as valid. Generally the question is so framed that the oracle will have to kill a fowl in the first test and spare another fowl in the corroborative test to give an affirmative reply, and to spare a fowl in the first test and kill another fowl in the corroborative test to give a negative reply . . . (Evans–Pritchard, 1937: 299).

The validations of such procedures are no doubt comforting to those involved who must act on the results.

We can turn now, briefly, to other varieties of divination. We look first to the chance type of internal or inspirational divination, which involves the use of dreams. Many societies, as previously mentioned, utilize dreams to discover hidden knowledge or to be apprised of the future. This became a central and important technique among the seventeenth-century Iroquois of northeastern North America. This was based, apparently, on the belief that a person's soul had hidden desires that it made known through the dream experience so they might be gratified (shades of Freud), lest the soul ultimately become frustrated and cause the death of the person whose body it inhabited. As a result the dreamer was naturally keen to dream and to have his dreams promptly interpreted (Wallace, 1958). Such interpretation was necessary since the content of the dream often obscured rather than revealed the true desires of the soul. Such dreams might be interpreted by the dreamer himself or by a special diviner (clairvoyant). Sometimes a second type of dream experience occurred in which it was felt that a supernatural being gave the message or supplied information. This revealed the supernatural being's wishes rather than those of the dreamer. It was imperative to understand and act upon these as well. This latter type was often a call to the individual to pursue a different life style, perhaps that of a supernatural practitioner.

Another variety of divination is that involving a more deliberate or manipulative internal source for knowledge. Here two examples may suffice, since we will cover some of these phenomena in detail in Chapter 7. The first case is what might be called a lower form—that of the ordeal. It occurs among the Bushong of Africa as reported by Jan Vansina (1969). This is one of their most important rituals and is employed when witch-caused misfortunes occur on a clan or village level. It involves administering poison to a woman who has been accused of witchcraft activities and is a complex rite typically involving the following procedures. The suspect is isolated, the officiant (diviner) is selected, and the accused is specially prepared. The diviner comes to the village and ritually prepares the poison while acting out how the witch will die. At this point the audience sings a series of songs relating to the practice of witchcraft. The diviner then holds two knives symbolic of danger and death and calls three times for the accused to appear. She answers his third call and comes to sit beside him. The accused swears an oath that if guilty the poison will kill her, or the diviner reinforces its effectiveness with a magical spell. Then further recitations occur, during which . . . "The accused drinks three small saucers of poison, followed by one of plain water . . . [and] . . . then goes out into the bush followed by the people. She chooses a place to sit and waits" (Vansina, 1969: 251, 253). If she began to die, she was (in the past) stomped to death. If she was able to vomit—a sign of innocence—she was saved and eventually underwent other rituals to reintegrate her back into the community.

A more high-powered form of external manipulative divination involves the direct intervention of spirits in possession. A classic world case of this comes from ancient Greece, represented by the famous oracle at Delphi. This site was a sacred place, especially to the god, Apollo, although perhaps earlier it was the abode of a mother goddess. Many city states sent representatives there to inquire as to the rightness or probable success of contemplated activities. "Greek states generally did not ask Apollo to originate their policy: They merely sought his sanction for what they had already determined upon, and invoked his blessing upon a project already conceived" (Dempsey, 1972: 40). Essentially, the procedures went about as follows. The diviner (priestess) would fast and then bathe in a sacred spring. She took omens, chewed laurel leaves, and drank from the spring. A small sacrifice (leaves and barley meal) was offered in the fire on a special altar, and then she mounted a special seat over a cleft in the floor of the cave from which, apparently, mephitic gas vapor escaped. Soon she would be overcome and would burst forth with prophetic utterances. These were felt to be given by the god, Apollo (or perhaps through him from Zeus himself), and were then either interpreted, or at least relayed, by an attendant priest. Such activities are also common in the primitive world in the form of shamanism, and additional examples are taken up later in this text. Likewise, additional material on divination such as its functions and results are dealt with when we return to a general consideration of supernaturalism in Chapter 10. We now turn to other general types of technological rituals, those that attempt control over the environment in a more direct fashion. These partly comprise those rituals Wallace calls *intensification*—food supply concerns.

OTHER TECHNOLOGICAL RITUALS: FOOD SUPPLY

We first examine rituals having to do with the hunting of wild animals. These range greatly from one society to another in emphasis, depending upon the degree of reliance upon such food resources. They also differ in complexity: from such simple observances as the wearing of good luck charms to increase hunting success or ward off danger, to lengthy rites dealing with the increase of the natural species, to the "worship" of those spirits thought to control their supply and abundance. An excellent example of this variety comes from Alaskan Eskimos as formerly exhibited in their *great hunting festivals*. "Everywhere in Eskimo Alaska impressive ceremonies under one name or another were given to honor and please the animals themselves or the supernatural beings that controlled them, so that the people would continue to have good hunting" (Lantis, 1947: 51). A number of such rituals occurred, all perhaps part of one big, supernatural complex associated with the concerns of hunting. This complex was believed essential for subsistence, since it placated those supernatural forces permitting success in such endeavors. All such rites apparently included fairly elaborate material paraphernalia as well as simulation of animal behavior and hunting techniques.

Perhaps the best-known ritual segment is the so-called Bladder Festival. The hunters of a particular group brought out inflated bladders of seals, walruses, and so forth that they had killed during the preceding year. These were painted and hung up in a special ritual structure. Wild plant material that had been dried was burned, the smoke purifying both the bladders and the male participants. At least some participants remained at all times in the ritual dwelling to keep a fire burning, and many taboos were observed so as not to frighten the "souls" of the animals involved. The hunters and boys took ritual baths each day and kept apart from women, who also were not participants in the direct sense. Dancing and singing, imitative of hunting and other activities, might take place over a several-day period. Small gifts of food and water were also offered to the souls of the animals and eaten ritually by the participants. Generally on the fourth day of the ritual the bladders were taken down, carried to a hole in the ice, deflated, and returned to the sea. On the return all group members apparently purified themselves in the smoke of a special fire, and the hunters themselves took a sweat bath in the ritual dwelling. Among many groups this festival would be combined with other ritual elements from the hunting complex. Periodically other types of hunting ritual occurred. Among one group, for example:

At the beginning of Winter an annual festival was given, lasting several days, which showed the products of the hunt. Mothers strung together the skins of birds and small mammals that their sons had killed during the year and hung them up, with a bird carved of wood placed in the middle of the [ritual dwelling] above a lighted lamp. The main part of the festival . . . was a distribution of gifts. A hunter danced, surrounded by his relatives, to an accompaniment of singing by everyone. At the end of his dance, he divided all the products of his labor . . . skins, foods, ornaments, etc. . . . After a feast, another man went through the same performance, and so on for all the strong hunters (Lantis, 1947: 60, quoting an earlier account).

Another variety of rituals dealing with wild food resources is well known in Australia as practiced among many Aborigine groups. These are called *increase rituals* and are part of a larger complex of behaviors generally known as *totemism*. Basically speaking, in these societies beliefs occur relating particular persons or groups to various natural species; such beliefs often imply a notion of supernatural descent from such totems and ritual obligations relating to their increase. Male individuals associated with a particular totem (i.e., witchetty grub or emu) perform rites intended to maintain or renew the numbers of the natural species. These may be quite simple but often attain great complexity. In the simple rite often just uttering the name or touching a rock painting of the species is sufficient. In more elaborate rites the miming of the behavior of the animal by masked or costumed dancers generally occurs, often accompanied by visiting sacred locations, uncovering sacred objects representing the totems, making drawings of them on a background of dried human blood, or shedding human blood from an opened arm vein onto the ground. Sexual cohabitation in a real or symbolic manner may also play a significant role in the attempt to increase the number or fertility of natural species.

All increase sites or objects, along with the ritual acts which are carried out, are associated with mythological and totemic characters. The general idea in all these rites is to get in touch with these beings, to draw on their power to achieve the particular goal the performers have in mind. . . .

Increase ritual need not concern only food. The goal may be rain; or it may be calm weather, as where rough conditions interfere with certain kinds of fishing. . . . Some rites can be performed on any suitable occasion. For others, the usual time is just before the period when the species concerned would normally increase—to make sure that they do. The Aborigines did not try to go contrary to nature . . . but simply to keep it going in a normal way (Berndt and Berndt, 1964: 230, 231).

For those people who have access to marine resources in great quantities, some of the focus of supernatural concerns may shift to fish and related foods and conditions of such a habitat. A typical example comes from the atoll of Ulithi in the Pacific (Micronesia). Among these people, "The ocean is a highway for travel and a major source of food, yet at the same time it is inconsistent and menacing. . . . It is noteworthy that of the four types of primary magicians recognized by Ulithians as being the most elevated of all, each has some involvement with the sea" (Lessa, 1966: 66). These supernatural leaders are those dealing with typhoons, navigation, fishing, and divination. We can briefly describe some activities of those who deal with attempts to insure the availability and supplies of fish.

Fishing rituals that are felt to benefit the entire society are carried out once yearly by specialists appointed by political leaders. Such rites begin in the main village. The specialists practice magic over a special canoe that is then taken to a special location where offerings are made to a sea spirit to help ensure that the rites will be effective. The various undertakings of the fish magician and his assistants now commence in earnest and last for two lunar months. Much of these rites consist of going out at night and attracting fish by dragging a sacred bundle tied at the back of the canoe through the water. Flying fish are attracted by the light from torches. The practitioners also engage in actual fishing expeditions and at all times are restricted by rather severe taboos: segregation from females, from eating certain foods, and the like. These continue after such magic has been completed, and the entire community is required to observe certain lesser taboos.

In still other societies, where the emphasis has shifted to dependence upon cultivated plants, there are agricultural rites. These types of rituals occur in an as-yet-unclassified variety of forms, but one can recognize (crudely) three major types. One is a type of ritual in which participants attempt to increase the food supply, generally by magic-oriented practices. The second involves giving thanks to the gods or spirits or nature itself for aid in food supply matters, and the third involves attempts to control other factors in crop growth— insects, rain, sun, and so forth. We may briefly give a few examples to demonstrate the somewhat different character of these rites.

The Apa Tanis of Northern Assam (India) exhibit ritual endeavors that fit into the first category. These people represent a society in which rice grown on irrigated terraces is a staple agricultural foodstuff along with other crops for variety. This is reflected in the fact that their two main public festivals have to do with crop success and are held at the beginning of the agricultural season. The first of these rituals, the *Morom,* is an annual affair and involves the welfare of all of the villages in Apa Tanis society. Basically, it involves the following procedures. Priests in ceremonial dress lead single file processions of young men and boys from village to village.

The priest waves a fan of feathers and scatters husked rice grains as he walks across the fields, and the boys and young men brandish swords and beat brass plates in the manner of gongs. As they lift the flashing blades of their Tibetan swords, they utter rhythmic shouts, but the priest keeps on chanting prayers until the procession reaches a village. An older man accompanies the procession carrying a basket of rice-flour, small quantities of which he distributes in the villages visited by the procession (Furer–Haimendorf, 1962: 138, 139).

Every so often as the processions move along, young boys will leave the file and gyrate around while holding huge bamboo phalli. Both the scattering of grain on the fields that are soon to be cultivated and the waving of symbolic sexual organs have functions in supernaturally ensuring the abundance and success of the agricultural growing process itself. Each of the processions spends the entire day visiting each of the Apa Tanis villages in turn, and in each they are entertained with food and drink. At the same time this ritual is held, there may also be rituals staged by individual wealthy men who wish thereby to increase their own prestige. This reminds us that many different elements may become intertwined in ritual contexts. Along these lines the other ritual, the *Mloko,* is held by each village only once in any three-year period—by rotation ensuring that it, too, is an annual event. Along with the gift exchanges and ritual games that occur:

The religious side of the Mloko consists mainly of sacrificial rites celebrated separately by the different clans, but intended for the general welfare of the people. The priest representing his clan . . . performs these rites at a clan-sanctuary in a garden inside the village; pigs, chickens and a dog are sacrificed. The deities involved are the divine pair . . . as well as . . . a deity associated with the earth. The timing of the Mloko at the beginning of the cultivating season, the performance of the sacrificial rites in a village garden, and the worship of an earth deity are obvious pointers to its character as a spring festival aimed at the enhancement of the fertility of the land (Furer–Haimendorf, 1962: 141).

As an example of the second variety of agricultural rite we can turn to the Iroquois people of New York State who in the past (and in part today) conducted a series of rituals of this general type. Six regular festivals along these lines took place each year in a cyclical fashion. One of these is of broader compass and will not be discussed in this context. The five in question were—in time of their yearly occurrence—the Maple Festival, Planting Festival, Berry Festival, Green Corn Festival, and the Harvest Festival, running from spring to fall respectively. We may examine some of this ritual cycle. The general idea of the *Maple Festival* was not only to give thanks to the maple itself for its sap, which was variously utilized, but to the major god himself for the gift of this remarkable tree. As in most rites the actual ritual was preceded by a confession of sins. On the main day women would prepare food, and games would be held until noon when everyone went inside the ritual structure (long house) in which the rituals were held. A religious official delivered an opening speech relating to the purpose of the ritual and to the associated deity. Other speakers gave talks on "spiritual guidance." The Great Feather dance followed as an outward expression of thanksgiving and involved dancers circling musicians in the center of the long house.

After the conclusion of this dance others followed, in which all participated. Before they were ended, the usual thanksgiving address to the Great Spirit, with the burning of tobacco, was made. In ancient times the Maple Festival was terminated with these dances. One of the keepers of the faith made a closing speech, after which the people partook of the feast, and separated for their respective homes (Morgan, 1954: 192).

When it was time to plant seeds, the *Planting Festival* was held to give thanks to the associated deity for the coming of the planting season itself and to invoke his blessing on the seeds. The format was very much like that of the Maple Festival. When wild strawberries had ripened, this was also noted in the performance of the *Berry Festival*, which, again, closely duplicated the ritual procedures of the first two festivals of the year.

At the first appearance of corn (indicating possibilities of abundance) a somewhat more involved ritual was held that lasted four days. This was the *Green Corn Festival*. The first day was generally like that of the previous rites. The second day involved a special thanksgiving dance. In its basic format it was ". . . like the Feather dance, the chief difference between them being the introduction of short thanksgiving speeches between the songs of the dance" (Morgan, 1954: 201). By the time of its conclusion all the important objects in nature had been taken notice of and honored. This was followed by other dances and the usual feast. On the third day, the highlight was a special thanksgiving concert in which different persons successively gave short speeches and songs. These again gave thanks to natural objects but also extended their praise to include human beings—their achievements, aid, and generosity during the past year. The fourth day concluded the ritual with games. At the time of gathering in the fall crops, there was another four-day ritual, the *Harvest Festival*. This was primarily to render thanks to/for the agricultural staples—corn, beans, and squash. The associated deities were also the object of praise. "Nature having matured and poured forth her stores for their sustenance, they instituted this ceremonial as a perpetual acknowledgment of their gratitude for each returning harvest" (Morgan, 1954: 206). This rite approximated that held for the appearance of green corn. We can turn now to the last major variety of agriculture-related rituals.

Among the Papago of the American Southwest, a rain-making ritual took place in July, coinciding with the usual advent of the rainy season and also marking the beginning of their yearly cycle. The chief behavior of this rite consisted of fermenting and drinking a mildly alcoholic beverage from the juice of the giant cactus of their region. The idea involved was that the saturation of the bodies of the participants with drink would magically produce the saturation of the earth with rain. The preparations for this rite consisted of the women going to groves of the cactus and collecting quantities of sap. As they did this, old men would recite speeches dealing with the origin of such activities. They would then return to their villages. Certain objects of great supernatural power (fetishes) were then brought to a special ceremonial house as aids in proper fermentation and eagle down was placed there as a special offering. A special person would be appointed to preside over the fermentation activities. Special songs were sung, and people danced outside to assist in this process. The dancing took place for two successive nights, and during pauses in the dance, shamans were called upon to make rain magic. "In former days the shamans often performed rain magic at this time. Tradition says that they would walk to the string of eagle feathers hanging over the dance place, shake it, and cause drops to fall" (Underhill, 1969: 49, 50). Some data exists concerning sexual license at this time. While some apparently kept their wives and daughters at home, there were women whose activities in this regard apparently furthered the ends of securing fertility. The fermentation itself was also carried on with great ritual inside the ceremonial house with magical spells, guards, and a special taster assisting the leaders.

At the main rite of consumption of the drink a local village representative plus three guests occupied the four directional positions (sometimes four shamans from the same village). They most probably represented the rain gods of these directions. The guests were invited by messengers who delivered formal speeches of invitation. After everyone had gathered near the ceremonial house and the guests had been seated, more formal recitations were delivered and special cup bearers brought the drink from the house to the main participants. They each drank a portion and sang four rain-charm songs. They also dripped the drink from their fingertips onto the ground, symbolizing rainfall. Two typical songs are given below:

> Am not I a shaman!
> I cause the wind to run.
> My elder brother the land it floods with water.
> Am not I doughty!
> I cause the cloud to fly.
> My younger brother the mountain it washes with water.
>
> [again]
>
> Just yonder a cloud comes forth,
> And here it trembles,
> Soft thundering.
> Just yonder a mist grows long,
> And here it trembles,
> Softly drizzling. (Underhill, 1969: 62)

Subsequent to this main rite, everyone went to their own houses and consumed the drink thay had fermented until the supply had been totally depleted. Men went visiting from house to house to aid in this endeavor. During the time of consumption, those who vomited were considered as "throwing up clouds" in keeping with the symbolism of this occasion. After the conclusion of this rite, both rain and crop growth were considered as generally assured.

The Papago rain-making rite was, of course, part of a larger ritual cycle of activities relating to food. For the sake of some completeness and as further examples of this variety of technological supernaturalism, we may briefly summarize some of these behaviors. In the past, planting occurred after the rain ritual, and the growing season itself had a number of rites and observances. Even before the crop cycle, pilgrimages were made by some village members to shrines (piled-up stones) to renew them so that winds and floods would not come and destroy the crops. These shrines appear in myth where children were sacrificed to prevent such occurrences. Men would whittle cactus sticks symbolic of cornstalks, take down the old fence around the shrine, and use these to erect a new one. The stones were unpiled, bead offerings deposited, and then the pile was rebuilt. A special speaker made a recitation to the four directions to ensure cultivated food crops as well as a plentiful supply of wild plant foods. After their return, the night was spent singing special songs in the ceremonial house. Those villages lacking such special shrines used the main village fetish in charge of the main ritual leader, who would smoke over it and recite the appropriate formula.

During the actual cycle of plant growth, a great deal of song magic took place. Some villages left this to the individual farmer; others utilized special leaders for this task; some used a community song approach. In all cases such singing encouraged growth and fertility of crops. Images were made, representing the crops expected. Legends were recited and shamans assisted.

After four songs the shaman took up one sample of each fruit in succession, blew upon it, held it up, and asked help of the rain houses of east, north, west, and south. As the singing proceeded, he looked about, as he would look for a war party, to see if danger threatened the crop from any direction. If he foresaw the coming of a pest, blight, or sorcery, the company sang the songs to avert evil . . . (Underhill, 1969: 83).

The images were later placed in the fields to ensure the success of crop growth.

Some villages also appear to have had a green corn festival at the time the ears were forming and the size of the expected harvest could be estimated. Again effigies representing crops were placed in the ceremonial house; rows of boys and girls danced, and the village fetish was ritually opened to lend its power also to continued growth. After harvest of the crops, still other rituals of the food cycle occurred. "Another ceremony which always took place in the Autumn just before the people moved to the winter village was called the deer dance or cleansing ceremony. Its object was to work magic over all the crops which had been gathered and over the first deer of the season, to make them safe for eating during the winter" (Underhill, 1940: 50). A special deer was hunted and killed. It was cooked along with plants from the harvest. Old men sang while younger men and women danced. The songs made deer easier to kill, and the speeches that were made had the function of sanctifying the food objects. During the dancing, shamans removed any evil from the foods by sucking it out of them. After the deer meat was distributed to the people, they rubbed it over their bodies to ensure good health. And still other rituals occurred. We can turn now to the last variety of technological rituals to be considered in this chapter.

OTHER TECHNOLOGICAL RITUALS: WORLD CONTROL

So far we have discussed a variety of technological rituals: those that gain information about the surrounding physical and social world via divination and those that deal more directly with the food supply in some manner—for hunting, agriculture, rain, and similar concerns. There are certainly many other supernatural rituals or observances practiced by peoples in most primitive societies today or in the past that fall into this general category. These include those rituals Wallace calls *protective* (to ward off dangers) as well as activities surrounding many aspects of life to make activities or things more effective—for example, in building a canoe or house, celebrating the first animal kill of a season or of a young hunter and the like. One class of rituals that are of some range of world distribution (but that Wallace's scheme seems to make no account of) are those that might be called *world control rituals*. These are attempts, either individual or collective, to gain power or control over the general circumstances of life or the world itself, thereby increasing human mastery over them. These may also have the function more specifically of renewing nature and the world. If technological rites are designed to control nature or aspects of it, it appears that these rather general-purpose rites belong in this category as well. We can examine two varieties of this type of general ritual.

Good examples of *individualistic world control rites* occurred in the past among many of the American Indian societies that occupied the Great Plains area. Here young boys grew up with the notion that to succeed in life—as a hunter, warrior, trader, whatever—one required a personal revelation or vision from one or more supernatural beings. If properly requested, these would appear and impart special knowledge and objects to the supplicant, which would give that person greater-than-normal abilities—hence, a better ability to deal with the world. Such experiences were usually sought during the period of youth but might well be repeated in later life if some crisis required special supernatural aid. The Crow Indians are an excellent example of this general ritual concern. In this society a youth would observe the following procedures.

Most probably he would set out for a lonely mountain peak, fast, thirst, and wail there. . . . Almost naked, the god-seeker covered himself with a buffalo robe at night as he lay on his back facing the east, his resting place being framed by rocks. Rising at day break, he sat down towards the east. As soon as the sun rose, he laid his left forefinger on a stick and chopped off a joint. This he put on a buffalo chip and held it out towards the sun, whom he addressed as follows: "Uncle . . . you see me. I am pitiable. Here is a part of my body, I give it, you eat it. Give me something good. Let me live to old age, may I own a horse, may I capture a gun, . . . Let me get good fortune without trouble" (Lowie, 1956: 239, 240).

Subsequent to this, a number of days and nights would be spent in fasting until the visionary spirit appeared. Other devices of self-torture and mortification of the flesh might also be used in an effort to convince a kindly spirit of the earnestness and sincerity of one's intentions. Sometimes such a vision might occur in an unsought fashion and without hardships. Sometimes more than a single spirit might render aid in this manner. The type of aid given also differed somewhat. Sometimes the spirit visitant would transmit some of its own powers, other times merely instructions on how to put together a sacred bundle containing objects that gave powers to their owner; sometimes all of these would be involved. Special spells and the necessity to observe lifelong taboos were also constant elements in such behaviors. In all cases, "Visions . . .

were the basic means of controlling life, and virtually every man tried to secure one" (Lowie, 1956: 248). In the event one tried and failed to secure his own vision experience, one could often purchase such powers from someone else, usually a relative. So power for general control over life or an aspect of it was transferable. Such vision activities generally duplicate the spirit quest of the shaman in most societies, and in fact if the powers gained here were extraordinary or along special lines the recipient would come to function in a professional capacity. Such more highly developed and continual behaviors are discussed in detail in Chapter 7.

There are also *collectivistic world control rites*. Although these give people control along the lines of those of a more individual nature, they often do so in a context of renewing or strengthening the world for another season or year. We may give two examples of varieties of such rites. The first comes from the American Southwest as part of the Hopi Indian (Pueblo) yearly religious cycle. This is the *Soyal* or winter solstice celebration. This is one of their key rituals, since the rather fixed schedule of Hopi annual rites is mostly determined by a special priest observing the positions of the sun. The year is divided into ritual seasons, and the period between the winter and summer solstices is the time for most important rites. Specifically, the Soyal emphasizes the annual cycle of the sun progressing from one solstice point to another, at this time starting back to its summer "home." This brings warm weather for plants and nature. The rite thus functions as an aid in the renewal of nature but also includes many other elements such as fertility, bravery, good health, crop germination, and general blessing for all Pueblo members. We can discuss its general format in simple terms, although Pueblo rituals are lengthy and complex rites.

The participants in this rite are those persons belonging to four general, tribal religious organizations. The rite itself is under the control of the village chief assisted by society leaders. Preliminary rites prior to its beginning include purification, prayer, and the manufacture of offerings. The first three days consist of relatively minor activities—the manufacture of more offerings and construction of altar paraphernalia. On the fourth day, war fetishes are taken into the chief religious structure (kiva), and offerings are deposited at shrines. A war priest impersonates a war god, and war "medicine" is made, which—during a series of songs—is smeared on the bodies of participants for bravery and blessing. During one song the priest is symbolically attacked and fends off attackers. Later, medicine water is drunk by participants who retain some to rub on kinsmen for health and bravery. More dances occur in the evening (see Titiev, 1944).

The fifth day is mainly comprised of a number of evening impersonations of the Hawk Man (war bird). In these a number of participants imitate the actions of a hawk. The dancers flop symbolic wings and ritually handle a bow and arrow, screeching all the time in a vigorous manner. The sixth and seventh days are mostly given over to preparing altar paraphernalia. On the eighth day, corn meal and pollen are taken throughout the pueblo so that people may breath on them, perhaps as a charm against illness. The altars are erected and corn ears are collected and brought to the kiva. Special dancers appear who pantomime sexual desire. "They began running among the spectators outside the kiva, taking a hold of a woman from behind here and there and going through the motion of copulation . . ." (Dorsey and Voth, 1901: 45). After these dancers leave (having aided fertility), the war priest repeats his medicine-making rites, and in the evening the hawk dance is repeated. Before dawn on the ninth day, some participants bring a screen fixed with the representation of the main god of germination into the kiva. This holds a grown cornstalk in one hand, and there are symbols of rain and lightning over his head. Moon and sun symbols are also represented, and a variety of seeds have been affixed to the screen, which are scraped off ritually by the main leader. Then a special priest enters and performs a dance while singing in accompaniment. His costume includes a headdress in the shape of a four-pointed star. His dance is climaxed by the twirling of the sun symbol—a disk with a face in the center and with feathers radiating out from its edges. The twirling of this symbol represents the going and coming of the sun. After this (which concludes prior to sunrise), the participants leave and deposit further offerings at shrines with prayers for success in hunting for males and long life and fertility for females. The seeds, now consecrated, are kept until spring planting. After this, the major dance cycles of the rest of the ritual calendar begin.

Another case of this type of renewal/control activities comes from the Near East where they were common in many ancient civilizations. Here the king was a major figure in an annual ceremony of this nature. The Babylonians may serve as a specific example. "In the New Year Festival in Babylon the celebration of the annual renewal in nature and society was enacted in very intimate association with the Creation Epic . . ." (James, 1963: 81). This myth recounted how the world was created out of chaos by the mingling of "sweet waters," personified by a male creator god (Marduk), with the salt waters of the ocean, represented by a consort female deity. This myth duplicated the flowing of the Tigris and Euphrates Rivers into the sea, producing luxuriant vegetation and fertility for crops. This story was recited during the rites, the Akitu festival.

The rites themselves were preceded by a variety of preparatory activities. The high priest purified himself and called upon Marduk to bless the city and look over his special temple. Paraphernalia were constructed by special craftsmen. On a subsequent day the priest continued prayers asking the god's blessing for the city and prayed also to the consort goddess, Sarpenit, to give life to the people and intercede with Marduk on their behalf. Later the priest recited the creation myth in its entirety, part of which concerned the death and rebirth of Marduk himself as part of his battle with chaos during the creation. In subsequent activities much symbolic action suggested the temporary death of Marduk (as well as the passing of the last year). The temple of Marduk was then purified and consecrated by being cleansed and sprinkled with holy water from the two rivers and having the sacrificed body of a sheep wiped over it and disposed of to remove evil. The king and the priest then entered the temple, and the priest struck the king and forced him to his knees in penance and expiation before Marduk (the king represented the people). This act was followed by a ritual confession by the king and the act of absolution and renewal blessing by the priest (acting for the god). These participants then made a major offering to Marduk. This constituted the major renewal ritual and suggested the mythic return to life of the god. Later processions and a feast—to which other gods were invited—were held for the king, priests, and attendants. At the end of the festival the king retired to ritually cohabit with his wife, symbolizing the union of god and goddess and reinforcing the creative process of spring in nature. "Generative force having been once more made to flow freely to sustain nature, the gods returned to their respective cities, the king went to his palace to continue his vital functions, and the men to the cultivation of the revitalized soil in sure and certain hope that now all would be well in the new year, the prosperity of which had been assured" (James, 1963: 88, 89). We can turn now to a second major category of ritual, which Wallace designates as *ideological rituals.*

REFERENCES

Beattie, John.
    1964. Divination in Bunyoro, Uganda.
        Sociologus 14: 44–61.
Berndt, Ronald, and Berndt, Catherine.
    1964. *The World of the First Australians.*
        Chicago: University of Chicago Press.
Dempsey, T.
    1972. *The Delphic Oracle.*
        New York: Benjamin Blom, Inc.
Dorsey, G. A., and Voth, H. R.
    1901. The Orabi Soyal Ceremony.
        Field Museum of Natural History Anthropology Publications 3: 5–59.
Evans–Pritchard, E. E.
    1937. *Witchcraft, Oracles and Magic Among the Azande.*
        Oxford: Clarendon Press.
Furer–Haimendorf, Christoph Von.
    1962. *The Apa Tanis and Their Neighbors.*
        London: Routledge and Kegan Paul.
James, Edwin Oliver.
    1963. *Seasonal Feasts and Festivals.*
        New York: Barnes and Noble, Inc.
Lantis, Margaret.
    1947. *Alaskan Eskimo Ceremonialism.*
        Seattle: University of Washington Press.
Lessa, William A.
    1966. *Ulithi: A Micronesian Design for Living.*
        New York: Holt, Rinehart and Winston.
Lessa, William A., and Vogt, Evon Z., eds.
    1965. *Reader in Comparative Religion.* 2nd ed.
        New York: Harper and Row.

Lowie, Robert H.
    1956.   *The Crow Indians.*
            New York: Holt, Rinehart and Winston.
Moore, Omar Khayyam.
    1957.   Divination, A New Perspective.
            American Anthropologist 59: 69–74.
Morgan, Lewis Henry.
    1954.   *League of the Ho-de-no-sau-nee or Iroquois.*
            New Haven: Human Relations Area Files Reprint.
Reynolds, Barrie.
    1963.   *Magic, Divination and Witchcraft Among the
            Barotse of Northern Rhodesia.*
            Berkeley: University of California Press.
Rose, H. J.
    N.D.   Divination (Introductory and Primitive).
            Hastings Encyclopedia of Religion and Ethics.
Titiev, Mischa.
    1944.   Old Orabi.
            Peabody Museum Papers 22: 1–277.
Underhill, Ruth.
    1969.   *Papago Indian Religion.*
            New York: AMS Press.
————. 1940.   The Papago Indians of Arizona and Their Relatives
            the Pima.
            Indian notes and customs pamphlets 3: 1–68.
Vansina, Jan.
    1969.   The Bushong Poison Ordeal.
            In *Man in Africa,* eds. Mary Douglas and Phillis
            Kaberry, pp. 245–275.
            London: Tavistock.
Wallace, Anthony F. C.
    1958.   Dreams and Wishes of the Soul: A type of psycho-
            analytic theory among the seventeenth century
            Iroquois.
            American Anthropologist 60: 234–248.

CHAPTER 4

Social Rituals

The technological rituals discussed in the previous chapter dealt with the control or understanding of the environment, including other humans as part of that environment. In the understanding of Wallace, ideological rituals have as their main thrust the specific control of human beings. It will be remembered that this is generally a conservative type of control in the attempt to further the interests of the community as a whole. As in the case of the first general ritual category, these rituals take many forms depending upon their intent and structure. In the present chapter we can discuss a number of general types. These are not entirely conceived along the same lines as in Wallace's scheme; so here they are designated simply as *social rituals*. It should also be understood that there are certainly more types than are discussed here. Anthropology has yet to progress to a stage in religious studies where adequate typology construction is possible for ritual types.

PASSAGE RITUALS

As used here, *passage rituals* will refer to those supernatural activities that may accompany the transition of a person or group from one status in society to another. Perhaps the most visual of these surrounds the physiological stages of birth, puberty and/or adulthood, and death. Few societies fail to mark at least some of these with appropriate rites. More purely social stages of "growth" may also require supernatural markings: marriage, ascension to political office, membership in secret societies, and the like. Generally speaking, it is in such passage rituals that the ritual phases discussed in Chapter 2 become most evident, since at least one major emphasis in such rites is to mark change. These and other functions are discussed in Chapter 10. We can illustrate examples of two types of passage rituals in the present chapter, those concerned with puberty—initiation rites—and those marking the physical demise of the individual—death rites. These are most common and generally the most elaborate of this general ritual category.

Since initiation rites for boys are more common and generally more elaborate than those for girls, we discuss these first. In Australia, classic examples of such rituals occur. Although various Aborigine societies undertake to perform different procedures, it is possible to construct a sort of amalgamated account of the general program of events that is adequate for the present illustrative purposes. The following description closely follows those of A. P. Elkin (1964) and Ronald and Catherine Berndt (1964). The general stages of ritual went as follows:

Preliminary Rituals—The Taking of the Novice: Subsequent to a decision that enough boys of the proper age exist for initiation, the young novices are taken from the living areas of the camp. Rituals at this time strongly suggest in symbolic terms that they must leave their youthful status behind. Adult males often attempt to physically drag them away and ". . . they take refuge with their mothers and the other women. As the men seize the boys, some of the women grab spears and pretend to defend them . . . others wail . . . and some of their close female relatives cry. Eventually, after this mock fight, the boys are removed to the sacred ground" (Berndt and Berndt, 1964: 139, 140). At this time other ritual procedures may also occur. These include painting the novices with red ocher or human blood, throwing fire over their heads, and piercing their nasal septa.

Further Preliminary Rituals—Arrival at the Sacred Area: In the past as various groups met at the sacred area, a ritual combat often took place, functioning at least partly to settle any past grievances before the parties to the ritual performed it, strengthening the attitude of cooperation and solidarity. This was usually followed by feasting—in some areas of a cannibalistic nature to dispose of anyone killed in the previous combat. The novices apparently did not usually take part in these activities.

Further Preliminary Rituals—Symbolic Death: These rites serve "magically" to separate the novices from their youthful status and involve their symbolic death. In many cases they act as though dead and are carried about and may be laid over the crossed spears of the men. Women cry as though their sons had been killed.

Main Ritual—Body Operations: As part of the transition portion of initiation rites, a number of manipulations of the bodies of the novices take place. There are a number of these, and depending upon the tribes in question, one usually is considered the main concern. These "operations" include the following: removal of body and face hair, knocking out one or more front teeth, scarification, circumcision, and sub-incision—this latter involving slitting the underside of the penis. These rites are stern tests of the manhood of the novices. Speaking of circumcision, ". . . men form a table on which the novice is held down: the foreskin, held by one man, is cut off with a stone flake . . . Nothing is done to stem the flow of blood, which soon dwindles: but the Wiranggu sometimes apply a fire stick to the bleeding penis" (Berndt and Berndt, 1964: 143). The foreskin may be eaten by a specially designated person, kept in a special container, or buried.

Main Ritual—Period of Seclusion: The novices are now indeed dead, and they spend a variable interval of time away from the camp and normally may not be seen by any of the women or uninitiated persons. They are in the world of the sacred. During this seclusion these "in-between" persons are given instruction in the sacred lore of the tribe, shown other rituals, and exhorted as to their adult responsibilities.

Main Ritual—Blood Ceremony: For most groups,

. . . at some part of the initiation series a blood rite is performed. It consists of anointing the newly initiated with arm-blood from the older men, or else giving them some of this to drink. The older men also anoint themselves or each other and drink blood. This blood is sacred; there is a secret name for it, and . . . it gives life, strength, and courage and so fits the candidates for the revelations . . . At the same time it unites them to the elders of whose blood they have partaken . . . (Elkin, 1964: 183).

Even beyond this, the drinking of the blood unites the novices with mythic ancestors and the world of the "timeless" sacred.

Main Ritual—Fire Ceremony: Among most groups, the novices are brought into contact in some manner with a ritual fire. They may stare at it until dazed, may be dropped into it, may have coals thrown on them, or may trample it out with their feet. This is generally regarded as effecting purification so that the novices, now men, can safely return to the world of profane life.

Final Activities—Washing and Return: At the end of the sequence of rites, some kind of washing ritual occurs to remove the last traces of paint and blood before the initiated come into contact with other group members. To complement the first phase of the ritual, the young men are welcomed back as though they had risen from the dead, and of course they indeed have been reborn as men.

As previously mentioned, initiation rites for males are more common and generally more elaborate than those for females. In some societies, however, due to social and/or technological considerations, comparable rituals for young girls gain the center of the ritual stage. Excellent examples of such female initiation rites are found among the various Apache groups in the American Southwest. We can briefly discuss such a rite among the Cibecue (Western) Apache of Arizona. In this society the ritual has ramifications beyond initiation itself. ". . . that which is performed on the most elaborate scale and which affects directly the greatest number of people is the girl's puberty rite" (Basso, 1970: 53). As is generally the case, the timing of this rite correlates with a girl's first menstrual period. At this time a date is selected by her family, a sponsor and other officials chosen (including a medicine man who knows the ritual chants appropriate to the rite), and other preparations begun. The sponsor is an older woman who is not kin to the girl and who is of excellent reputation. A dance area is constructed, and buildings for cooking and other activities are set up along with a special structure for the girl.

On the day prior to the beginning of the ritual, the medicine man prepares paraphernalia that includes, among other things, a special cane for the girl to use in dancing, a scratching stick, and a drinking tube for use by her during and after the ritual while she has to observe taboos on ordinary behaviors. At this time, too, the sponsor and other participants undergo purification. The next day the rite begins with the creation—shortly before sunrise—of a special dancing place for the girl. This is done by placing blankets on the ground and covering them with buckskin. An exhortative address is given to all present by a male kinsman of the girl; the medicine man and some musicians take their place adjacent to the dance area, and chanting begins. The girl emerges from the ritual structure and stands on the buckskin facing the rising sun.

As interpreted by Apaches, the primary objective of the puberty ceremonial is to transform the pubescent girl into the mythological figure . . . Changing Woman. At the request of the presiding medicine man, and "Traveling on his chants," the power of Changing Woman enters the girl's body and resides there for four days. During this time, the girl acquires all the desirable qualities of Changing Woman herself, and is thereby prepared for a useful and rewarding life as an adult (Basso, 1970: 64).

Changing Woman is a chief mythic figure for these peoples. She gives long life and good qualities to the girl, and the various phases of the rite itself reflect aspects of this deity and/or her mythic adventures.

Following Basso, the various phases can be briefly summarized as follows. At first the girl dances in place on the buckskin by herself. The accompanying chants refer to the contribution of Changing Woman to creation, and at the end of this action the power of the deity has entered the girl's body. The sponsor now comes forward and gives instruction as well as moral support (which continues for the rest of the ritual). In the next phase the girl kneels on the buckskin and raises her hands. She looks toward the sun and sways from side to side. This represents the impregnation of Changing Woman by the sun in myth. The girl now lies on the buckskin and is massaged by the sponsor so that she will grow up to be a strong and energetic adult. Next the girl's dance cane is set up some distance away, and as the chants continue she runs to it, circles it, and returns. She is followed in this course by the sponsor who returns the cane so that she can now dance in place. This sequence is repeated four times, each trip representing one phase of life, through old age. This assures the girl of long life, since she has symbolically gone through all life stages. More running now takes place as the cane is next set in each of the four directions to ensure that the girl will never feel fatigue. In the next phase, the medi-

cine man blesses the girl and ". . . picks up a small basket
filled with candy, corn kernels, and . . . coins . . . Standing
on the buckskin, directly in front of the girl, he pours these
contents over her head" (Basso, 1970: 67). These sacred
objects represent food and wealth, and the crowd of observers is encouraged to take some of them, too.

The girl and her sponsor next dance in place, as those onlookers who wish to do so repeat the blessing previously given
by the medicine man. This blessing is at the same time a
request to Changing Woman to grant them their own, personal wishes. Now the pubescent girl steps off the buckskin,
throws it to the east, and throws one blanket in each of the
other directions. This action partly ensures material wealth for
herself as well as good fortune for everyone. The girl and her
sponsor now retire, which concludes the ceremony; but the
power of Changing Woman is felt to remain with the girl for
four more days, and she may apply her power for health or
rain purposes, just like a medicine man. "The puberty ceremony may be interpreted as isolating symbolically four critical
life-objectives towards which all Apache girls on the threshold
of adulthood should aspire. These are physical strength, an
even temperament, prosperity, and a sound, healthy old age"
(Basso, 1970: 68). It should be mentioned here that while
body operations and tests of courage do not occur for Apache
girls, they often do become part of female initiation rituals
elsewhere.

As a final example of initiation rites, we can examine a situation where rites for both sexes occur but with emphasis
upon extra ritual attention for males. The Ona and the Yahgan
formerly pursued simple hunting-and-gathering existences at
the foot of South America on the island of Tierra del Fuego.
Among both of these groups at the time of puberty (first
menses) a girl would fast for several days and would be
painted appropriate to this change in her condition. Apparently they remained out of the way of other group members
for some time and were given counsel on their forthcoming
duties as adults and as potential wives and mothers. After this,
among the Yahgan, they and young boys as well took part
in the *ciexaus* rite, as did all those who had previously been
initiated. This was a local group affair and was probably
their major ritual activity. It was presided over by a super-

natural leader and other officials as well as several sponsors for each novice.

The candidates were subjected to certain endurance restrictions: little sleep, food, and drink, hard work, a daily bath in cold sea water, cross-legged posture during much of the time. They had to drink through a hollow bird bone. The boys were given a sort of temporary tattoo. Much vocational instruction was given, and particularly an elaborate moral instruction in the native code, with very concrete counsels on the obligations of altruistic behavior, respect for the aged . . . and so forth. This moral instruction was given by the mentor, sponsors, and other elders as the will of Watauinewa, the Supreme Being, who saw everything and who would punish delinquents with shortened life . . . (Cooper, 1963a: 99).

Dances and songs were another important aspect of the ritual along with a mock battle between men and women and a feast. Those who passed through the rite were considered full-fledged group members.

Often after the ciexaus rite, men who had passed through it at least twice participated in further supernatural activities, the *kina* rite. This involved building a special structure and impersonating, with masks and body painting, various spirits. It also included active threatening of women. A similar rite among the Ona is better known, the *kloketen* rite. Here, in addition to telling the women that they would be punished by supernaturals if they didn't listen to them, and impersonating spirits, the men further initiated the young boys. ". . . the boy candidates stayed at night in the large hut, had to do with little sleep and little food, to talk little, to assume a cramped posture, and to make long travels afoot. They were further given long and intensive instruction and training in their vocational as well as their social obligations and responsibilities" (Cooper, 1963b: 121). No formal feast terminated this more exclusive rite. We can turn now to another variety of passage rituals.

In addition to initiation rites that "make" adults for a society, perhaps the most elaborate passage rituals are those surrounding death. Certainly the overt rationale of such rites is to ease the dead person out of this life and into the next world. Death rituals reflect a feeling—probably universal —that at least some part of a person (his or her soul or animating principle) does not perish at death but continues in some manner to exist. This continued existence varies greatly from society to society. The soul may linger about the domain of the living as a ghost, which may or may not be harmful. The soul may go to some sort of afterlife, quite often passing through tests or hells first. Once there, it may or may not continue its existence, often dependent upon the ritual attentions of its descendants. In such cases it may or may not be capable and/or willing to act as a beneficent spiritual force on behalf of its living descendants. Such possibilities are described further in Chapter 8. Finally, such a soul-force may eventually reincarnate in another living person. In such cases, the reincarnation may be quite informal and beyond human manipulation—as when the soul merely comes to inhabit a newborn—or it may become quite formal and develop considerable theological sophistication. An example of the latter possibility are the various South Asian creeds stipulating that depending on how one behaved in this life and on the amount of good works (karma) accrued, one would be reborn after death as a person occupying a higher or lower social category. Such conceptions go beyond the concerns of an introductory text, but the student must remain aware of the fact that beliefs relating to the ultimate testing of the soul strongly influence both the form and content of death rituals.

It should also be kept in mind that death rituals not only provide transition for the deceased to some future existence, but they may also involve:

. . . a matter of the living renouncing their attachment for the dead. Psychologically, this is absolutely necessary; the living cannot go on and on sorrowing, and failing to disentangle themselves from the non-living, or the society would become morbid. And yet this cannot be done too cheerfully or quickly. . . . they act to emphasize the acknowledgement by the group and its members that they have lost something significant and are in an unsettled state, trying to reform their ranks. And these customs do it with propriety, and adjust the degree of mourning for different mourners according to their nearness to the departed, although involving all of the immediate group (Howells, 1948: 164).

It must also be pointed out that ideas relative to the very nature of the soul may condition many aspects of death rituals. It is possible for complexity to arise here, even in societies that are not otherwise elaborate in their belief systems. Usually the notion of the soul is conceptualized in multiple terms. For example, among the Nunamiut Eskimos of North Alaska (Gubser, 1965) what might be called the *spiritual substance* of an individual had three aspects. The *ishuma* or "mind" of a person developed by age four or five and was a special part of that person but was lost prior to death. The *inua* or "spirit" was the soul in the more classic sense. It was the life essence itself, which came with the first breath and lived on (in poorly defined fashion) after death. Finally, there was the mysterious *taganiga* or "shadow," which seems to have been a kind of alter ego.

Among the Konyak Nagas of Assam in India:

. . . man himself split at death into several distinct invisible entities. Immediately after the funeral the "soul" (yaha), to which a large portion of the individual's personality was attached, set out on a lengthy journey to Yimbu, the land of the dead. . . . Shamans were believed to enter the land of the dead in dreams and trance, and there were credited with the ability to recover and lead back to earth a yaha which, straying from a sleeping body, had been kidnapped by some spirit. The absence of a yaha from the earthly body, . . . did not immediately result in death, but its separation from the body could not last longer than a few days if death was not to occur (Furer–Haimendorf, 1969: 93).

In addition to the yaha, another spiritual force remained in the skull and could be of value to the living group members. This was called the *mio*, and belief in its potency resulted in skulls of relatives and enemies being kept and fed periodically to utilize its benefits. A third "soul" was called the *hiba*. This apparently was the ghost of the deceased, which lingered for a time among the living.

We can now examine a few rituals occasioned by death, choosing both relatively simple and complex practices as examples. The Konyak Nagas cited above believed that proper ritual was necessary for conveying the yaha to its existence in the land of the dead. On the morning after death, female members of a person's age group association would erect a monument consisting of a carved human figure and a bamboo structure, as a last gesture of friendship. Relatives observed taboos on work, and all morning the corpse remained in its house while female relatives ritually wailed. Relatives and friends brought gifts of food. In the afternoon, elders from a men's association brought a bamboo bier into the house.

"One of them sacrificed a chicken, saying to the dead man, 'this fowl which like you will be eaten by worms, is now your companion, do not look behind at your daughters and kinsmen'" (Furer–Haimendorf, 1969: 90). The deceased was then invoked to enter the land of the dead, placed on the bier, and removed from the house to the accompaniment of increased wailing. The bier was then placed on a corpse platform and the body covered with a cloth and palm leaves. Packets of food were placed on the platform. The corpse was then left to decompose. After six days the head was taken from the body and cleaned and placed in an urn on the edge of the village. It was ritually fed for three years, so that the mio soul would aid the living and feel no resentment. The other bones were ignored.

A second example comes from the Island of Wogeo near New Guinea. Here, when it becomes obvious that death is at hand, the close relatives assemble. At the moment of death they utter piercing shrieks, and one relative goes outside and hits a village drum (slit gong). This sound is relayed from village to village, informing all of the more distant relatives and friends of the deceased of his demise. The death rites vary in elaboration, depending on the status of the deceased. Close relatives are obligated to ritually wail and prepare the corpse for burial and are referred to at this time by the term used for spirits of the dead. They wash the corpse, dress it, and place it on a bed of palm leaves. They smear their own faces and chests with ashes, and for the rest of the day and through the night they wail over the corpse while hanging on to its feet and legs. They invoke the ancestral spirits to welcome the deceased to their ranks. Less close relatives symbolically display their anger at losing the companionship of the deceased, as may close friends. The members of other groups show their resentment at the deceased's lack of concern for the living (because he died) by destroying his property—often working a hardship on his surviving relatives.

Preparation for burial begins the next morning, a grave is dug under the house, and the body is placed in it.

While the burial is in progress one of the close . . . [relatives] . . . drives the spirit out of the land of the living. . . . He fills his mouth with ginger and, holding a spear in one hand and a flaming torch in the other, prances through the settlement before and behind the dwellings and around and among the groups of bystanders. . . . At each step he grimaces horribly, grinds his teeth, flourishes spear and torch, and spits a fine spray of gingery saliva. As he reaches the point from which he started he utters a blood-curdling yell, hurls the weapon after the ghost, and follows this with the torch. The spirit is said to make its way to a headland at the extreme east of the island and thence take flight for the afterworld (Hogbin, 1970: 162, 163).

This is followed by lengthy purifications on the part of the mourners that involve their being shut up in the house of death for twenty-four hours without food or drink and having to observe other taboos. The widow of the deceased remains in semiseclusion for a year and also observes taboos. If the deceased was a mature man, a close relative later digs up the jaw and some other bones. These are placed in a basket and are thought to enhance the effectiveness of any magic forms that were inherited from the deceased.

Somewhat more involved rituals and conceptualizations relating to death formerly typified societies in the Far East. In China, for example, an assumption that the living and dead were interdependent was well developed—the dead requiring periodic sacrifices and bestowing blessings on the living in return. This ancestral cult made "family" religion a basic supernatural concern and transformed the household and the greater descent group into an actual religious corporation. The basic assumptions here were not only the survival of the soul after death but the possibility of continual contact along lines of the original kinship relation, i.e., remaining a spiritual father to a surviving son. Such beliefs translated themselves into action with funeral rites and mourning as well as continuing sacrifices to maintain the contact and relationship. A now classic account of such activities in China is given by Francis L. K. Hsu (1967) for the village of West Town.

General belief has it that every person has a spirit (*huei*), and when death occurs this goes on to the spirit world. If death is unusual (for example, as punishment for a crime), this spirit becomes a ghost and must be specially uplifted via priestly procedures. Also, depending upon the previous behavior of the deceased, the spirit may go straight to the next life in heaven or may have to go through underworld hells. The spirit worlds themselves are organized along human lines.

. . . the worlds of spirits are places where human beings go after death. In broad outline they are organized similarly to the world of the living, with a head of the government and a bureaucracy, power to punish and reward, and encouragement for individual achievements. But these spiritual worlds are more than a mere counterpart to the world of the living. The former are really a necessary supplement to the latter. This is especially made clear by the fact that the achievements or sins for which the individual is rewarded or punished in the spirit world correspond closely to virtues or evils upheld or condemned in the world of the living (Hsu, 1967: 153).

The funerals are as elaborate as the economic circumstances of the relatives and family permit and reflect the social status of the deceased. Calendar divination takes place to determine if the death occurred on an unlucky day, which will cause another family death if special rites are not observed. A diviner also determines the most propitious place for the location of the grave, usually in the family graveyard. Some personal articles of the deceased are burned for use in the next life, along with quantities of paper money. Offerings are also made to a local patron god, since this is the first spirit the soul will meet in its travels. Priests recite scriptures to ensure the safe passage of the soul, and such recitations continue periodically for some period of time, as do taboos for close relatives. At the time of death, sorrow is expressed by wailing and wearing special clothing of coarse white cloth. The deceased is placed in a coffin, often constructed years in advance by elderly persons, and this is borne off to the graveyard in a funeral procession to the accompaniment of exploding firecrackers to ward off ghosts. Also at the time of death a wooden spirit tablet is made to represent the deceased and is placed in front of the coffin. After burial it is placed on the family altar.

Of equal or greater complexity are subsequent rituals to maintain communion with ancestral spirits. These encompass three motives. "Some rites are designed to gain knowledge about the dead . . . Some rites are intended to provide comfort for the dead: the offering of food, clothing, and money. Still other rites are performed to invoke the dead to discharge their duties which were practiced in life . . . (Hsu, 1967: 67). Perhaps the most typical of such rituals are periodic ancestor festivals taking place in the household or greater descent group shrine. In these the ancestors are represented on the spirit tablets or on scrolls. Representation of other major gods may also be kept in these shrines, and part of the festivals seems also to honor them. Incense is burned daily before these images, and the festivals are the foci of such ritual attention.

Prior to the rite, a priest may be hired to report the names of the deceased to the higher gods via incantations. This helps to maintain the souls of the dead in the next life. Also if a family member had died within a year of the rite, a special pilgrimage to his grave will be made and offerings will be deposited. In the main rite the members of the various household branches may perform together with joint offerings, or they may perform separately. The offerings consist of various food dishes and wine, paper money, and paper clothing. Offerings are placed on an altar before which the celebrants ritually prostrate themselves (kowtow) four or more times, each person one after the other. After all have paid such individual homage to the ancestors, the offerings are taken to the shrine of the greater kin group and offered at its main altar and then returned to the house. All the household members now consume the food offerings. After this feast, bags containing silver ingots bearing the names of the male ancestors of the group (and their wives and descendants) are burned with a request to the ancestors to accept them. This rite may take considerable time. A young household member takes each bag in turn—beginning with that for the most anciently departed male relative—reads everything inscribed on the ingot, and then puts it into a fire (to which other offerings are also added). After all of these are consumed, the ashes are poured into a stream. In such rituals we see that not just death but continuity and the concerns of the living may become prominent. In cases such as Chinese ancestor worship, the death emphasis is present but the ritual intent is less that of passage and more what Wallace has called *social intensification*. In this light we can turn now to types of this variety of social rituals.

SOCIAL INTENSIFICATION

Rituals of social intensification are those supernatural activities that remind people of the general nature of the sacred world and of their obligations to it, as well as of what blessings or other reciprocations they can expect from it. Such rituals frequently also remind people of their obligations to each other. It is true, of course, that almost any ritual will serve as such a symbolic prop to the belief system. It is simply that these rites seem most expressly designed to activate such responses. Here again, although the general category is recognized, no real attempts at creating subgroupings are possible at present. We can simply illustrate one example here of this general ritual category.

Our example briefly describes the Bear Festival of the Ainu of Northern Japan as reported by, Joseph Kitagawa (1960). This ritual, apparently widespread in the Northern Hemisphere at one time, is still preserved among these people. The Ainu hold the belief that their gods (kamui) periodically visit the profane world of humans but that to do so, they must wear some kind of disguise—generally animal. Further, there is the notion that they cannot return to their own world unless somehow human beings rob them of these disguises.

In this process, the Kamui give their flesh, and/or furs, to men as souvenirs, and they can return . . . with all kinds of offerings from men. The Kamui thus emancipated from their disguise, however, do not disappear altogether from the world of men. Their seremak [soul or spirit . . .] remain . . . in or around the person who did the favor of "releasing" the Kamui from the bondage of this world and watch over him and protect him in his daily life. (Kitagawa, 1960: 131).

The bear is the most exalted such god disguise, and in an annual rite it is killed to release the god within. While some power is, of course, gained in the process for the human participants, the overall notion of the rite appears to serve as a reminder of the general theme of god and human interdependence.

About the end of winter a bear cub is caught alive and kept until about the following October when a three-day ritual is held. The preparations for the rite are obviously lengthy and chiefly involve keeping the bear in a cage and caring for it in an exacting manner. Millet wine is prepared along with sacred arrows. On the first day of the actual ritual guests arrive, and all are dressed in special clothing. Sacred wooden wands (Inau) are placed in the ground as offerings, and prayers are offered to the bear in apology for having to kill him and asking the god within to notify the other gods that it is about to return. Participants then dance before the cage and then partake in an all-night feast. The second day begins with the participants gathering about a sacred hearth as a ritual elder, who functions throughout the rite as the leader, prays to the gods, asking their assistance in the correct performance of the ritual. Then the person who "owns" the bear—the host who obtained it in the first place—goes to the cage and prays to the god inside the bear relative to its return to the sacred world. The participants then dance around the cage. About noon a young man climbs to the top of the cage and places a rope around the bear in such a fashion that men can hold it on both sides of the animal. The bear is then pulled from the cage and is led in several circuits around the whole area. This is a bidding of farewell to the human participants. The bear is then tied to a tree. As the bear passes in front of the par- ticipants, they shoot blunt arrows at it that can then be taken home as good luck charms. As the shooting occurs, there is great shouting and confusion.

Finally the bear is seized and held by a number of men, and a wand is stuck in its mouth and a sharp arrow shot into its heart. The blood is collected and drunk by the elders. At the same time or slightly afterwards, two poles are clamped on the neck of the bear, and it is strangled while the women chant in a mournful manner. After the death of the bear it is skinned, carried into a hut, and placed on a mat. Prayers of all types are offered to it, and women sing and dance. This is followed by the placing of offerings, sacred wands, food, and wine beside the carcass. The ritual elder prays to the god, beseeching it to take the offerings to the sacred world and to share them with the other gods. It is also requested to depart in peace. The head of the bear is removed and the skull cleaned out and decorated. While this ritual phase occurs, a number of other dances are being performed. These have various symbolic referents, among them being pantomimes of animals and the driving away of evil spirits. Finally, a last farewell occurs. The bear skull is placed on the top of a spe- cial pole, and the elder, bidding it farewell, turns it to the east; a sacred arrow is shot in that direction. This signifies its safe departure. The skull is then rotated to face west, and the main ritual phases are concluded.

This supernatural activity ". . . is the most significant communal ritual that solidifies the organic unity of the Ainu people since in this rite the people are made to realize that they are not simply men confined to the bondage of this earthly existence. Rather, they are made to feel the organic unity between this world of man and all other worlds of the kamui . . ." (Kitagawa, 1960: 151). We can turn now to yet another variety of social rituals, those that deal with hostilities between human beings.

WARFARE RITUALS

Warfare rituals are a type of socially oriented supernaturalism, although it could be argued that they should be included under the heading of technological rituals. The intent of such rites is to gain control over fellow humans in some other group or society. This may be done by the supernatural strategy of strengthening one's own group prior to battle or purifying one's own participants afterwards—in effect gaining control over the enemy and securing oneself from ghostly or other supernatural revenge. Such rites may also include brief observances during a battle and may even include rather lengthy rituals long after a particular battle has been conducted.

Among the Ifugao of northern Luzon in the Philippine Islands there were a series of rites connected with head-hunting. Prior to a head-hunting raid, a ritual was held at the house of the person who was its leader. Gods who had to do with war were invoked (see Chapter 8), and several chickens were sacrificed. The gods were asked to cripple the enemy's ability to fight, and the chickens were offerings to special gods who supply omens as to the favorable outcome of the activity. The men slept the night beneath the house, and myths were recited by supernatural leaders—myths that had to do with "contests" as well as those of sorcery. If a good omen was received in the morning, they set forth, going only to the limits of their own region and then constructing a small hut. They again sacrificed chickens to the omen deities and placed some pieces of ginger on a special shelf. ". . . the priest prays that, should the head-hunting party be fated to any misfortune, then some of the pieces of ginger . . . shall be lost" (Barton, 1946: 143). That night a fire was also built for divinatory inspection. The warriors slept with their spears, and the priest observed the position of these, too, as an omen of success or failure. Each man placed a piece of ginger on his person and set out the next morning to enter enemy territory. At the first sign of danger the ginger was touched to the head for success.

After killing a victim, the head was severed, and the head-taker licked some of the blood to make the victim a blood brother to the slayer and thus forestall vengeance. The head was now carried back home and the war party welcomed by speeches of old men. The warriors entered the house of the leader and jumped out the back door in the magical attempt to shake off any undesirable spirits that might have attached themselves to the expedition. Members of the war party slept on their shields under their own houses until the head feast rites had been completed; they also had to observe numerous taboos on sex, certain foods, and other acts. Meanwhile the head was set on a stake, and speech making and dancing occurred to celebrate the victory. Ancestral spirits were invoked, and the activities continued into the night.

On the next day the *lopad* rite occurred to counteract the vengeance rites being performed by the losing side. Appropriate gods were invoked and myths recited to befuddle and worry the enemy. That night old men invoked special gods to affect the enemy with physical infirmities. Now every participant performed the *binangyu* rite. Gods were invoked to bewitch the enemy, and pigs and chickens were sacrificed. After various prayers those gods receiving the offerings possessed the supernatural leaders. While these people brandished spears over the carcasses of pigs, the gods spoke through them and told of how they would punish the human enemies of the participants. These possession rites were lengthy and complex and involved further varieties of supernatural attempts to gain control over the enemy and safety from them. Eventually the head was buried, and days later final purification of the participants was completed and their taboos lifted. It can be seen from the Ifugao that war rites before and after a battle to aid the combatants in supernatural ways may become complex and may for a time become the focal points of ritual endeavors. We now examine a more specific war ritual, that of purification.

In former times, the Papago of Arizona held victory dances after a return from a successful war expedition. If they were able to take scalps from the slain enemy, these were tied to a long pole and sent ahead via a messenger who would shout out the names of the killers so that they could be segregated apart for sixteen days while other individuals participated in a special scalp dance and song cycles could be sung from myths. "The taking of a scalp or a trophy was the ritual act which brought a man into contact with the supernatural. . . . The warrior who had taken such a trophy became instantly at the mercy of supernatural power" (Underhill, 1969: 192, 193).

When a person took a scalp he had to retire immediately from battle. When enough warriors had so retired, the leader would call a retreat, and an old man who had experienced such activities before was appointed as a guardian to the slayers. He tied up their hair and made speeches to them describing various supernatural experiences. The killers were now supposed to receive visions in which they themselves would see these experiences (aided, no doubt, by the previous suggestions). Taboos were placed on the killers, and the party now started for home, keeping at some remove from the other warriors. When they arrived at their village they were led to an area some distance away, and they began their period of segregation. They ate and slept little and talked only to their guardian. Black paint was applied to their bodies and then washed off every four days. The guardian also taught them war rituals and revealed to them his own past visions and supernatural experiences.

While this purification continued, the scalps were prepared as powerful supernatural objects (fetishes) and placed in the dance area of the village in a basket. On the day of the victory dance itself, the killers were brought into the presence of the other participants and seated near the dance area. They had to spend the entire night without moving. Men who had undergone purifications on some previous occasion now sang special songs and danced with the weapons of the new killers to purify them. At dawn the basket was held up to catch the rays of the rising sun and handed to the slayers. Apparently the soul of the enemy now resided in the scalp.

This treatment made the trophy his servant and added the dead (person's) power to his own, but if he were lax in his attentions, he and his whole family would be open to misfortune. He could, now, touch a dead enemy or an enemy's possessions without fear. The songs he had dreamed, or learned from his guardian during purification, could be used to purify other warriors . . . He would expect to sit in the council . . . and to be generally regarded as a "ripe man" (Underhill, 1969: 210).

We now examine another purification/power aspect of war rituals.

The Jivaro of eastern Ecuador in South America are also a good example of the above kinds of activities and famous in anthropological and popular literature for their past custom of shrinking the heads of their slain enemies. If the Jivaro were successful in battle they would cut a head from a body; after they had gone a sufficient distance to prevent pursuit, they would shrink the head to temporarily trap the soul of the slain man inside. Some rituals occurred during this process. There were also rituals on the return of the successful expedition. The most important rites, however, were undertaken somewhat later. Three or four months later the "feast of painting" would occur. This involved washing the shrunken head trophy in a magic solution that would help to make the soul of the slain man inside the willing slave of the killer. It would then supernaturally aid the killer in his preparations for the victory feast.

At or before this time, the killer was also painted black and had to observe various taboos until this had worn off and he could go back to ordinary life. Some taboos lasted until the conclusion of the victory feast. The victory feast (*tsantsas* feast, after their name for the shrunken head) would take place about one and a half years later, after many preparations by the slayer and his kinsmen. It opened with a dance lasting for four nights before the ritual itself began. These preliminary rituals had the intent of preventing any danger from the head—from the enemy soul within. The slayer himself, while remaining awake each night, did not participate in these dances; they only involved young men and women. Alcoholic beverages were prepared, and the slayer transmitted some of the supernatural power he was thought to have at this time into the brew in a special rite of consecration. The slayer also spent some time alone in the forest. A four-day ritual followed.

On the first day all those participants who have come as guests enter the house of the host prior to dawn, and a ritual welcome occurs with each guest shouting greetings to the relatives of the killer and consuming a quantity of alcoholic beverages. Some of the older warriors take the head out of the house, and two warriors rush into it, acting as if they are charging the enemy; the slayer enters. All of these acts are to help protect the slayer against the spirit of the slain enemy until it is finally rendered harmless. There are many variations of ritual at this point. The slayer, his wife, and daughter perform a dance of purification that is followed by a general drinking bout and a feast. At dusk a general dance takes place involving everyone. This dance is called "the killing of the enemy," and in it

The dancers hold each other by the hands and circle around the three central pillars of the house . . . and moving alternately to the right and to the left. . . . foremost among them is the slayer who . . . is standing nearest to his wife and daughter. He carries the tsantsa hanging on his back during the whole time. . . . The dance is accompanied by a chant . . . When the dance reaches its climax the men also chant or shout and the dancers seem sometimes almost to reach a state of ecstasy. Each time the men, during the dance, reach one of the doors . . . they stop . . . stamping on the ground and shouting . . . are trying to keep off the spirit of the killed enemy, who, it is believed, is trying to enter through one of the doors to kill the victor (Karsten, 1923: 68).

The name of the enemy and those of his relatives are repeatedly mentioned. This dance continues until dawn.

On the morning of the second day the slayer prepares a sacred drink with elaborate ritual. This is a narcotic beverage, and all who partake of it vomit and repeat the process three times. The drinkers then go into the forest and dream, returning eventually to inform the other participants of their dreams and visions. This is partially an act of purification and partially a divination technique to foresee the future of the slayer. After this another drinking bout occurs, and then in the evening the dancing activities of the first night are repeated. On the third day, in the morning, the trophy is washed by the slayer, his wife, and a supernatural practitioner and is placed on a shield. The main ritual manipulation (of many at this pint) involves coating the head with tobacco juice and cutting the neck in symbolic fashion. The head is then washed in a pot containing a sacred liquid, which is then poured on the ground and speared by warriors to keep away the dangerous spirit. The washing has also dispensed with any hate still left in the spirit and made it the supernatural slave of the killer. The slayer again dances with his wife and daughter, and this is followed by the drinking bout, feast, and all-night dancing activity.

Early on the fourth day the head is immersed in tobacco juice, and the neck skin is all cut off. The killer, his wife, and daughter go into the house and break all the remaining taboos they had to observe during the ritual. All the older warriors consume alcoholic beverages, and there is a general feast. The slayer has his hair cut short and his face painted black. There is a final drinking bout and all-night dance, and the guests depart the next morning.

If we analyze the numerous ceremonies described above we find that all of them are founded upon certain fundamental ideas: 1. That in the trophy . . . the spirit or soul of the killed enemy is seated; 2. that the spirit . . . is thirsting for revenge and is trying to harm the slayer in every possible way; 3. that in case this danger is paralyzed through the different rites of the feast, the trophy is changed into a fetish, a thing charged with supernatural power which the victor may make use of in different ways and in different departments of life (Karsten, 1923: 87).

Although we have indicated just the barest outline of this highly complex rite, it still may serve as an excellent example of some of the intentions and procedures involved in war ritual. We can now turn to the final variety of social rituals discussed in this text, those of rebellion.

REBELLION RITUALS

According to Wallace, rites of rebellion permit or require participants to express in rituals otherwise inappropriate behavior. He believes that by so doing, such rituals actually help maintain the order and conventions of society by enabling individuals to temporarily express behavior patterns that are otherwise frustrated. They become, psychologically speaking, a kind of catharsis. Numerous scholars have also claimed that such rites function to maintain order in that, by permitting deviance, they remind people of what is considered correct and important by the society. Whether such rites highlight the requirements and norms of life or whether they simply allow people to blow off steam, these rituals obviously take a great number of forms. For example, ". . . in which persons in authority are mocked and reviled; those to whom one is normally polite and deferential are ridiculed . . . serious acts of ritual are mocked by buffoons; obscenity and sexual license meet with social approval; women who are normally weak . . . assume masculine roles to become rude, domineering, shouting braggarts or parody wanton lewdness; and valued conventions are flouted in other ways" (Norbeck, 1961: 204). Elsewhere (1963) Norbeck has divided such rites more concretely into those expressing social conflict —for example, between rulers and subjects, males and females, and so forth—and other reversals from everyday behavior—for example, sexual license. It should also be understood that such rites of rebellion may encompass the entire ritual itself or be simply an adjunct to some ritual of a different categorical type. We give here two brief examples of these cases.

In ancient Rome, a well-known ritual celebration was the Saturnalia, held for some days during the last month of the Roman year. It was held in honor of a reputed early political leader who, over time, developed agriculture-god functions. During the time of the ritual, all social distinctions were held in abeyance and normal business, schooling, and political–legal functions were terminated. Life for all classes was given over to gambling and feasting as well as many role reversals. "Slaves were served by their masters and sat at tables with them, railing at them, wearing the pilleus, the badge of freedom, and clad in their master's clothes" (James, 1961: 176). High political leaders also wore peasant clothing, and in some regions mock kings were selected who become Saturn for the duration of the ritual. These behaved in a comic manner as "lords of misrule." Though this ritual may well have had agricultural origins, its overall cast would seem to be that of rebellion.

A somewhat more limited case, where "rebellion" is merely an adjunct to other procedures, occurred among American Indian Societies, which permitted small groups of performers (or societies) to burlesque other ritual participants, to engage in role reversal and obscene behavior. Such persons are usually referred to as *clowns*. "Ritual clowns are known to have existed in a great number of tribes in North America. Ethnographic descriptions of ritual clowns in the greater Southwest . . . have provided data for nearly all explanations of ritual clowning" (Heib, 1972: 163). Classic examples of these types occur among the Pueblo Indians, especially the Zuni, who seem to have had the most complicated variety of Pueblo supernaturalism. Among these people clown behavior accompanied a number of ritual activities, including dances at which Katcina spirits having to do with rain were impersonated. There were several clown groups, but the Newekwe appear to have been more expressive of behavior contrary to norm and custom.

While the Newekwe are considered great theurgists, one of the organization is seldom called upon except in extreme cases, from the fact that the invalid, if cured, is expected to join the fraternity and one naturally hates to indulge in its filthy practices . . .

To add to the amusement of the spectators, members of the Newekwe frequently appear in the plaza . . . between the dances of the gods, and whenever this occurs they play the fool generally, but it is when the Newekwe appear in large numbers that their conduct is shocking.

Each man endeavors to excel his fellows in buffoonery and in eating repulsive things, such as bits of old blankets or splinters of wood. They bite off the heads of living mice and chew them, tear dogs limb from limb, eat the intestines and fight over the liver like hungry wolves (Stevenson, 1904: 430, 437).

One can easily see why such rebellion rites occupy the attention of students of comparative religion, even if we do not fully understand their whys and wherefores. It can, of course, also be mentioned that such reversals and license need not be confined to a context of supernatural importance. Quite clearly, such secular behaviors as Halloween for children and New Year's for their parents approach many of the ritual forms. All such behaviors remain the object of great attention for the student of human behavior. We can now turn to the third major ritual category considered in this text, rituals involving the health of human beings.

REFERENCES

Barton, R. F.
   1946. *The Religion of the Ifugaos.*
   American Anthropological Association Memoir #65.
   Menasha, Wisconsin.

Basso, Keigh H.
> 1970. *The Cibecue Apache.*
> New York: Holt, Rinehart and Winston.

Berndt, Ronald, and Berndt, Catherine.
> 1964. *The World of the First Australians.*
> Chicago: University of Chicago Press.

Cooper, John M.
> 1963*a*. The Yahgan. In *Handbook of South American Indians*, ed. Julian Steward, Vol. 1, pp. 81–106.
> New York: Cooper Square Press.

———. 1963*b*. The Ona. In *Handbook of South American Indians*, ed. Julian Steward, Vol. 1, pp. 107–125.
> New York: Cooper Square Press.

Elkin, A. P.
> 1964. *The Australian Aborigines.*
> Garden City: Doubleday and Company.

Furer–Haimendorf, Christoff von.
> 1969. *The Konyak Nagas.*
> New York: Holt, Rinehart and Winston.

Gubser, Nicholas J.
> 1965. *The Nunamiut Eskimos: Hunters of Caribou.*
> New Haven: Yale University Press.

Heib, Louis A.
> 1972. Meaning and Mismeaning: Toward an Understanding of Ritual Clown. In *New Perspectives on the Pueblos*, ed. Alfonso Ortiz, pp. 163–195.
> Albuquerque: University of New Mexico Press.

Hogbin, Ian.
> 1970. *The Island of Menstruating Men.*
> Scranton: Chandler Publishing Company.

Howells, William W.
> 1948. *The Heathens.*
> Garden City: Doubleday and Company.

Hsu, Francis L. K.
> 1967. *Under the Ancestor's Shadow.*
> Garden City: Doubleday and Company.

James, Edwin Oliver.
> 1961. *Seasonal Feasts and Festivals.*
> New York: Barnes and Noble.

Karsten, Rafael.
> 1923. *Blood Revenge, War, and Victory Feasts Among the Jibaro Indians of Eastern Ecuador.*
> Washington, D.C.: Bureau of American Ethnology Bulletin #79.

Kitagawa, Joseph.
> 1960. Ainu Bear Festival (Iyomante).
> *History of Religions* 1:95–151.

Norbeck, Edward.
      1963. African Rituals of Conflict.
          American Anthropologist 65:1254–1279.
————. 1961. *Religion Among the Primitives.*
          New York: Harper and Brothers.
Stevenson, M. C.
      1904. *The Zuni Indians.*
          Washington, D.C.: Bureau of American Ethnology
          Annual Report #23:13–608.
Underhill, Ruth.
      1969. *Papago Indian Religion.*
          New York: AMS Press.

CHAPTER 5

Health Rituals

Health rituals include those supernatural practices or beliefs that are employed either to secure or aid in the recovery of illness—as in curing and related rituals—or that are employed to cause such illness in the first place—as in activities that are usually designated as witchcraft and sorcery. Although the damaging of human health or its reconstitution may well be served by natural means in primitive societies, supernatural attempts of one variety or another are often resorted to in such cases. Since health rituals fall into the above extremes (both cause and cure), the present chapter divides itself along similar lines. It deals first with types of supernatural illness and possible cures and then with witchcraft and sorcery as an in-depth consideration of one type of such misfortune; that caused by human agency.

SUPERNATURAL ILLNESS AND ITS CURE

What are the causes of disease as seen by primitive peoples? Many scholars have remarked that primitive peoples lean quite heavily to supernatural beliefs and manipulations in this realm, emphasizing not only a magical or religious interpretation for the causes of disease or illness but resorting to supernaturalism for diagnosis of specific ailments and for their cures. So cause, effect, and cure tend to fall away from the natural pole of existence in such societies. Years ago in a pioneering and still valuable study of primitive disease, F. E. Clements made the following observations:

Examining the disease concepts of peoples the world over, we shall find them all similar in one respect; disease is never regarded as a normal thing but always as abnormal even though its etiology may be held natural. Aside from this similarity, by no means as psychologically natural as it seems, the concepts will fall roughly into three broad categories; first, *natural causes,* which include the modern medical theory . . . second, *human agency,* i.e. disease is considered directly due to the malefic action of some human being, embracing sorcery in all of its phases; and third, *supernatural agency,* i.e. sickness is regarded as due to the action of supernatural factors. All three of these categories occur among both civilized and primitive peoples. . . . Among primitive people and, perhaps to a lesser extent, among the nations of antiquity the latter two categories attain the greatest adherence (Clements, 1932: 186).

We can follow the lead of Clements in delineating five major categories of primitive disease concepts.

The first interpretation of illness is that it is the result of *sorcery* (including witchcraft). Theories of causation of this variety share in common the notion that human ill health can be caused by other human beings who have supernatural powers. These they gain either by ritual manipulations or by virtue of having been born possessing special capabilities or qualities beyond those of ordinary persons. Common ritual techniques involve the use of the victim's hair or nail clippings and other "magical" procedures. Harm may be done in some cases simply by such mechanisms as the "evil eye." We will considerably expand on this explanation and its varieties in the latter portion of this chapter. Clements believes sorcery as an explanation of disease to be of almost universal distribution in the primitive world, and this would seemingly point to its antiquity as a human belief or at least to its being a basic human assumption (and of repeated invention).

The second disease type is *breach of taboo.* Some variation in this notion occurs from society to society; the main principle involved is that human illness comes in response to the violation of some prohibition of a supernatural sort, backed up by spirit powers. A taboo is a kind of supernatural "no-no" and if violated will lead to retaliation by the world of the supernatural. This usually comes in the form of illness, often as environmental difficulties such as bad weather or lack of rain, or at the very least with a run of bad luck. The specific taboos vary widely—from a specific injunction not to mix together the bones of sea and land animals in many Eskimo groups to a more widespread prohibition against mentioning the name of a recently deceased individual. What makes matters worse in most taboo situations is that such a contravention may be unintentional or unknown to the violator but still bring harm to the violator, and its effects may well spread to other members of a group. Lack of rain may affect everyone, and a disease may be contagious! Clements plots a world-wide, but rather scattered, distribution of this disease mechanism (it has heavy importance only in some Old World regions) and assumes it to be a notion of rather recent development.

The third widely recognized primitive disease concept is that of *disease-object intrusion*. This idea presupposes that an illness is caused by the presence of some kind of object in the body of the sick person. This foreign substance may be hair, a splinter of bone, a small grub, or the like; either the presence of the material object itself causes suffering, or the supernatural essence contained within that object is the responsible cause. Obviously, if something is in the body that does not belong there, unfortunate consequences will result. This theory is not unlike our germ theory of disease in its logical assumptions. The disease object itself apparently enters the body of the victim either by human agency—sent by a sorcerer —or by a supernatural act of a spirit being. Clements sees this concept as an extremely old notion, going back to the Old Stone Age. It is extremely common in northeast Asia and in the New World among American Indians.

The fourth disease concept is similar to the above and is called *spirit intrusion*. In this case, the disease or suffering is caused not by a foreign object inside the body but is ". . . due to the presence in the body of evil spirits, ghosts, or demons" (Clements, 1932: 188). It must be pointed out here that spirit intrusion of this nature is of the sort we should call *involuntary possession;* the human subject has not solicited the presence of such beings inside his or her body. This is a different realm of supernatural experience from the voluntary possession of the shaman or other supernatural professional. This distinction is dealt with further in Chapter 7. The concept of disease obviously depends upon belief in the existence of evil spirits or in spirits that may become ill-intentioned towards humans, upon belief in ghosts of one sort or another and in demons. Certainly by their own volition such supernaturals may enter a human body to cause harm, but they may also apparently be motivated to do so by some human agency. Spirit intrusion is assumed by Clements to be fairly old and to have a rather continuous world distribution, perhaps of heaviest importance in the Old World. It is conspicuously lacking in some areas.

The last concept of disease is that of *soul loss,* also extremely widespread, although most common in the Northern Hemisphere. This concept depends upon belief in a soul—certainly an old human belief—and itself is generally attributed considerable antiquity. The notion that one's soul can leave the body is a logical lead-in to the idea that its loss causes harm. This works on the reverse principle of object and spirit intrusion. The soul may leave because of attraction by spirits or evil-minded humans or apparently may just leave of its own volition—often wandering about during sleep. In any case sickness results, and if the soul is not somehow returned death will eventually occur.

In sum, then, primitive explanations of disease include the work of sorcerer types, disease-object or spirit intrusion, loss of soul, and breach of taboo. These can be represented in diagram form as follows:

Mechanism (reason)

Origination	*Magic Manipulation*	*Disease-Object Intrusion*	*Spirit Intrusion*	*Soul Loss*	*Breach of Taboo*
Human	X	X	X	X	
Nonhuman		X	X	X	X

Potentially, all of these can occur in a given society. In actuality, only some appear to be considered, and generally one or two are the most common or emphasized. It should again be mentioned that such diseases or forms of human suffering may be accurately known from the symptoms expressed. For example, apathy indicates soul loss, and shaking may mean the intrusion of some spirit. It is quite commonly the case, however, that the indication of the specific cause of misfortune may be revealed only after undertaking extensive divination procedures, themselves supernatural activities. Further, divination may also occur after the cure has been administered in the attempt to determine the success of its outcome.

Before moving on to descriptions of actual curing rituals and to some of the other theoretical issues involved, we will very briefly indicate some of the range of the procedures represented in this ritual category and discuss the legitimacy of such procedures. Basically speaking, each of the above disease categories is handled supernaturally in a slightly different manner. In sorcery, attempts may be made to purify the patient, counter the evil influences, and/or send the magic power back to the sorcerer by reversing the spell. Attempts often are also made to discover the evil person and force him to stop his practices. In the case of witches, those who are proven guilty of such activities may be killed. Remember the Bushong ordeal described in Chapter 3. In the case of breach of taboo, the patient generally is made to repent the infraction (often by public confession), the offended spirits must be placated, penance may be necessary, and of course the patient purified. In disease-object intrusion, the object is commonly sucked out by the lips of the curer or through a special tube and is disposed of ritually. This is usually accompanied by massage and other ritual manipulations. Spirit intrusion is somewhat more variable cross-culturally with respect to even its common supernatural therapies. The spirit may be bribed into leaving the body, good spirits (the helping spirits of the shaman) may be placed in the patient's body to drive out the evil spirit, and mechanical means of exorcism may be employed. The evil spirit may also be transferred into the body of the curer, which is, of course, capable of dealing with it. Massage, purification, and other stock curing procedures may also accompany such procedures. Finally, soul loss is generally treated by attempting to coax the soul back into the body from the spirits who have taken it or from the land of the dead. This treatment may involve the curer sending his own soul or helping spirit to accomplish this, or it may simply require the appropriate spell, offering, and ritual manipulation.

As will presently be demonstrated, the actual procedures in any given case are a great deal more complicated than those indicated above, but these do give a brief suggestion of some of the more common techniques employed. They also, of course, raise the issue of the genuineness and effectiveness of such techniques. We will take up the latter question presently. With regard to fraud, Erwin Ackerknecht has dealt with this question in considerable detail in a series of papers (for example 1942, 1946). Following his lead we may suggest the following. First, it is probably true that frauds exist in primitive curing situations in the same proportion as quack doctors exist in our own. Honest curers in either situation may seek to expose them, or at least intelligent laymen may recognize such fraud when they see it. In fact, some primitive societies even have names for such people. The Eskimo of St. Lawrence Island (Alaska) designate a type of shaman as "foolish shaman" or quack! In my own field experience a story was related concerning a situation in which a supernatural practitioner from another group visited and performed a ritual for the host group. Later, people of his own group exposed him as a fraud. When he returned to the host group he was dealt with accordingly.

In a more specific sense, however, we might ask if the serious practitioners are not frauds. Do they really believe in the efficacy of cures that involve sucking out disease objects and restoring lost souls? Much depends, of course, on the angle of one's beliefs. As Ackerknecht points out (in the case of object sucking), it may be realized that the object removed was done so by sleight of hand; it is considered simply as a receptacle—"an invisible force is dealt with by means that are meant and understood to be symbolic" (Ackerknecht, 1942: 510). Whether the patient or other observers recognize the symbolism of the situation or not, the shaman or curer may be said to do so. And both curer, patient, and observers are party to the same cognitive system of supernatural beliefs regarding ill health and its relief. It must also be added here that since many cures do take place, for reasons given presently, this is a positive reinforcer for the whole activity.

Along the lines of the above discussion, a delightful narrative speaks strongly to this question. Claude Levi–Strauss reminds us of the case of Quesalid, a Kwakiutl Indian from the Pacific coast for whom we possess autobiographical details. This individual apparently did not believe in the curers in his own society but did associate with them out of a sense of curiosity. Finally one offered to teach him the supernatural curing arts, and he began to learn the various techniques involved, finding his fears of fraud realized. He was taught to pantomime, to simulate fainting, how to induce vomiting, and how to hide a tuft of hair in his mouth and bite his tongue to bloody before extracting this "disease object." He was at this point convinced of the duplicity of the curing fraternity, yet he continued to learn more.

His worst suspicions confirmed, Quesalid wanted to continue his inquiry. But he was no longer free. His apprenticeship among the shamans began to be noised about and one day he was summoned by the family to a sick person who had dreamed of Quesalid as his healer. The first treatment . . . was an outstanding success. Although Quesalid came to be known from that moment on as a great shaman, he did not lose his critical faculties. He interpreted his success in psychological terms . . .

He then adventures further.

While visiting the neighboring Koskimo Indians, Quesalid attends a curing ceremony of his illustrious colleagues of the other tribe. To his great astonishment he observes a difference in their technique. . . . What is the value of this method? . . . Quesalid requests and obtains permission to try his method in an instance where the Koskimo method has failed. The sick woman then declares herself cured (Levi–Strauss, 1963: 175, 176).

Since it is hard to argue with success, he then became a practicing shaman, losing sight of his earlier critical feelings about curing activities. "Thus his original attitude has changed considerably. The radical negativism of the freethinker has given way to more moderate feelings. Real shamans do exist?" (Levi–Strauss, 1963: 178). In sum then, such curing procedures are genuine given the belief context, the symbolism involved, the proof of success, and the recognition on the part of the people themselves that outright frauds can and do occasionally occur. Against this background we may now sketch some specific descriptions of curing rites.

SPECIFIC CURING RITUALS

We can give our first example of a curing ritual, a brief summary of a classic account by John Gillen (1965) of *soul loss* (espanto) in the Guatemalan community of San Luis Jiltopeque. This is a widespread disease type in peasant societies in Latin America. Basically, the soul is lost during some kind of fright situation, and this is revealed in such physical symptoms as depression, withdrawal from social life, generalized pains, and the like. Gillen observed such a case of "magical fright" in a sixty-three-year-old Pokoman Indian woman, and his account of the curing situation is paraphrased below.

A curer was engaged to hold a divination session to diagnose the trouble, which, of course, was already suspected to be soul loss. He arrived at the house of the patient; and after some preliminary conversation, he took her pulse—a common technique for ascertaining illness in this part of the world. From such activity he confirmed that soul loss was indeed the cause of her difficulties. Further conversation revolved around the occasion for the loss itself, and it was determined that it had occurred when she had seen her husband with another woman—probably the real cause of her difficulties (see the next section). She also admitted some marital difficulties at this point. The curer then declared himself confident of his ability to remedy her illness situation and gave her detailed instructions on preparations for the actual curing ritual and for inviting friends and an important local dignitary.

The curing ritual began four days later in the late afternoon, also at the house of the patient. The curer arrived, checked the preparations, and assumed control of the activities. First there were refreshments and light conversation. At dusk, a delegation including the local political leader went to the local church to burn candles to the saints and to plead for their aid (so they would not interfere with a pagan rite). They returned to the patient, and a large meal was served. The curer then made wax images of the chief of the evil spirits and his wife (who control the lost soul). The patient stood up, and the curer passed eggs over her body in various ways and directions to take some of the illness out of her body—this being the illness that accompanies soul loss. Then the curer, the political leader, and two assistants went to the place where the soul had first been lost, taking with them the eggs, images of the evil spirits, and offerings for them. A hole was dug, and the curer talked to the spirits, presenting the offerings and requesting that the soul be returned. Then all these things were buried, and the curer and the other participants returned to the house, taking some of the earth along so that the newly released soul would follow. "This step in the cure was the crucial one from the native point of view. The theory is that the evil spirits . . . had a disembodied soul somewhere in the mountains. Only a medicine man who has established friendly relations with these occult powers is able to persuade them to release the soul" (Gillen, 1965: 407).

When they returned they explained what they had done and set up a ground altar outside the house. The curer prayed to the four directions. The patient now stripped down to a brief loin cloth and came outside, and the other observers formed a square around her and the curer. The curer offered her a bowl filled with a magical potion from which she took a drink. Then,

The curer put his lips to the bowl and took a large mouthful, stepping back from the patient about three feet. . . . Suddenly and without warning a blast of fine spray burst from the curer's mouth straight into the face of the patient. The shock of the alcoholic liquid in the cold air rocked her. He continued, systematically spraying her whole body . . . with the medicine, ignoring her protests and her shivering. A stool was brought and the patient sat down trembling while the curer rinsed his mouth with a bowl of water. After she had sat for about ten minutes the curer gave her a bowl of the mixture and she drank it all, about a pint. Then everyone returned to the house (Gillen, 1965: 408).

Back inside the house the patient reclined on a mat on the floor, and the curer vigorously massaged her body ritually for some period of time. The patient then dressed and got into her bed and was covered with blankets. A pot full of smoking coals was placed under the bed as was the earth that had been brought back by the curer from the location of the earlier rituals. As the curer placed this earth there the coals flared, and the curer announced the return of the soul. A water-filled bowl was then brought to the curer, who then broke into it the eggs used in massaging the patient. The resultant patterns of these were then used to divine the success of the cure. At this point (5 A.M.) the patient fell asleep, and the curer and other participants and observers retired. Gillen reported the cure to have been a success.

A second example comes from the Pueblo of Sia, a Keresan-speaking Pueblo in New Mexico. Here the context and rituals of curing are a more complex affair. Classes of illness range from the purely natural—such as sore eyes—which almost anyone may attempt to treat, to sterility, wounds in warfare, snakebite, and the like—all treated by special medicine societies. Then there are bad dreams and prolonged anxiety (also conceived of in supernatural terms), treated by medicine societies, and illnesses induced by witches—evil persons born with two hearts, one of which is evil and brings the witch the desire to harm fellow humans. Witches are the main cause of serious illness at Sia, and they too are dealt with by medicine societies. Witches do harm by stealing hearts or by projecting disease objects into someone's body.

The members of the medicine societies (a common Southwestern Indian phenomenon) have curing abilities because of powers they receive from certain animal spirits, especially that of the bear. They have their own ritual houses with altars and much ritual paraphernalia. Some societies are capable of performing all kinds of curing rituals; others have more limited and specific abilities. There are (or were) apparently eight or ten such societies in all. Curing activities themselves are basically divided into two major types: clearing away and all the way rites. In the first case we observe a rather simple rite that fundamentally is to strengthen and purify the patient. A single curer visits the patient at his or her house in the evening. He sings a few songs and examines the patient. Treatments consist mostly of brushing away evil influences with eagle wing feathers, which are later deposited along with some food by the curer as an offering to his helping spirits. This may be repeated four successive nights. "Medicine" is also left for the patient to drink.

All the way techniques are used in the event of more serious illnesses such as witchcraft, and group curing takes place. Permission to cure in such cases must be secured from political leaders, and the members of the medicine society involved meet in their house for four days previous to attempting the cure to purify themselves and to sing and pray for the recovery of the sick person. On the fourth evening they visit the sick person (or bring him to their house) and construct their altar. They then sing and pray for a considerable time while some of their number blow, brush, or whip away the evil influences. This continues until all members have taken their turn at each activity. They now diagnose the patient, feeling his or her body for foreign objects. If there are some, these are either sucked out or brushed out with the tips of feathers. The patient is given medicine to drink and may be bathed with it. Special offerings are also deposited at shrines for the recovery of the patient. If witchcraft is involved, still further rites are performed.

After all the doctors have cured the patient, they turn their attention to witches. If they discover that they have stolen the patient's heart, they must go out and find it and bring it back. . . . The doctors prepare themselves to go out into the pueblo and battle with the witches. . . . Those who are to go . . . pick up a flint knife in the right hand and set out. They run out into the town, or outside the village looking for witches. Sometimes they fight them: "You can hear them fighting in the dark . . ." . . . If they have been out after the patient's stolen heart they invariably return with it. The heart is a ball of rags, in the center of which is a kernel of corn; the corn is the real heart. The doctors unwrap the rags and examine the corn closely. If they find it "burned or mouldy" the patient will remain sick, or even die. If the corn is unblemished, the patient will get well promptly. In either case he is given the corn to swallow and a draught from the medicine bowl (White, 1962: 298).

It should also be mentioned that an annual curing ceremony was also held toward the end of winter to purify the entire village by driving away evil spirits and witches. This was engaged in by all the medicine societies, and procedures were comparable to those for individual patients, with a main political leader acting as the symbolic patient.

As will be seen in these two examples, curing rituals may be lengthy, complex, and may involve one or more curers working individually or in joint practice. They may work their cures on behalf of a single patient or for the benefit of an entire social group. We discuss the types of curers themselves in detail in Chapter 7. We can conclude our present discussion of the curing variety of health rituals by examining the success of such endeavors.

SUCCESS OF CURING RITUALS

Why are attempts to cure the sick in primitive societies often successful? One can approach this question from at least two perspectives. First, they may be seen as successful by the people involved; that is to say that no one questions the effectiveness of the cures themselves. This is because in the event of failure, rationalizations may be made. Counter-magic, failure to be in the correct ritual condition, and omission of some ritual content are common excuses of a practitioner who fails. Here it is not the efficacy of the cure that is called into question, but the means of its application that has invalidated the proceedings. Along the same lines is the notion that such supernatural techniques may not even be applied in some cases of real disease. If some affliction is very common, it may not be recognized as a disease at all and hence not put curing techniques into question. Even in our own society, "Research on the history of malaria in the Mississippi Valley, for instance, has shown that at the peak of its endemicity during the 19th century, malaria was no longer regarded by man there as a disease either. We should not forget that what is mental and even bodily disease is primarily defined not by nature but by society" (Ackerknecht, 1946: 473). One also assumes the rejection of hopeless cases by the curer as common practice.

The second approach to the question of success in primitive medicine concerns itself not with application or rationalization but with actual cases of proven efficacy. Why specifically is it successful? Here there are answers on perhaps two levels. First, it is fairly certain that some cures work because the treatments involve some certain—sometimes unconsciously —"rational" (medically effective) elements. The use of massage, hot baths, physical shock, and potions may be of actual therapeutic value to the patient. In the last case it has been estimated (Ackerknecht, 1942) that perhaps 25 to 50 percent of the plant derivatives used in primitive curing are "objectively active," including such things as opium and eucalyptus, which do have advantageous effects even in our own medical pharmacopoeia.

It can also be suggested that even where the cure attempt is purely of a supernatural order it may be successful, because many of the illnesses to which it is applied are of the mental nature—to which mental manipulations and therapies are best applied. Most specifically here many recent studies have pointed out the great similarities between the techniques and often the substance of modern psychotherapy and the practices of many primitive curers. "Examining methods of religious and magical healing . . . the core of their effectiveness seems to lie in their ability to elicit hope by capitalizing on the patient's dependence on others and on the expectation of help aroused by the healer's personal attributes and his paraphernalia which gain their power from culturally determined symbolic meaning" (Kiev, 1964: 8). It will be recalled that the case of soul loss in Guatemala involved a mental difficulty and withdrawal from normal social life and was cured by reinvolvement with others by the patient, discussion of her difficulties, mental and physical manipulations, and basic statements of confidence by the curer that he could cure and that in fact he had been successful.

Even in cases where some physical aspects are involved, the role of the primitive healer may have beneficial mental aspects. As Frank has put it:

In all cultures, phenomena called "mental illnesses" disturb all levels of the person's functioning: bodily, psychological and spiritual. . . . These disorders result from or express the interaction of sociocultural stresses . . . The healer, whether psychiatrist or shaman, derives his healing powers from his status and role in the sufferer's society and functions, among other ways, as an evoker of the healing forces, a mentor, a role model, and a mediator between the sufferer and his group. His task is to help the patient . . . to mobilize his psychological and spiritual as well as his bodily resources (Frank, 1964: xii).

Many specific studies of primitive curing under actual conditions have described in great detail the specific psychotherapeutic elements involved. Jane Murphey (1964), for example, in her study of shamanism on St. Lawrence Island, Alaska, has pointed out the following techniques: gaining acceptance by the patient of the shaman himself and of the possibility for cure, involvement of the group (not only for public support of the patient but again as a way to underwrite the overall validity of the techniques), focusing attention on the shaman as a person of extraordinary power to enhance the expectations of the patient as to the success of the outcome, and involvement of the patient in the activities (by confession and so forth). "The commission of these acts has the psychological effect of enabling the patient to believe himself rid of the cause of his illness" (Murphey, 1964: 81). Of course, some actual "rational" treatments are also included. In sum, then, the notion is that primitive curing in the main is successful because it employs many mental remedies to what are quite often mental kinds of illnesses, as well as for the other reasons cited. We can now turn to a specific consideration of one variety of illness; that caused by witchcraft and sorcery.

WITCHCRAFT AND SORCERY

The belief in the doings of evil persons called *witches* or *sorcerers* is extremely common, with perhaps only a few societies lacking the belief. Those beliefs of historic Europe and New England, however, together with the rise of witch cults in modern society, must be regarded as changed concepts with new identifications (for example, compacts with the devil). Although not exactly comprising a unity, such beliefs in primitive societies are of a somewhat different nature. Generally speaking, witchcraft and sorcery are conceived of as rather separate types of operations, a division that carries over to the quality of persons involved.

Witchcraft

Witchcraft is the employment on the part of a special kind of person of supernatural power to work harm on other human beings. The character of the witch is quite important. Such supernatural powers for evil are felt to be derived from within the individual. Such a person incorporates a power that is not entirely human, and it is not a power that has to be learned or otherwise acquired; it is simply there! One is born a witch or one is not. Of course the power may not immediately be recognized. It may lay dormant, so to speak, and not be used. Once discovered, it may even increase its potency with practice, like building up a muscle or honing a talent. As such, a born witch, one may be recognized as such by other persons. There may be external signs such as red eyes. Or, it may be that the only difference between the witch and a normal person is internal. It may be found in the special aspect that creates the witch in the first place, possession of two hearts and so forth.

Secondly, and along pretty much the same lines, the use of the power may be a conscious activity, that is, the witch is aware of his or her powers and uses them willfully to harm others. Or it may largely be an unconscious activity; one may harm others inadvertently without realizing it. Generally, however, witches are adults whose powers and realization of them have come to fruition. Thirdly, whether cognizant of their innate capacities or not, witches are helplessly addicted to their evil ways. They cannot really help themselves from harming their fellow humans, either in their own group or in some distant group. It should be mentioned here that a tendency does appear to exist in which friends and relatives may be the chief target of such activities. At any rate, they do harm others, their behavior is immoral, and such powers are apparently never used for good or to the benefit of other people. They are immoral by habit as well as by birth. This may simply be the outpouring of their inner nature, or it may result from particular envy or malice on the part of a witch concerned in a given situation. It is not, then, simply due to a desire for material gain.

A fourth characteristic, generally speaking, of witches is that not only are they evil, but they often reverse the standards and values by which other members of their society live. In particular, they engage in practices repugnant to those who are normal; they commit incest, have intercourse with corpses, practice cannibalism, and so forth. It is in light of the aspect of witchcraft beliefs that we should interpret the great hate and fear in which such suspected persons are held and the eventual treatment accorded them. A fifth aspect of witchcraft is that its practitioners generally do their antisocial activities at night when secrecy can be maintained and when human defenses, perhaps, are at their weakest. The witch may project the evil influences, or they themselves may go to perform the evil deeds directly, often assuming animal or fantastic forms in the process. Philip Mayer has nicely summarized the basis of witchcraft beliefs:

I would suggest that the essence of the witchcraft idea is simply this: People believe that the blame for some of their sufferings rests upon a peculiar evil power, embodied in certain individuals in their midst; although no material connection can be empirically demonstrated between those individuals and the ills they are supposed to have caused. The witch then is held to be a person in whom dwells a distinctive evilness, whereby he harms his own fellows in mysteriously secret ways. To this central mystical idea each society adds its own embellishments (Mayer, 1970: 46, 47).

This identification adds another dimension to witchcraft beliefs. This is the notion that the results of witch activities are generally things that are out of the ordinary—special illnesses or misfortunes that otherwise have no explanation or are somehow unaccountable. They may also be calamities that do not yield to ordinary countermeasures. The substance of these is taken up further in Chapter 9.

Sorcery

The position of the sorcerer or sorcery is usually accounted for differently. Sorcerers are often thought to be individuals who have had to learn their technique for evil or at least to have gained power through contact with supernatural beings of some nature. They are not even equipped with the ability to work harm on their companions. As a natural consequence of this, they are generally believed to use such powers only in a conscious manner. They always know what they are doing, and they do it not so much as a slave to their special inner nature but because they do have desires—normal human desires for material gain, jealousy, and the like that they are able to gratify by engaging in such activities. They are ordinary people driven by motives that are disapproved but at least understood. As a consequence of this conscious and learned basis for their activities, sorcerers are usually conceived of as at least potentially capable of using their power for some beneficial purpose, if only to harm the people in some enemy group. If they have access to "black" magic they may be able to convert it to "white" magic! Sorcerers, unlike witches, are thought to be capable of redemption and may even be dealt with less harshly.

Finally, based on the above criteria and on the fact that sorcerers may function more openly (day witches?) in their societies since their identities may be known, many scholars have suggested that although neither type of evil practitioners are actually able to accomplish what it is believed they do, at least the sorcerer does possess paraphernalia, spells, and so on and does engage in the attempt. Witches and witchcraft, on the other hand, may be only limited to the realm of ideas. Sorcery is observable, but witchcraft never actually takes place! This, of course, does not make the fear of it any less real or the functions of the belief (see Chapter 9) any less potent.

Obviously an overlap does occur between these two varieties of practitioners of evil, at least in terms of results. "Because both witches and sorcerers incur social disapproval, generalizations about both are often made. This fact calls for a generic term which includes both" (Marwick, 1970: 13). That this is suggested is due also to the fact of a mixing of such activities in many primitive societies, or impreciseness in recognition and translation of anthropologists. Most often the term *wizardry* is substituted for both kinds of practices. And yet there are some fairly consistent patterned differences between such practices in most societies. Some differentiation, even if simpler than that outlined above, does seem to be a comparative necessity.

So it is impossible to specify that only persons with a particular combination of qualities are to be called witches; the name would have no usefulness. Some would prefer to drop the name . . . or to invent some new word that would subsume all the characteristics that have been associated with both. I would suggest that, even if it is rarely practicable to divide supposed evil-doers sharply into witches and sorcerers, it is still useful to distinguish types of evil-doing on these lines. The distinction I would make is a simple one— that the sorcerer uses material objects and the witch does not. It is by no means insignificant, since it is possible to find evidence of sorcery . . . But there can never be evidence of witchcraft, and so accusations of witchcraft can only be pursued by means as mystical as the supposed offence (Mair, 1969: 22, 23).

Along such lines, then, we turn to some actual descriptive data both to highlight the nature of the difficulties in clearly separating the witch from the sorcerer and to add substantive data to the presentation of these concepts.

EXAMPLES OF WITCHCRAFT AND SORCERY

An excellent example of the actual practices of witchcraft and sorcery, as well as a specific test of the conceptual differences between them, occurs among the Cebuano of the Philippine Islands as reported by Richard Lieban (1967). Among these people the sorcerer generally learns the methods of bad magic or sorcery through an apprenticeship to an established sorcerer. Such individuals are thought to vary greatly in their command of such knowledge. Learning is not enough, however; the would-be sorcerer must also originally establish contact and relations with a special spirit (Ingkanto) who will supernaturally support such endeavors. This is done by offerings that—after originally accepted—must be repeated at least once a year. There is also an obligation to kill at least one person a year, lest the sorcerer himself become victim to his own powers of destruction. It should be mentioned that in performance of these antihealth rituals no part of the procedures can be omitted, lest the effects turn on the sorcerer or at the very least be ineffectual.

Sorcerers have a variety of motives. They use their powers as an outlet for aggression against those who antagonize them, having the power is apparently an attraction in itself. Most often it is done with a view toward financial gain, since such individuals exist as specialists in their community—available for hire. Of considerable interest is the notion that sometimes such persons are also healers. "Sorcerers are supposed to be able to cure illnesses which they inflict, and this is not surprising considering the deadly nature of the forces with which the sorcerer deals and that he is subject to attack or counterattack by other sorcerers" (Lieban, 1967: 29). This good–bad nature for some such practitioners is partially rationalized in terms of the fact that they are supposed to be hired only as the agents of "rightful vengeance," that is, to harm only people who have wronged others. In fact, it is sometimes even held that they cannot harm truly innocent people! Lieban remarks that actual practice often runs counter to this proposition.

There appear to be six main sorcery techniques. One is called *Barang* and involves the use of insects and related animals, although not ordinary specimens. The sorcerer keeps some of these in a bamboo tube and can command them to do harm. He drops a slip of paper with the victim's name into the tube, and if it is consumed, the animals are interpreted as having accepted their assignment. They are then removed and given orders to go and do their job—being thought to invisibly enter the body of the victim. A second variety, *Usik*, also employs the use of insects but apparently uses different incantations and is thought to work more slowly. An alternative here is the use of objects such as pins or bits of glass that are also made to magically enter a body to do harm.

A third sorcery technique is called *Hilo* and is so potent that if learned, one must first employ it on a person within his own household to render it effective in the future. This involves a special offering to a spirit and a request for it to bring snakes to a certain location. Here a special altar is set up containing bamboo stakes. The snakes leave blood and poison on the bamboo, and those parts so covered are cut into shavings and then mixed with other poisonous materials. The mixture is put in the food or drink of the victim, placed on his body, or buried in the ground over which the unfortunate is apt to walk.

Still another variety, *Paktol,* comes in two forms. In one, the sorcerer employs a human skull placed on a table, along with an offering to a spirit. Along with other things a slip of paper bearing the name of the victim is placed on the skull, and the spirit of the skull is invoked to go and kill the victim. As an alternative a small wooden doll may be employed. Holes are bored into it, representing the joints of the victim's body, and nails are placed in the holes to the accompaniment of the proper incantations.

La-ga, a fifth sorcery possibility, works evil by securing part of the victim or some of his possessions ". . . such as his hair, urine, feces, saliva, footprints, or garment—which serves as a representation of the victim" (Lieban, 1967: 58). These things are wrapped in a special leaf and poisons are added; then they are carried to a special place, put in a pot, a fire is lighted beneath it, and a spirit is invoked to help harm the victim.

Finally, there is the *Sampal* technique in which the sorcerer places representations of a person inside a sea animal along with poisons and other objects of malign influence and returns it to the sea (or leaves it to dry out on a beach). In Lieban's analysis these and other sorcery techniques employ the use of an agent—some object or spirit being—to harm the victim, along with contagious magical representations.

Witchcraft beliefs for the Cebuano involve activities more rooted in the individual. These fall into two categories. The *Aswang* is a person who looks normal; but once he gains power—either by heredity or by being contaminated soon after birth by another witch—he can become a real menace in his community. "Waylaying people at night in isolated places, he may try to suffocate them by getting his long hair in their nostrils and overcoming them with the bad odor of a special oil he applies to himself when he attacks people. He may bite live men or feed on their dead flesh after killing them. His attacks may come after he has changed his body into that of an animal . . ." (Lieban, 1967: 67). The other general technique of the Aswang is to hurt others by merely looking at them or, on occasion, to contaminate them with poison along sorcery lines.

The other variety of witch is the *Buyagan*. This type kills victims by cursing them (by word power alone) and in some cases even by the expression of evil thoughts. Such a person is thought to be stigmatized as an evil practitioner by his possession of a dark tongue and works most of the time from malice. So it would seem, basically, that such notions highlight the general distinction between practitioners of evil previously suggested, although less than absolutely.

Witches can act because they are socially provoked, and sorcerers or their clients can be regarded as intrinsically wicked. But the evil of the witch assumes the form of an aberrant power that often is activated for no reason other than because it exists, whereas when the wickedness of the sorcerer or his client is expressed in sorcery this is usually because of a social stimulus, dissension between the instigator of the attack and the object of the attack (Lieban, 1967: 77).

We can turn now to a different example.

The Quiche of Guatemala (Santiago El Palmar Village) also express a dichotomous belief in the existence of witches and sorcerers, heavily overlaid with Christian beliefs. Basically speaking, the witch (*Win*) is a lazy and greedy person who has the ability to transform himself into animal form (*Nagual*) to enter the homes of villagers to rob them, engage in sex with sleeping women, or to sadistically enjoy the sufferings of innocent persons. Such a witch is ". . . the polar opposite of the good man. He is at the same time a stereotype of loathsome evil and an example of the possible consequences of an indolent disposition" (Saler, 1964: 312). The witch obtains his powers by sleeping for nine nights in a cemetery and by praying to the devil, who finally appears and gives battle.

If the human can wound the devil in the process he gains transforming powers and is launched upon his career.

The sorcerer in Quiche society, the *Ajitz,* is a person who employs the use of magical practices in his attempts to harm other people. He recites incantations and performs rituals he has learned from other sorcerers. He engages in no special compact with the devil. Dolls representing the victim may be buried or their possessions harmed; such activities generally occur at night. Some of the motives for such activities may be the same as those mentioned for the witch, but:

> . . . his canons of selection are likely to have a different focus. The sorcerer is usually motivated by personal feelings directed against specific individuals, some of whom may even, by local standards, be adjudged deserving of punishment because of their own immoral or imprudent actions. The intended victim is, in any case, his or his client's private enemy. The witch, on the other hand, is animated by a perverse delight in harming or harassing any person of virtue and is thus at war with society at large. From a social point of view his transgression is manifestly greater (Saler, 1964: 322).

So the sorcerer remains basically a human being, whereas the witch not only transforms himself into an animal but becomes a nonhuman in the process. We can turn now to a final example along these lines.

The Navaho Indians of the American Southwest also have well-developed beliefs in the existence of evil supernatural practitioners. One of the sources of evil that profoundly disturbs the Navaho is that emanating from witches.

> The Navaho Indians . . . believe there are human wolves; or more especially, that men and women disguised in wolf or mountain lion skins go about practicing witchcraft. . . .

> There is myth and tale material about these human wolves; and stories, delusions, hallucinations. Diagnosticians find them to be the cause of sickness and there are songs for protection and songs for cure. Sandpaintings, prayers, herbs, and rituals free the patient and send the harmful influences back upon the witch (Morgan, 1936: 3).

Witches are generally active at night, and they cause sickness and death in a number of ways. Kluckhohn (1944) has distinguished four basic formats for such evil practices. In *witchery,* a preparation is made from the flesh of corpses, and after being ground into a powder it is placed on people and things. Thus it works by contamination. These people, apparently, are the most typical human wolves and meet together to plan and carry out their terrible activities, have intercourse with corpses, and the like. What Kluckhohn calls *sorcery*, perhaps a branch of the above, gains its ends via enchantment by spell—reciting evil words over the possessions of the intended victim and then burying them with material from a grave. These practitioners may also have special spirit powers to aid them. In *wizardry* the evil activity consists of projecting a disease object into the victim. This is accomplished by placing it on an animal skin or in a basket and intoning the correct spell to make it travel into the victim. Usually one has to kill a close relative to become a practitioner of the above categories. The last type is *frenzy witchcraft* and involves the use of love magic to gain unfair advantages. It employs ground up plants of a special nature that are placed in food. This is also used in trading and gambling.

One gains protection from such evil persons by using charms and by possessing ceremonial knowledge. One can undergo protective rituals. There is also the notion that a strong and well-protected person can cause the evil of such individuals to backfire.

All ceremonial cures, if successful, are believed to cause the death of the witch before long, and various deaths are accounted for in this way. Some Navahos also believe that witches are commonly struck down by lightning. When public feeling is sufficiently aroused, the supposed witch is made to confess, which ensures his "magical" death within a year or he is actually put to death, sometimes by bloody and brutal means (Kluckhohn and Leighton, 1946: 129, 130).

Certainly the belief in types of "witches" among the Navaho leads to an amount of fear and caution in their daily lives. This example brings us to a consideration of still other facets in such antihealth concepts. We can turn now to some of these behaviors.

OTHER ASPECTS OF EVIL SUPERNATURALISM

Considered both as an explanation for particular types of illnesses and generally as the cause of a wider variety of misfortunes as well, witchcraft and sorcery do indeed engender a great deal of fear, or at the very least uneasiness. In response to such feelings there are a number of alternatives that may be employed in the sense of protection and revenge. Two basic possibilities are suggested. In the first, a would-be or actual victim essentially has to rely upon *private means*. Here a variety of courses of action exist. As pure protection, an individual may wear amulets or other physical objects thought to have the supernatural power to keep practitioners of evil supernaturalism (as well as evil spirits) at their distance. Along these lines a person may also utter special, protective phrases—often drawn from curing rites used against such evils—from time to time or when a situation renders a person especially susceptible to malign influences. There may also be special taboos—not going out at night when witches or sorcerers are about or eating foods that weaken one's resistance to evil. These obviously vary in quantity and variety from society to society. Among people where, like the Navaho, one's relatives may be the evil persons, it may even lead to extra "tender loving care" for such persons—lest resentment lead to attack.

A second private means is to employ one or more of the divination techniques described in detail earlier in this text. This is either to discover the presence of witches and sorcerers, to determine whether a specific ailment or misfortune is their doing, or to elicit the name or identity of a specific suspect. Finally, and therapeutically, an actual curing ritual (as described earlier in the present chapter) may be resorted to in the attempt to restore an individual so attacked to his or her proper state of health. Such attempts at relief may not only cure the sick person but may also try to send the bad influences back to the point of their origination, to harm the witch or sorcerer responsible.

The second basic alternative relies more on *public action* than on private means. Here in some kind of wider social context, often in addition to personal action, evil supernatural practitioners are dealt with or held in check. An excellent example of such practices is given for the Nupe of Africa by S. F. Nadel (1954). His account is very briefly summarized here, since it is discussed again in Chapter 10. Among the Nupe there was an annual "witch hunt" performed by the members of a secret antiwitch society composed of males. This society predicated its activities on the notion that it possessed a certain type of supernatural power as well as control of specific spirits. Members would go out to the various villages and engage in a special dance while wearing a unique type of mask covering the body as well as the head of the dancer. A spirit in each mask had the power to detect witches in the village. The women of the village (only women were witches) were understandably frightened by the sudden appearance of such dancers, and some were either discovered to be witches or they were able to bribe their way to innocence. At the very least, such a society was able to keep witches on the run for the benefit of the entire community.

Whether the response by people to the presumed existence of evil persons in their midst is private or public, means of detection and treatment generally are along similar lines. Detection, in addition to supernatural means, might also involve more purely secular involvements. A classic study along these lines is that of Beatrice Whiting (1950). Among the Paiute Indians of North America, an accused sorcerer would be made to confess his evil activities or would run away, really another sort of admission of guilt. What is interesting are the steps leading up to such an accusation. First of all, a person would get a reputation for being mean and uncooperative in everyday social relations and as such would come to antagonize the community. Second, gossip then revolved around such an antisocial person—why is he that way? Could it be that sorcery has made him mean and uncooperative? Third, some unfortunate event occurred, one to which circumstantial evidence tied the person around whom such discussions took place. The result of antisocial acts, gossip, and circumstances was a direct accusation and the discovery of a sorcerer! So here it is a case more of reputation than of divination.

Finally, we may mention that usually rather dramatic treatment is accorded the "convicted" witch or sorcerer. Generally such persons were killed, often in a most violent manner. Clubbing, stomping, and burning were common, and excommunication from their own society (social death) also appears a possibility, along with confiscation of the property of the guilty party. Sorcerers, because of their redeemability, seem to fare somewhat better. Overall, however, treatment is harsh due to the fear engendered by such individuals. It should also be mentioned that there is often an obligation on the kin of an afflicted individual to seek vengeance (especially if killed by a practitioner of evil), and this responsibility may also contribute to the usually terminal treatment of such persons. Having now briefly discussed health rituals from both a positive and negative perspective we can turn to the last major ritual category discussed in this book.

REFERENCES

Ackerknecht, Erwin.
> 1946. Natural Diseases and Ritual Treatment in Primitive Medicine.
> *Bulletin of the History of Medicine* 19:467–497.
——. 1942. Problems of Primitive Medicine.
> *Bulletin of the History of Medicine* 19:503–521.
Clements, Forest E.
> 1932. *Primitive Concept of Disease.*
> University of California Publications in Archaeology and Ethnology 32:185–241.
Frank, Jerome D.
> 1964. Foreward.
> In *Magic, Faith and Healing*, ed. Ari Kiev.
> Glencoe: The Free Press.
Gillen, John.
> 1965. Magical Fright.
> Reprinted in *Reader in Comparative Religion*, eds. William A. Lessa and Evon Z. Vogt, pp. 402–410.
> New York: Harper and Row.
Kiev, Ari, ed.
> 1964. *Magic, Faith and Healing.*
> Glencoe: The Free Press.
Kluckhohn, Clyde.
> 1944. *Navaho Witchcraft.*
> Peabody Museum Papers 22:1–149.
Kluckhohn, Clyde, and Leighton, Dorthea.
> 1946. *The Navaho.*
> Cambridge: Harvard University Press.
Levi–Strauss, Claude.
> 1963. *Structural Anthropology.*
> New York: Basic Books Inc.
Lieban, Richard W.
> 1967. *Cebuano Sorcery.*
> Berkeley: University of California Press.
Mair, Lucy.
> 1969. *Witchcraft.*
> New York: McGraw–Hill.

Marwick, Max, ed.
        1970. *Witchcraft and Sorcery.*
                Harmondsworth, England: Penguin Books.
Mayer, Philip.
        1970. *Witches.* In *Witchcraft and Sorcery,* ed. Max Mar-
                wick, pp. 45–64.
                Harmondsworth, England: Penguin Books.
Morgan, William.
        1936. *Human Wolves Among the Navaho.*
                Yale University Publications in Anthropology 11:1–
                43.
Murphey, Jane M.
        1964. Psychotherapeutic Aspects of Shamanism on St.
                Lawrence Island, Alaska. In *Magic, Faith and Heal-
                ing,* ed. Ari Kiev, pp. 53–83.
                Glencoe: The Free Press.
Nadel, Siegfried F.
        1954. *Nupe Religion.*
                Chicago–Glencoe: The Free Press.
Saler, Benson.
        1964. Nagual, Witch, and Sorcerer in a Quiche Village.
                Ethnology 3:305–328.
White, Leslie A.
        1962. *The Pueblo of Sia, New Mexico.*
                Bureau of American Ethnology Bulletin #184.
Whiting, Beatrice B.
        1950. *Paiute Sorcery.*
                Viking Fund Publications in Anthropology #15.

CHAPTER 6

Revitalization Rituals

The last major ritual category to be discussed is that of revitalization rituals. These, it will be recalled, were considered in the Wallace scheme as attempts on a level beyond the individual to solve some kind of group "identity crisis." Such rituals are often referred to in the literature as *religious movements* or *cult movements*, because of their group nature and due to the generally new aspects of behavior involved and the resistance they often engender from their own or some other society. This will become clear shortly. The first step in trying to understand such a ritual category is to engage in the attempt to classify these ritual types.

TYPES OF REVITALIZATION RITUALS

There exists a number of attempts to classify revitalization rituals. In fact, more discussion has occurred on this type with respect to forms and contexts and causes than on any of the other major ritual categories. This is partly due to the dynamic nature of such movements and partly due to their appeal to a wider range of interest than just that of the anthropologist, since quite often they are a social change phenomenon. It is too early for a consensus typology to have emerged, so we may simply summarize a few such attempts —each taking a somewhat different perspective—to illustrate the range of such supernatural activities and all thinking relative to them.

Linton Classification

The first example, and one of the oldest attempts, is that of Ralph Linton (1943), which was developed primarily to cata- logue movements of primitive peoples arising in response to threats from more powerful ("modern") societies. Such ac- tivities Linton called *nativistic movements,* and he defined them as "Any conscious, organized attempt on the part of a society's members to revive or perpetuate selected aspects of its culture" (Linton, 1943: 230). By such a definition Linton implied that such a movement could never manipulate their entire culture, only particular aspects or elements within it— generally those elements that have symbolic value or that are distinctive with respect to other cultures. He also suggested that the society involved must be aware of the existence of other societies and feel threatened by them. So nativism hinges on dominance-and-submission behavior. "Conscious, or- ganized efforts to perpetuate a culture can arise only when a society becomes conscious that there are cultures other than its own and that the existence of its own culture is threat- ened. Such consciousness, in turn, is a by-product of close and continuous contact with other societies . . ." (Linton, 1943: 230).

Based upon these considerations, this writer felt that there were two main axes along which such nativistic attempts might develop. The first of these was what he called *magical* or *rational* attempts. In *magical* nativism, the people lean most heavily on supernatural mechanisms and assume miracu- lous and unusual events will occur for the participants—resur- rection of ancestors, for example. In *rational* nativism, the element or behaviors involved are chosen more "realistically," although this does not preclude the use of supernatural sym- bols or behaviors; there may still be a ritualistic format. The difference might well be that between assuming the immi- nence of a cataclysm that will destroy the oppressors and save the elect of the movement versus simply maintaining some ritual that provides solidarity and integrity for the threatened group. The second axis is based on whether the at- tempt is to revive or perpetuate certain behaviors. In the first case the reference point lies in the past—behaving like the ancestors or keeping the past as a reference point (psycho- logically) or simply attempting to retain some aspect of pres-

ent behavior; again, this is generally something that sets the
society off from others. In Linton's scheme of classification
these two over-all aspects yield up four basic possibilities as
indicated in the chart below.

	Revive	*Perpetuate*
Magical	1	2
Rational	3	4

It should be mentioned that Linton had difficulty in finding
a case of type 2, magical nativism apparently having only
revivalistic aspects. He also emphasized the ideal nature of
such a classification, a given movement being only mostly
based on type 1, 3, or 4 behaviors.

Among other problems, the major criticism of this scheme is
that it did not take into account the possibility—widely documented—that movements may take place within a society.
Frustration and oppression (or whatever sets them off) are
not always caused by external sources. In light of this we
may turn to a somewhat broader scheme and one arranged
on a different basis.

Smith Classification

In a comprehensive effort at classification published in 1959,
Marian W. Smith considered such behaviors as cult movements. These movements were felt to be both deliberate, conscious, and organized (unlike many change phenomena) and
to originate as responses to social and economic dissatisfaction. The implication is that such movements are not always
engendered by disruptive culture contact.

Cults have often arisen during conditions of stress not immediately
triggered off by contacts with a foreign culture. All these movements are, however, portents of, or vehicles for, culture change and
they involve the society in a choice between widely accepted or
strongly supported values or practices, or both, and newly phrased
or validated ones. Thinking of them in this way, one is less apt to
accept "nativistic" as either the only one or the most inclusive of
cult categories (Smith, 1959: 9).

Since change is involved in some manner, Smith proposes
that such movements can be divided up in terms of this basic

aspect. *Nativism* seeks to revive or perpetuate aspects of a particular cultural system. It seeks to draw upon internal resources, so to speak. *Vitalism* places the stress more on external sources, recognizing newly perceived aspects of culture brought in from outside—beliefs, behaviors, and so on. As such, "Vitalism and nativism become parallel terms, emphasizing whether or not the changes proposed are in the direction of the acceptance and reorientation of traits or their continuance. Vitalistic movements tend to be productive in a positive sense and pave the way for new developments and growth, whereas nativistic ones are often . . . regressive" (Smith, 1959: 9). Finally, there are cases of *synthetism,* which stresses both internal and external sources by attempting to combine—in the same deliberate, conscious, and organized way—selected aspects of two cultures. The example given of this last possibility is that of Sikhism, which developed in South Asia as an attempt to blend Islam and Hinduism. Voodooism in Haiti, a blend of West African religion and Catholicism, also comes to mind.

In the Smith scheme, the scope for such movements is opened up based upon the materials of change being within, without, or both. Such movements cover a wider range than those of the Linton scheme, or at least they cover the same ground more adequately. As in the case of the first scheme, however, these categories are also conceived of as ideal. A given movement may involve more than one format. Smith also points out that there will be various "contextual features" that can be considered in the attempt to classify cult movements. Any basic type, nativism, vitalism, or synthetism may also feature any of the following possibilities. They may be, for example, *messianic.* They may stress the coming of some sort of messiah or savior. They may be *millenarian* in that they may stress the coming of a new age or cataclysmic events. They may also incorporate *militancy.* The participants may have the feeling that the ends involved necessitate aggression against those who oppose them (rather than passiveness) and may assert the need for the destruction of older or newer behaviors. Cult movements may have *reformative* aspects; that is, specific behaviors may be singled out and changed to help people achieve new meanings and realizations. Finally, such activities may also display what Smith called the character of *revivalism,* ". . . excessive exhibitions of personal behavior" (Smith, 1959: 10). This may involve dance behavior, seizures, and trance and is a common accompaniment to many such movements.

Aberle Classification

Still another classification of this ritual category is that of David F. Aberle (1966) and concerns what he calls *social movements*. He also considers these different from regular change in a society. He defines such movements as ". . . an organized effort by a group of human beings to effect change in the face of resistance by other human beings" (Aberle, 1966: 315). In his conceptualization of the type of such movements Aberle focuses his attention upon two main dimensions. The first of these concerns the location of the change that is being sought. It may be on an individual level—in people—or it may be beyond the individual—attempting to effect change in some major institution or in society itself. Second, Aberle is concerned with the amount of change involved—partial or total. These concepts of change, both with respect to focus and amount, are different from the perspective on change considered important by Smith. There are four possible types here (as in the Linton scheme), and they can be represented as follows in the chart below; the names given them by Aberle are supplied and discussed.

	Supraindividual Change	*Individual Change*
Total Change	1	3
Partial Change	2	4

The first type of movement, aiming at a complete change in supraindividual behavior is called a *transformative* movement, since its overall aim is to transform society. Such movements tend very strongly to be of the nature that Linton called *magical*, although Aberle would include revolutionary movements here as well. Certainly a major feature is often militancy. The second type is a *reformative* movement. This approach aims at only a partial change in society. As such, these are much more limited in scope (i.e., the women's rights movement). They appear most often to take forms that do not emphasize supernatural means of accomplishment. The third type, movements aiming at total changes in individuals, are called *redemptive* movements. The attempt is made here to effect behavioral changes more by the creation of a new inner state, by the means of psychological salvation and redemption. As in the other cases, the goal need not always be reached by supernatural means; witness psychoanalysis! The final movement type (number four in the chart) is an *alternative* movement. This type has as its aim only a partial change in individuals. "Many of the nativistic, revitalistic, millenarian, cargo, and other movements studied by anthropologists may be classified as transformative or redemptive . . ." (Aberle, 1966: 318). It should also be pointed out that Aberle feels his classification to be of the ideal type, although some movements may in fact be close to "pure types." A given type may also change its fundamental character over time. "A transformative movement may shift to the quest for individual salvation and thereby fall into the redemptive class" (Aberle, 1966: 317).

From a brief consideration of merely three of the dozens of classifications of revitalization rituals (or nativistic, cult, or social, depending upon the terminology of the individual writer) it becomes clear that both the range of activities and even more so the various criteria employed to define and categorize them seem endless. See also, for example, Clemhout (1964), Kopytoff (1964), and Wallace (1956). No further attempt at theoretical synthesis is attempted here. The student is simply reminded that any such scheme, basically, is merely a device to initiate thought and comparison. The statements of all scholars that their classifications are at best ideal warns us against "hardening of the categories." Probably all of the descriptive materials that we are shortly to examine can be fit more or less sufficiently into most such classificatory schemes.

Related Issues

One cannot, however, resist including two further comments of a theoretical nature at this point. First, anthropologists have not fully undertaken to include sociological analysis and categorization of sectarianism when discussing such phenomena in primitive societies. Bryan R. Wilson, for example (1969), has classified sects into seven fundamental types of which only two are very common in so-called primitive societies. He has also discussed these two types (1973) in great detail. If there is ever to be an overall science of supernaturalism, all scholars must become less limited in their approach, and some basic commonalities must be agreed upon. Second, it is clear from the obvious difficulties most classifiers have with the boundaries of their subject matter that it is also necessary to study comparable movements without fundamental supernatural orientations, for example, those of a political nature. We need to pay close attention to at least the literature on radical types of change in human societies. We need to study all kinds of social movements and then, from an interdisciplinary perspective, especially those of a supernatural nature to understand those exhibited in societies focused upon in anthropological research. We have a long way to go in our understanding and classification of such activities.

As suggested above, there are a great many revitalization rituals. They are deliberate attempts, and they involve some kind of organizational procedures. They are responses to some kind of dissatisfaction or problems on the part of at least some of the individuals in a given society (as are presumably all kinds of movements). And, whether the problems are caused by the society in question or by some other society as is perhaps most often the primitive case, such movements are associated in some way with change. "Radical political, social, or religious movements are usually seen as results of or reactions to fundamental social disruption and the extreme personal disorientation associated with radical change. Participants are therefore assumed to be groups suffering from a particular form of social disorganization or from some type of deprivation in the existing order" (Gerlach and Hine, 1970: xiii). Such movements may also cause change as well as being its result.

STAGES OF REVITALIZATION

Of considerable interest in the understanding of revitalization are the activities that might be called the internal dynamics of such movements. What are the stages of development that they pass through during the course of their existence? With his usual ability for synthesis, Anthony F. C. Wallace (1956) has, after careful comparison, suggested five stages of development for these movements. We indicate these to present another theoretical perspective on revitalization.

Steady State

This represents a base line, so to speak, the point in time when at least most individuals in a society are content with their state of existence. That is to say ". . . culturally recognized techniques for satisfying needs operate with such efficiency that chronic stress within the system varies within tolerable limits" (Wallace, 1956: 268).

Period of Increased Individual Stress

During this time there is an increase in the stress experienced by at least some individuals in the society. In other words, existing mechanisms for stress reduction become less effective. This may be due entirely to internal affairs or changes within the society or may result from contact with and influence from outside sources.

Period of Cultural Distortion

If the experience of stress is continued ". . . the culture is internally distorted, the elements are not harmoniously related but are mutually inconsistent and interfering. For this reason alone, stress continues to rise" (Wallace, 1956: 269). Many individuals develop ways to cope with this situation, including such regressions as alcoholism and apathy.

Period of Revitalization

As a solution to such problems, the possibility now exists for a revitalization movement that, Wallace believes, must perform at least six tasks. First, some kind of leader or "prophet" must combine or recombine—revive, perpetuate, import, whatever—some cultural elements into some sort of consistent structure. This often occurs by insight or revelation. Second, this leader has to spread his individualistic experience to others in the society along with the notion that ". . . the convert will come under the care and protection of certain supernatural beings; and that both he and his society will benefit materially from an identification with some definable new cultural system . . ." (Wallace, 1956: 273). Third, organization must take place, often stimulated by the first followers (disciples) of the leader. Next, adaptation must occur. Since most such movements are of a radical nature and may be opposed by those in power or by the members of a dominating society, "Those who desire the change, therefore, must mobilize for collective power to oppose the power vested in existing structures" (Gerlach and Hine, 1970: xiii). Such adaptations may involve militaristic aspects or the restructuring of doctrine to be more compatible with things as they are. If successful at this point, cultural transformation—the task of revitalization—occurs in which many members of the society accept the new rites and cultural formulations, and the previous levels of stress are reduced. Of course, many such movements fail before this task has been completed. This may be due to their unrealistic (magical) nature or to the application of force sufficient to terminate them. Finally, if all has been successful, what Wallace calls *routinization* occurs. The movement loses its dynamic qualities, and its suppositions are established as normal in the society.

New Steady State

"Once cultural transformation has been accomplished and the new cultural system has proved itself viable, and once the movement organization has solved its problems of routinization, a new steady state may be said to exist" (Wallace, 1956: 275).

Having now discussed various aspects of revitalization, we can now deal with several such movements in a more descriptive manner.

EXAMPLES OF REVITALIZATION

We may draw our first descriptive example of revitalization movements from the Pacific Islands where a variety of such activities, commonly called *cargo cults,* continue to occur even at the present time. Many of these movements were generated in response to outside contact and many involve at least some importation of outside materials as well as some millennial aspects. Certainly the island peoples of the Pacific and adjacent regions were subjected to a variety of foreign influences ever since the early 1500s and often experienced severe disruptions as a result. The first contacts were with explorers. By the late 1700s, whalers, traders, and missionaries had made their appearance. Then came planters, merchants, and slavers. In the early 1900s, mining proved to be a profitable activity. World War II brought still further contact and disruption to many island areas. Altogether, much foreign influence occurred, setting off destruction, profound dissatisfaction on the part of native peoples, and a fertile area for revitalization activities. One such movement was the Vailala Madness, which occurred in the Territory of Papua in New Guinea. For some general surveys of such movements in this world region see Burridge (1970), Cochrane (1970), and Worsley (1968).

The Vailala Madness

The Vailala Madness is chiefly known through the work of F. E. Williams (1923) and seems to have originated about 1919 among the people of the Village of Vailala. There were two main aspects to this movement. The first was that it was characterized by considerable display of "nervous and physical" behaviors. "In practically every village will be found a certain number of men who are from time to time overtaken by the Madness; and for lack of a better term, these may be called by their pidgin English name of 'Head-he-go-round Men' . . ." (Williams, 1923: 4). Such individuals exhibited swaying back and forth, rolling of the eyes, strange talking; such behavior was often interpreted as the result of spirit contact or influence. Williams, himself an observer of the movement, felt that some individuals were involuntarily seized by such symptoms, that some faked them so as not to be left out of the proceedings, and that others, the leaders, appeared to have the gift of inducing such a state when required. Certainly many of these unusual behaviors spread by emotional contagion, and the populations of entire villages were observed acting in such a manner.

The second main aspect of this movement was the doctrine that the dead were shortly expected to return to life. They were to arrive in a large boat of European type and would bring with them all manner of gifts intended for their living descendants. This element was no doubt stimulated by the Europeans themselves who appeared in native eyes to receive many gifts by boat and to have to do nothing to earn them. The reception of such valuables is the origin of the term "cargo cult" so often applied to such movements in the Pacific region. At any rate, villagers collected food, neglected their gardens and work, and awaited the coming of the ancestors and their gifts. Such beliefs varied somewhat from village to village. In some, the revived and returning ancestors were expected to be white, and in some the Europeans already present were considered as ancestors. In some cases, the gifts were expected to include rifles to drive the whites away, a militaristic notion quickly discouraged by the foreign power structure. There were ritual aspects to this movement.

The really fundamental fact in the whole cult is the tremendous interest in the dead; and perhaps the most important regular duty connected with it is the making of mortuary feasts. In all the affected villages are to be seen roughly-made tables, usually with benches surrounding them. These tables and benches are always fixtures and usually placed in some central position in the village. The relatives of a deceased person make a series of mortuary feasts which are set out upon the tables and consumed . . . by men and women alike (Williams, 1923: 19).

Such mortuary feasts were an older cultural feature to honor the dead, but in cargo cults they now became much more important, given the eventual return of the dead. In many villages daily food offerings were also given for such purposes. These were offered in special cult structures called "hot houses" after the notion that persons entering one would become "hot," that is to say, would be inspired with the symptoms of the "madness." The usual interpretation given for this was that the souls of the dead were attracted to such locations. Flagpoles were a part of these structures and (like European radio antennas) were considered as a medium for receiving messages from the dead. As part of such activities it should also be mentioned that new ethics were developed with many "thou shalt nots," especially an injunction not to neglect the feasts for the dead. Fines and public confession of such sins also developed as features of this cult.

Certainly such magical aspects of the Vailala Madness doomed it to failure; ancestors and gifts failed to materialize! After a while the majority of people in each village reverted to more normal behavior. A few individuals, however, seem to have maintained the cult behaviors and in the process came to exert considerable influence along secular as well as sacred lines.

Now in certain villages, at any rate, these men enjoy very considerable power; and it sometimes appears that they have superseded the former Chiefs. . . . In most instances there seems to be a small clique of such men in the village whose power will naturally vary according to their personalities, but who are to no small extent respected and obeyed. It is not too much to say that in many villages there is a "Head-he-go-round" regime. . . . It is especially in the detection of thieves, adulterers, and so forth, that the divinatory powers of these men are exercised . . . (Williams, 1923: 32, 33).

Such divinatory procedures were apparently often employed to enhance the position of such men by inspiring fear. In divination, long, battering-ramlike poles were carried on their shoulders, and such a pole "directed" itself to smash down the houses of "sinners" in the village. In so doing they continued to bluff the majority of villagers long after the movement had lost its immediacy. So even though this movement may be said on the whole to have failed, some participants carried on some associated behaviors past the point of inspiration and original excitement. By 1934 the movement was simply a memory, but one can recognize the dimension of hope offered by such movements to those suffering dissatisfactions.

The Ghost Dance

Another magically oriented (transformative) revitalization movement, one with pronounced millennial aspects, occurred on the part of various American Indian peoples and has been called the *Ghost Dance*. For some other types of American Indian revitalization consult Lanternari (1963). The movement in question first appeared among the Paviotsos of Nevada in 1870. This phase of activity was begun by a prophet, Wodziwob, who had received a vision exhibiting a railroad train carrying Indian ancestors. They were returning to life and would announce their coming with a great explosion. In the prophetic vision it was also suggested that the world would be subjected to a great cataclysm and would open up to engulf the Whites, who would disappear. White material culture—tools, wealth, and so on—would remain for the use of the Indians. Apparently, Indians would also be destroyed in the cataclysm, but those who followed the ways of the Ghost Dance were to be reborn shortly thereafter and would live in the company of the Great Spirit in a deathless existence.

Like the peoples of the Pacific, American Indians had been subjected to hostile outside influences and occupation of their lands by Whites. Loss of land, destruction of aboriginal culture, and outright genocide were the unfortunate results of these contacts, and by the nineteenth century Indian culture was shattered, and most groups were literally locked up on reservations. Feelings of helplessness and despair were rampant, so such an idea found an encouraging reception among Wodziwob's people. The basic ritual consisted of men and women dancing around a pole. The dances to be performed were traditional supernatural performances, but the songs that were to be sung at this time were new. They were taught to the dancers by Wodziwob, who had learned them while in a state of trance. This early phase of the Ghost Dance had only local significance for a time and then spread to other Indian societies west of the Mississippi River. Such revitalization procedures may also have spawned a number of other comparable movements among Western American Indians at this time, most of which also predicted great destruction and advised new ritual activities. As previously suggested, such groups were fertile fields for such movements at this point in their history.

Around 1890 a new prophet, Wovoka (John Wilson), infused new life into the Ghost Dance and caused an extraordinary spread of this cult. His tribal affiliation was Paiute, and he had originally been a supernatural leader among them.

His own vision was gained during a period of sickness and did not fundamentally differ from that of Wodziwob, although Wovoka appeared to have been less hostile towards Whites. James Mooney gives us the classic account of the Ghost Dance, and we can extensively quote him on its doctrine.

The great underlying principle of the Ghost Dance doctrine is that the time will come when the whole Indian race, living and dead, will be reunited upon a regenerated earth, to live a life of aboriginal happiness, forever free from death, disease, and misery. . . . The White race, being alone and secondary, and hardly real, has no part in this scheme of aboriginal regeneration, and will be left behind with the other things of earth that have served their temporary purpose, or else will cease entirely to exist. . . . All this is to be brought about by an overruling spiritual power that needs no assistance from human creatures. . . . On the contrary, all believers were exhorted to make themselves worthy of the predicted happiness by discarding all things warlike and practicing honesty, peace and good will, not only among themselves, but also towards the Whites, so long as they were together (Mooney, 1965: 19).

The suggestion here was that the dead were returning to life and were close to earth. Their final return would be signaled by earthquakes, and immortality would be the reward of the faithful.

An ethical code was also part of the doctrine propounded by Wovoka. Chiefly, injunctions were placed upon harming others, lying, and stealing. Adherents were admonished to love one another, to work hard, and not to engage in the destructive rituals for mourning the dead that had been a part of their original culture (destruction of property to show grief and so on). It especially preached that Indians should remain at peace with the Whites until the day of deliverance was at hand, when Whites would automatically disappear. Such forbidding of war was a basic alteration of traditional culture, and not all groups accepted the relevancy of such a doctrine. In fact the Sioux developed the idea that the "ghost shirt" (a special garment worn by dancers in the cult) had properties of a supernatural nature so as to be impenetrable to weapons of any sort, including the bullets of Whites. This led to a less than conciliatory attitude with respect to Whites, even though Wovoka himself did not feel that the ghost shirt idea was valid.

As in the 1870 phase, the dance was the major ritual endeavor. Men and women danced in concentric circles (over a four- or five-day period). Leaders invoked the ancestors in an opening song and were joined by the other participants, who formed a circle containing up to hundreds of dancers. A song was sung repeatedly as the participants circled around, although in the case of many dancers it would be sung only once. Rest periods might occur between songs and dance circuits. During such opportunities, leaders might relate their trance experiences or engage in sermonizing activity. No musical instruments were employed in this dance, which was also a departure from original custom. As the dancers circled around singing and dancing, the level of excitement slowly increased (partly by emotional contagion as in the Vailala Madness); as some participants became very affected (with muscular tremors and so forth), a leader hastened to them and waved a feather or a handkerchief rapidly in front of his or her eyes to enhance this condition. "For a while the woman continues to move around with the circle of dancers, singing the song with the others, but usually before the circuit is completed she loses control of herself entirely, and, breaking away from the partners who have hold of her hands on either side, she staggers into the ring, while the circle at once closes up again behind her" (Mooney, 1965: 198). The leader then continued to "hypnotize" such a person, and eventually they became rigid and passed into a trance state for an interval of time. Apparently such people were thought to be in contact with the dead.

Obviously, as with many movements of this variety, the Ghost Dance was doomed to failure. The overall vision of the millennium and the return of the ancestors failed to materialize. Yet, despite failure, the Ghost Dance did lead to a revival of much of native culture in some groups. The Pawnee were a good example of this occurrence. As elsewhere the movement held out hope for these people; hope of throwing off the influence of the White oppressors and recovery of their original freedoms.

The Ghost Dance doctrine brought hope. It promised a destruction of the invading white man, a return of the buffalo and old Indian ways, and a reunion of the Indians and their deceased forebearers. The last may well have been a Christian element, as well as the moral precept accompanying it . . . But the sanction for this hope was native to the Indian mind. It was based on the vision, on the direct supernatural experience. In the vision a message came from the deceased, telling the living what to do, telling the living what would happen (Lesser, 1933: 109).

This vision failed; but in the process of the ritual, Pawnee visionaries in their trances saw the ancestors practicing the older way of life—a way of life largely forgotten or lost for one or another reason at this particular point in time. Such visions led to a resurrection of these older elements of Pawnee culture.

This effect occurred in the following way: In a vision the subject would "see" some old way of life which had come to be disregarded. He would "remember" it. His vision then became a command upon those alive who knew how it must be carried out to do so. Sometimes there were men alive who knew the thing thoroughly and were persuaded by the demand of a supernatural message to begin it again. But often a ritual or dance was only partially remembered. Then many men would get together and pool their memories to revive the affair (Lesser, 1933: 112).

If one had such a vision, this was the only sanction necessary to perform such a rite—unlike the past where only direct learning was permissible. The final result of all of this was to give the Pawnee a new sense of integrity and solidarity. So one might observe that at least in one sense this revitalization movement did lead to some positive effects.

The Peyote Cult

Among the many revitalization movements among American Indians, one movement—the peyote cult—stands out as being rather remarkably successful. It is an example of a more rational and redemptive type of cult movement and involves the use of a rather remarkable plant.

Peyote . . . is a small, spineless, carrot-shaped cactus growing in Rio Grande Valley and southward. It contains nine narcotic alkaloids . . . some of them strychnine-like in physiological action, the rest morphine-like. In pre-Columbian times the Aztec, Huichol, and other Mexican Indians ate the plant ceremonially either in the dried or green state. This produces profound sensory and psychic derangements lasting twenty-four hours, a property which led the natives to value and use it religiously (LaBarre, 1938: 7).

The use of peyote is fairly widespread in Western North America today, and—as will be indicated later—it has been a factor in the continuation by these various tribal groups of their traditions and sense of identity and self-worth in the face of the national society.

Our example of the ritual of peyotism is taken from the Taos Indians of New Mexico (Collins, 1967, 1968). The Taos live in the Northeast near the upper Rio Grande and the Sangre de Cristo Mountains. They are the most northern of those groups residing in the Southwest who are grouped together by anthropologists as the Pueblo Indians. Peyote practices among the Taos are generally comparable to such activities among other tribal groups.

At Taos Pueblo the peyote ritual is almost always performed in response to a vow made by one of its participants. The only exceptions are cases of emergency, such as a special sickness, when time is lacking for the complex vowing procedures. In such cases the ritual may be performed on any night, whereas a vowed performance regularly occurs on a Saturday night. Vows to hold a performance are made by individuals for various, but usually specific, reasons. As it has been put, "You've got to have a good reason, more than just to eat the peyote." Analysis of these reasons suggests that there are three basic reason possibilities. It should be noted that the differences in vowing reasons does not substantially alter the nature of the ritual; only prayers are changed to fit the purpose. The first possibility can be called a *favor performance*. In this case the purpose is specific; the ritual is held in response to some difficulty. An individual vows to hold a ceremony in the hope of gaining a solution to some personal problem through supernatural means. Specific reasons vary widely and may include relief from sickness, success of crops, or related matters. An *appreciation performance* is held to offer thanks when a specific favor has been granted. The individual vows to hold a ceremony to express thanks for the resolution of his difficulty. The giving of such thanks may, however, be delayed until a number of things have accrued that require such a response. Finally, there are *blessing performances*. In these cases the purpose is more general. An individual vows such a ritual to insure ordinary good luck or to express general thanks. In a sense this is taking out a kind of supernatural insurance policy.

Such performances may coincide with national holidays but may occur just to keep participants active, that is, to provide an excuse for holding the ritual.

The person who vows to hold the ritual becomes its sponsor and will set a date for "his" particular performance. At this point three things must be accomplished. A leader (often called the "Road Chief") is selected, participants are invited, and food and other supplies are obtained. On Friday night preceding the ritual the poles for building the tepee in which the rite is held are erected and the ground cleared. On Saturday afternoon the tepee itself is set up, blankets and pillows are placed inside, the peyote is prepared, an altar is erected, and a supply of wood is collected. The altar is built of special sand in a crescent shape (usually called a "moon"); the fire will be built adjacent to it. The symbolism is very complex and cannot be taken up here (see Collins, 1968, for details). These tasks are divided between the sponsor and the leader. Other officials are also selected at this time—a fire chief to tend the fire, a drum chief to make the music for the leader, and a cedar chief to place cedar incense on the fire at selected points in the ritual. A woman is also selected to function in the ritual; she is usually the wife of the sponsor.

Preparations by the other participants are variable and individualistic, but there is a general feeling that behavior should be circumspect on the day of the ritual. One should maintain a serious frame of mind, not quarrel, and not use alcoholic beverages. In the evening all the peyote members who are to participate in the ritual assemble near the meeting place about six o'clock. Some purely secular discussion may occur at this time, but most participants quietly await the start of the ritual. The first official step occurs when the fireman goes inside the tepee and lights the fire. When he returns, all the participants line up in a systematic fashion consisting in order of the leader, the drummer, the cedar man, the congregation, and finally the fireman. Within the congregation older men, who are given their choice of seats, pick their places in the line accordingly. Then the leader offers a formal prayer that is fairly standardized and makes reference to the fact that the participants are there for good purposes. After this prayer the participants file clockwise into their positions inside the tepee.

Inside, the cedar man places some cedar incense on the fire for purification, and the leader "warms up" the peyote by the fire. He also does this to tobacco that will be used in special cigarettes. All this is believed to have beneficial effects on both the participants and the paraphernalia. Next the leader passes the tobacco, which is made into cigarettes. During this preparation the leader offers another formal prayer in which he states the specific purpose of the performance. He then delivers a series of instructions—to think only of God and the purpose of the rite. After these preliminaries the cigarettes are lighted. The fireman lights his cigarette first and then passes a burning twig from the fire clockwise around the tepee. The leader again offers a formal prayer to ensure the success of the ritual. At this time the congregation also offers private prayers.

The next task of the leader is to circulate the peyote. He takes four portions, gives four to the drummer, and then passes it clockwise around the tepee until it returns to him. The peyote is consumed by the participants as soon as they obtain it. The leader may again remind the participants of the sanctity of the occasion at this point and may welcome any visitors from other tribal groups. He then announces that singing will begin. He signs a special *Starting Song* and three others that accompany it. Next the drummer and the cedar man sing their four songs and the right to sing and drum passes clockwise (the man to the right of a singer accompanying him on the drum). These activities continue until about midnight, and the number of circuits depends upon the number of participants. During this time the leader may smoke and pray again, and participants may request more tobacco, pray, and/or request more peyote. After his own prayer, a participant may pass a cigarette to the leader and request the latter to pray for him. The tobacco smoke is thought to ensure truth and that the "prayers will be heard." At midnight the leader recalls the drum (and other paraphernalia) and sings another special song (the *Water Call Song*). He blows a special whistle and the fireman leaves to obtain water. The leader concludes his songs, again blows his whistle, and the fireman returns with the water, which is passed to the participants. The leader offers a formal prayer. The fireman removes the water from the tepee, and the leader goes outside to pray. He returns and instructs the participants to continue

with the drumming and the singing, returning the paraphernalia to the position of their recall. These activities then
continue until about sunrise.

When it is almost sunrise the leader again calls for water.
He blows his whistle and sings the *Morning Water Call Song*
and others that accompany it. This time he sends the fireman to bring the water woman who enters the tepee and
places the water by the door. The leader then requests that
the cedar man burn incense and offer a formal prayer. During
this prayer the water woman fans herself with the smoke
from the burning cedar. Next the drummer rolls a cigarette
for her; she smokes it and offers a formal prayer relating to
the purpose of the ritual. She may also pray for other things
at this time. When she has finished the fireman takes her
cigarette to the leader who also prays to ensure that the
prayers of the water woman will be answered. The water
woman then passes the water, and it moves clockwise until
it reaches her again. Each participant drinks; and after all
have finished, the water woman walks the circuit that the
water took, picks up the bucket, and leaves the tepee. As she
exits, the leader asks her to bring in a special "breakfast."
This breakfast, like the water itself, is symbolic of the necessi-
ties of life.

The water woman now brings in the breakfast, and the
leader usually asks an old man or a visitor to offer a formal
prayer. The breakfast foods and water are passed around
the tepee. After the foods have been consumed the leader
sings the special *Quitting Song* and some other songs and then
picks up the paraphernalia. Participants may sprinkle water
from inside the drum on themselves and on the floor as a
final blessing. Just prior to leaving the tepee the leader reminds them of the good they have accomplished by the
performance of the ceremony, and he—or one or more older
men—may engage in preaching activity. Occasionally a dona-
tion of money is requested to permit the secular peyote organization to replenish the supply of peyote.

When the participants leave the meeting place, the fireman
exits first; and the others leave clockwise, according to their
sitting positions. They remain in the immediate areas until
about noon, when a special meal is served. Before it is consumed, the participants pray over the food; the main prayer
is delivered by the sponsor, the leader, or someone desig-

nated by the latter. This prayer relates back to the purpose of the ceremony, is concerned with the experiences of the participants, and concludes with some reference to their unity as a group. After the prayer, the meal is consumed and the participants disperse.

The peyote cult is, as one might expect from the above description, an extremely personal kind of experience. One derives from participation in its ritual pretty much what one wishes. It is (as many participants have put it) a kind of road that one can follow. As LaBarre has so aptly summarized:

Peyotism functions in many other ways as a living religion. . . . Throughout life, peyote offers consolation for troubles, chastens for bad deeds or thoughts, advises and directs behavior through the drug-induced vision, and serves as the focus nowadays for both tribal and intertribal life, thus preserving and reinforcing many of the old cultural and religious values. . . . In this too, one tribe reinforces another against encroaching white culture. Thus peyote makes a major contribution toward the preservation of morale of the present day generation, torn as it is between loyalty to two cultures, the native and the white (LaBarre, 1947: 300, 301).

These general functions have been observed in a number of specific cases. For example, among the Delaware, "The younger generation is assimilating more White than Delaware culture. . . . They were facing a spiritual crisis and their religion appeared powerless to help them. Some turned to Peyotism and . . . more and more have been converted to the new religion . . ." (Petrullo, 1934: 25–27). The Taos Indians are themselves a case in point of this process. The old aboriginal religious organization that in the past gave solidarity and unity requires a long period of initiation, one scarcely possible today due to the insistence upon white schooling and work. The result is that for the greatest part, only older Pueblo members are very involved in it, and as they die its secrets are also lost. Younger people at the Pueblo not only do not join but often consider the aboriginal practices as "old hat" and criticize their elders for being out of step with reality. The old religion is not completely valid to younger population elements. These young people, on the other hand, are more active in the local Catholic church. This often becomes a way to be more modern and up to date. The older people, while nominally Catholic, do not really consider such new practices as being authentically Indian. In the peyote cult, however, all are offered a common ground for supernatural participation. For older people it is a way to remain at least partially Indian without being subjected to criticism for being rooted in the obsolete past (since this is an Indian movement). For the younger participants, disillusioned with the more traditional practices and looking toward the national society, it is something new and valuable. As such, peyotism among the Taos is a way for both old and young people to participate together in a meaningful, supernatural fashion and to reinforce their common cultural and social identity. We may now examine one last example of such revitalization activities.

The Jamaa Movement

Another revitalization format is demonstrated in Africa. These activities (redemptive, rational) are in some respects like peyotism but involve a different type of origin, a somewhat different doctrine, different rites, and they began much more recently. Like peyotism, it is a contemporary movement. These revitalization procedures are called the Jamaa movement (*Jamaa* meaning family). The movement was begun prior to 1960 by a Franciscan missionary originally from Belgium who had come to Katanga. This man, Placide Tempels, had originally come to Africa as a typical Christian missionary in support of colonialism. After a time he came to feel that his own ideas and Christianity per se did not fit very well in the context of African peoples. Early on, he became impressed with the thought of African Bantu tribes, which culminated in 1945 in a book on their philosophy. He questioned not only the idea of colonialism but sought to promote respect for the native culture, considering them as equals rather than as "helpless children." In particular he felt that if they could be enlightened about their own conceptions their response would immediately be enthusiastic. In his book on Bantu philosophy, he stated:

We do not claim, of course, that the Bantu are capable of formulating a philosophical treatise. . . . It is our job to proceed to such systematic development. It is we who will be able to tell them . . . what their inmost concept of being is. . . . More than that, if we can adapt our teaching of true religion to what is worthy of respect in their ontology, we shall hear, in the same way in which it was given to me, such testimony as was given to me. "Now you deceive yourself no longer, you speak as our fathers speak, it always seemed to us that we might be right" (Fabian, 1971: 31).

In the task of recasting Christianity in native terms, he stressed personal involvement as the way to accomplish this task.

In 1953 Tempels was appointed pastor at a mining settlement near Kolwezi in Katanga and began to initiate discussions along the above lines, formulating Christian ideas in the context of Bantu categories of thought. His message found a good response due to the emergence of self-awareness and desire for liberation of the peoples involved. These miners were dissatisfied and lacked hope and felt inferior to Whites. The Jamaa doctrine held out the idea of human dignity—*Umuntu* (being man). The cult spread rapidly after 1960 due to the independence of the Congo and the secession of Katanga, although Tempels himself left Africa for health reasons in 1962.

The basic pattern of organization of this movement is for a leader to attract followers (originally Tempels, later disciples) who develop their own followers as they are trained in the doctrines. Most recruits were Catholic mission Christians and married. It should be understood that what might be seen as a lack of many distinct rituals is partly due to the fact that Jamaa is basically grafted onto Christian doctrine and practice. A Jamaa group is definable due to its engagement in certain other activities based on their extra beliefs. Basically, three types of such activities occur. The first is a weekly meeting, the *Mafundisho*, which involves an introductory prayer and hymn, instruction in the doctrine by leaders, announcements relative to current affairs, and a concluding prayer. Comparable activities may occur on almost any other occasion of importance, for example, a wedding. Second is the *Pulan*, an intergroup meeting that includes the presentation of candidates (so that all can see them) for the first and second degrees. The last ritual is the *Ku-ingisha* rite, which is performed by a priest who, like Tempels in the beginning, is a member of the movement. This ritual involves some revelation of secrets and examination of the awareness of candidates; it instructs them in the meaning of belonging to the Jamaa, prophesies about what initiates can expect, and gives direction about the *initiatory experience* to be undertaken by them.

To become a fully initiated member requires at least three years of instruction—some public and more on a private basis. It is also required that secrecy be maintained concerning the doctrine. There are three degrees or "ways" in the doctrine. Each degree actualizes one of these ways in the Ku-ingisha ritual, depending upon the level of knowledge attained by the candidates. In the first way, the candidates receive the thought of *life/force*. They receive a consciousness of their vocation by uniting themselves with Jesus Christ and the Virgin Mary. They are told to prepare for this with prayer and meditation. "The proof of their admission to the first degree will be their initiatory experience, union with . . . [Jesus and Mary] . . . in a dream" (Fabian, 1971: 169). In the second degree or way, the candidates receive the thought of *union in love;* that is to say, between husband and wife. Again, prayer and meditation are involved, and the initiatory experience consists of ritual intercourse between the husband and wife. At this point they realize "complete union," and the marriage is elevated to the Jamaa level for group unity as well. In the third degree or way the candidates receive the thought of *fertility/fecundity.* At this point they also gain full integration into the Jamaa.

Husband and wife, now in the roles of Mary and Joseph, are to give birth to Jesus Christ, represented by the priest. This is the point where the ritualized "encounter" between priest and candidates is supposed to happen: the "exchange" of their deepest feelings and wishes, of the story of their lives, and their conversion. The idea is that in this "confession" the priest humiliates himself before his parishioners to become their child. He re-enacts God's descent on the Holy Family . . . Having given birth to the priest, the initiates have now acquired . . . parenthood, which gives them the right to introduce other candidates to the movement (Fabian, 1971: 170).

The initiatory experience here is the ritual confession. Through such ritual activities and in terms of their doctrine, a sense of hope and identity is given followers, a development accomplished without the agency of militancy (although friction with nonmember priests does occur). A sense of continuity is also guaranteed via the bringing of new members into the movement. For some other African movements with somewhat different dimensions, see Bengt Sundkler (1961).

We have examined four specific cases of revitalization ritual—the Vailala Madness and the Ghost Dance, as examples of more dramatic types of movements, and Peyotism and the Jamaa activities as cases of more moderate degree. These are somewhat, but not entirely, representative of such movements as a whole. We have also indicated some of the many classifications of revitalization attempts and given one perspective on the stages that they pass through in the course of their development. These are deliberate courses of action undertaken by groups to solve some kind of "identity crisis," to overcome dissatisfaction and to provide hope. As such, these have increased in the world as the more "modern" nations have come to disrupt those of a "primitive" nature. Many revitalization movements occur in the context of modern societies as well, since many aspects of contemporary life have apparently caused despair for groups of people (see Zaretsky and Leone, 1974).

Revitalization rituals are only one of four major types; technological rituals, health rituals, and social rituals also occur in a variety of possibilities. The specific functions of supernatural experience are discussed in Chapter 10, but it can be suggested that the relationship of all such activities to human life is wide and penetrating. They help us to control such various aspects of nature as our physical environment. They help us to control the social environment of our fellow human beings, and—either positively or negatively—they permit human beings to gain access to the health process—to cure or harm, as the case might be. Finally, we have the solutions provided by revitalization rituals as discussed in the present chapter. It could be argued, of course, that all of supernaturalism is geared to revitalization, that its ultimate function is one of hope and identity. This is perhaps true; we must avoid imposing too many categories on supernaturalism or at least remain aware of their artificiality. For the present, however, we can keep these four ritual categories in mind and move on in Part 3 to a consideration of some other aspects of supernaturalism and other accounts possessing supernatural content. These dimensions of supernaturalism will add substance to the ritual types previously discussed.

REFERENCES

Aberle, David F.
  1966. *The Peyote Religion Among the Navaho.*
    Chicago: Aldine Publishing Company.
Burridge, Kenelm.
  1970. *Mambu.*
    New York: Harper and Row.
Clemhout, Simone.
  1964. Typology of Nativistic Movements.
    Man No. 64:14–15.
Cochrane, Glynn.
  1970. *Big Men and Cargo Cults.*
    Oxford: Clarendon Press.
Collins, John J.
  1968. A Descriptive Introduction to the Taos Peyote
    Ceremony.
    Ethnology 7:427–449.
———. 1967. Peyotism and Religious Membership at Taos
    Pueblo, New Mexico.
    Southwestern Social Science Quarterly 48:183–191.
Fabian, Johannes.
  1971. *Jamaa: A Charismatic Movement in Katanga.*
    Evanston: Northwestern University Press.
Gerlach, Luther P., and Hine, Virginia H.
  1970. *People, Power, Change: Movements of Social Trans-
    formation.*
    New York: Bobbs–Merrill Co.
Kopytoff, Igor.
  1964. Classifications of Religious Movements: Analytical
    and Synthetic. In *Symposium on New Approaches
    to the Study of Religion,* ed. June Helm, pp. 77–90.
    Seattle: University of Washington Press.
LaBarre, Weston.
  1947. Primitive Psychotherapy in Native American Cul-
    tures: Peyotism and Confession.
    Journal of Abnormal and Social Psychology 42:294–
    309.
———. 1938. *The Peyote Cult.*
    New Haven: Yale University Press.
Lanternari, Vittorio.
  1963. *The Religions of the Oppressed.*
    New York: Alfred A. Knopf.
Lesser, Alexander.
  1933. Cultural Significance of the Ghost Dance.
    American Anthropologist 35:108–115.

Linton, Ralph.
　　　1943.　Nativistic Movements.
　　　　　　American Anthropologist 45:230–240.
Mooney, James.
　　　1965.　*The Ghost Dance Religion and the Sioux Outbreak
　　　　　　of 1890* (first published 1896).
　　　　　　Chicago: University of Chicago Press.
Petrullo, Vincenzo.
　　　1934.　*The Diabolic Root.*
　　　　　　Philadelphia: University of Pennsylvania Press.
Smith, Marian W.
　　　1959.　Towards a Classification of Cult Movements.
　　　　　　Man No. 51: 8–12.
Sundkler, Bengt G. M.
　　　1961.　*Bantu Prophets in South Africa.*
　　　　　　New York: Oxford University Press.
Wallace, Anthony F. C.
　　　1956.　Revitalization Movements.
　　　　　　American Anthropologist 58:264–281.
Williams, F. E.
　　　1923.　*The Vailala Madness and the Destruction of Native
　　　　　　Ceremonies in the Gulf Division of Papua.*
　　　　　　Papuan Anthropological Reports #4.
Wilson, Bryan R.
　　　1973.　*Magic and the Millennium.*
　　　　　　New York: Harper and Row.
————. 1969.　A Typology of Sects.
　　　　　　In *Sociology of Religion,* ed., R. Robertson, pp. 361–
　　　　　　383.
　　　　　　Harmondsworth, England: Penguin Books.
Worsley, Peter.
　　　1968.　*The Trumpet Shall Sound.*
　　　　　　New York: Schocken Books.
Zaretsky, Irving I., and Leone, Mark P., eds.
　　　1974.　*Religious Movements in Contemporary America.*
　　　　　　Princeton: University of Princeton Press.

PART III

RELATED ISSUES

CHAPTER 7

Practitioners and Participation

One of the dimensions of supernaturalism that we have mentioned but not yet explored systematically is the issue of human involvement in supernaturalism. What kinds of supernatural leaders exist, and how does one come to occupy such a position? What other kinds of involvement and/or participation are available to the supernatural layman or to the congregation? As suggested, some notions relating to this topic have already been presented. In Chapter 1 a distinction was drawn in ideal terms between the professional and his client and the shepherd and his flock. In Chapter 2 we presented ways in which the supernatural "impulse" obtains expression —personal apprehension of the holy, myth and ritual, harmony with cosmic law, and freedom through spiritual insight (or mysticism). We also dealt with the ideological, intellectual, emotional, ritualistic, and consequential dimensions of such experiences as well as the basic confirming, responsive, ecstatic, and revelational natures possible in such experiences. We have also dealt in Chapters 3, 4, 5, and 6 with leaders and participants in action, so to speak. To put, at the very least, the leaders and followers in their proper contexts, we may now examine some of their basic types. At the same time we can introduce some other aspects of this arena of supernaturalism.

Anthropologists, by and large, have not made any substantial theoretical progress in delimiting the types of supernatural leaders beyond the rather obvious, logical distinction between those persons who conduct rituals and those who in some way as individuals or groups are thought to benefit from those rituals. It is assumed that leaders have special attributes (training, call to office, powers, and so forth) and that laymen become somehow dependent upon them as clients and congregations. Yet such nonspecialists may perform some activities entirely for themselves (magic or prayer); they may have to participate to ensure the success of some supernatural endeavor, the entire population of some society may aspire to a leadership role, and many leaders may not function as such in any full-time role. Hence this distinction must be drawn carefully; it is perhaps less logical than it first appears.

TYPES OF SUPERNATURAL INVOLVEMENT

An older attempt at making a comprehensive scheme along these lines was that of Paul Radin (1957). This scheme has been largely neglected due to the theoretical bias on which much of Radin's work was based, but it does appear to be a fairly good attempt at an overall beginning.

If religious feeling is to be characterized as far more than normal sensitiveness to certain customs, beliefs, and superstitions, it is fairly clear that no individual can remain in this state continuously. In some individuals, however, it can be called up easily. These are the truly religious people. They have always been few in number. From these to the essentially unreligious individual the gradations are numerous. If these gradations are arranged in the order of their religious intensity, we have three types: the truly religious, the intermittently religious, and the indifferently religious. The intermittently religious really fall into two groups—those who may be weakly religious at almost any moment; and those who may be strongly religious at certain moments, such as at temperamental upheavals and crises (Radin, 1957: 9, 10).

The truly religious person is, of course, the individual most often called to positions of supernatural leadership in his or her society. This person Radin calls the "Priest–Thinker," the person most often involved in or theologizing about the nature of the supernatural world. Intermittently religious people are those who become clients and congregations. Indifferently religious people may well become "believers," especially during times of crisis, but the implication is that they supply the ranks of those suspicious sorts who deny the validity of supernaturalism. Such nonbelievers surely occur in primitive societies as they do in our own. Such categories of participation are surely in need of expansion and refinement, and this task should be an immediate concern of anthropologists involved with the study of religion.

Another older approach is that of Joachim Wach (originally in 1944), who distinguished between the person possessing one or another variety of religious authority and the audience, the types of groups who respond to that authority. Such authority is thought to be based on the possession of certain qualities lacked by other individuals, which makes leaders "Homo religious." Such qualities might be derived from the personal nature of the leader or from the office or position held by that person. In either case, such persons are thought to be closer to the supernatural world than others in their societies. Wach went on to distinguish some basic types of religious authority as manifested in leadership types.

The founder is a person who bases his authority on preaching and teaching. The reformer has less creative religious power than the founder and does not develop a great faith, but still has some authority along preaching and teaching lines. The prophet is a third type:

The prophetic authority is distinctly secondary, a derived authority, more distinctly so than the authority of the founder. . . . Visions, dreams, trances, or ecstasies are not infrequently encountered, and by these the prophet is prepared to receive and interpret manifestations of the divine. He shares this privilege with other types of religious leaders . . . His interpretation, however, is "authorized", a fact which distinguishes him . . . It is characteristic of prophetic revelations that they are usually not induced by methodical or casual manipulation, but arise spontaneously and are received passively. This differentiates prophecy and divination (Wach, 1962: 347).

The seer is characterized as a sort of junior-grade prophet and is a person who also has contact with gods or spirits. He is, however, less general in his predictions and statements; he is more individualistic in his relevancy and deals more with personal situations than the prophet type of leader. He still has a spirit-message type of authority. Other types of leaders suggested by Wach are magicians, diviners, and priests. As he himself points out, however, there is a profound overlap between all of these leadership types, their actions, and bases of authority. As such, most anthropologists have been content to make a simpler somewhat ideal distinction between two general types widespread in primitive societies, the shaman and the priest.

THE SHAMAN

The position of supernatural leadership that anthropologists have designated "shaman" is apparently found quite commonly in primitive societies. The term itself, however, is used to cover a host of phenomena not all of which are currently agreed upon by those writers who employ the term. We can give here only an indication of what might be called the "classic" manifestations of this type of behavior, illustrate it with some descriptive accounts, and indicate some of the difficulties connected with its usage.

The term *shaman* itself is taken from the North Asian Tungus people who call one of their leader types the *Saman*, meaning "one who is excited or raised." This term possibly derives from the area of South Asia from the Pali word, *Samana*. The classic area of shamanism is in Siberia, Central Asia, and Arctic North America, where such a person ". . . has mastered spirits and who can at will introduce them into his own body. Often in fact, he permanently incarnates these spirits and controls their manifestations, going into controlled states of trance in appropriate circumstances" (Lewis, 1971: 51). A somewhat more restricted view is that of Mircea Eliade (1972) who holds that shamanism basically is a technique of ecstasy, an engaging in trances during which the shaman's soul can leave his body and ascend to the sky or descend to the underworld. A somewhat fuller statement defining shamanism occurs in the *Hastings Encyclopedia of Religion and Ethics:*

While the shaman exercises certain priestly functions, his main powers are connected with healing and divination. These he exercises by virtue of his intimate relations with the supernatural world. Certain spirits aid him, possess him, are at his command. He has direct intercourse with spirits and actual (bodily or spiritual) access to the spirit world. With the aid of these he obtains knowledge superior to that of ordinary men, and can overcome or drive out hostile spirits or powers. . . . And generally, during the exercise of his powers, the altered mental state of the shaman is in evidence (MacCulloch, 1924: 441).

These statements or views give a general indication of the type behavior of shamans, even though the emphasis may be slightly different. In the attempt to generally indicate the character of shamanism we can offer the following list of basic characteristics (even though they are not universally agreed upon by scholars).

1. First of all, the powers of the shaman are derived from some sort of direct contact with the world of the supernatural —most specifically, with one or more spirits or deities residing within it. These spirits may be rather highly placed gods (in some cases the most powerful), they may be spirits of a more minor nature, or they may in fact be the spirits of deceased shamans—often one's own kin. These beings give a shaman enhanced qualities beyond those of purely magical technique or, at the very least, enhancement of magical effectiveness.

2. These powers are gained by the shaman (originally) in a variety of ways that basically reduce to two. The shaman may—especially in the classic area for this phenomenon—gain the powers by hereditary right because of being a kinsman of a former shaman. Or, one may respond to a "call or election" from the spirits in general. It may be, as Eliade has put it, a case of spontaneous vocation. Along these lines, although not overlapping with them completely, is the notion that such inheritance or free election may result from a deliberate quest or may come unsought. In either case, the pattern for obtaining such power appears to be fairly standardized. It involves some kind of interaction with the spirits and some kind of apprenticeship to practicing shamans to learn the various techniques through which the power gains expression. "This twofold course of instruction, given by the spirits and the old master shamans, is equivalent to an initiation. Sometimes the initiation is public and constitutes an autonomous ritual in itself. But absence of this kind of ritual in no sense implies absence of an initiation; the latter can perfectly well occur in dreams or in the neophyte's ecstatic experience" (Eliade, 1972: 13). The content of the spirit contact aspect of all this usually involves the "death" of the would-be shaman at the hands of the spirits, renewal or rearrangement of his internal organs or addition of special substances to his body, and revelations of special knowledge. Such an experience, coupled with later apprenticeship, converts the shaman

into a person of an extraordinary nature. We will presently examine some descriptive details of such proceedings.

3. A third characteristic commonly found in shamanism is that this type of supernatural practitioner can actually "traffic" in the sacred world. Because of the powers bestowed upon him and honed by experience, he can accomplish tasks beyond the abilities of ordinary people. Of all the special tasks the shaman may be called upon to perform, those connected with curing the sick (from supernatural maladies) and divination (for the whereabouts of game, the enemy, and so forth) seem to be the most common. It should also be noted that other practitioners may also engage in these types of activities; but lacking the shaman's special nature, they are apt to be less successful in dealing with them. Shamans sometimes also serve as mediums; they may be mouthpieces for the spirits to speak directly to other individuals. Likewise, shamans are thought to be able to send their souls to ascertain information, coax back a lost soul, and accomplish other supernatural errands. They may utilize the power of their helping spirits to increase what they themselves have gained. The actual application of shamanism and its variety are great. With some significant exceptions—perhaps an embarrassing number—shamans are generally thought to function in situations of a more critical and unscheduled nature than those of some other types of supernatural practitioners.

4. Another seemingly general characteristic of the shaman concerns his or her position or context in their society. Shamans strongly tend to be males, and in contrast to some other specialists they are generally part-time practitioners. This is to say that though they may take some compensation for their endeavors, they do not usually make a complete living off the proceeds of such activities. They themselves may have to participate in the direct quest for food, as do the other members of their society not so exceptionally gifted. In fact, in many cases such a person may function chiefly (or only?) on behalf of his own kinsmen, although a shaman of great repute may be sought out by other people—as is also the case where shamans have acquired more specialized abilities. It has also been a general observation of anthropologists that shamans tend to be associated with some of the simpler primitive societies: hunters and gatherers, herders, and horticulturalists. In such societies there is a tendency for shamans

to operate rather individualistically in their practice, and in fact, numerous accounts exist of their actually competing with and attempting to harm one another. Certainly shamans exist in more complicated societies. In such situations there appears to be a trend toward more collective activities with "group practices" involving societies of shamans (recall the Pueblo curing society discussed in Chapter 3). In such social situations, other types of supernatural leaders also emerge; and where society becomes even more complex, these other leaders may come to occupy the center of the supernatural stage. The shaman types may begin to recede into the background, or at least lose their more exclusive franchise.

5. Another character usually conceded to shamans is their association with unusual psychological and physiological behaviors. As previously mentioned, the trance state appears to be a hallmark of shamanistic practice. This is a condition of dissociation and lack of movement. Such a trance state, however, may be complete or only partial; it may run from mere, quiet contemplation (or mystical rapport) through rather hysterical seizures, to a state of deep withdrawal from all surrounding circumstances. Such behavior, the ability to go into and, importantly, come out of a trance experience, clearly demarcates the shaman as a very special kind of person. In the societies where shamans exist, the trance state is overwhelmingly interpreted as either the result of the departure of the shaman's soul on some sacred journey or as evidence of the possession of his body by his spiritual associates. It is very important to note at this point that the spirit possession involving the shaman is quite a different phenomenon from spirit possession as illness involving other individuals. Above all, in the case of possession, it is—for the shaman—a voluntary experience. The shaman, in becoming a "master of spirits," can control the situation for his own purposes. To be a shaman is to render the spirits obedient to human beings. Theoretically the shaman is in the "driver's seat," whereas the nonshamanic involvement in spirit possession is a case of being at the mercy of the spirits; it occurs in involuntary fashion. So it must be stressed that the shaman is unique not just because of trance but due to his supposed abilities to harness such experiences for his own ends. Lewis (1971), along social context lines, would characterize supernatural systems that feature such voluntary–involuntary contrasts as

central possession religions. This could be added to the social characters discussed under number 4 above. How is the state of trance actually accomplished?

As is well known, trance states can be readily induced in most normal people by a wide range of stimuli, applied either separately or in combination. Time-honored techniques include the use of alcoholic spirits, hypnotic suggestion, rapid over-breathing, the inhalation of smoke and vapours, music and dancing; and the ingestion of such drugs as mescaline or lysergic acid and other psychotrophic alkaloids. Even without these aids, much the same effect can be produced, although usually in the nature of things more slowly, by such self-inflicted or externally imposed mortifications and privations as fasting and ascetic contemplation . . . (Lewis, 1971: 39).

As a simplification it can be suggested that such techniques fall into two main classes. *External* techniques could include such stimuli as music, chanting, dancing, use of incense or smoke, alcohol, and various drugs. *Internal* devices could involve control of respiration, fasting, lack of sleep, and things not requiring outside objects. An excellent series of accounts on one specific trance aid is that found in Harner (1973). It should also be mentioned that the possibility exists that the trance is part of shaman behavior in some cases, because the individual involved is not normal. That is, he suffers from epilepsy or schizophrenia. This may be the case in some instances, however, the fact that such practitioners seem in good control of their "abnormal" behaviors suggests that most are normal persons or, if suffering from some impairment originally, have managed through shamanism to cure themselves.

Still another unusual behavior associated with shamanism and often exhibited by other supernatural participants as well is the phenomenon of speaking in tongues, or *glossolalia* as it is often called. This is often an accompaniment of trance and consists of verbal articulation of a variety of utterances that depart seriously from normal speech patterns. These may range from grunts and groans to singsong syllables. They may include a few recognizable words, often drawn from languages not native to the speaker. Such unusual speech is to be considered differently from the use of sacred languages (like Latin in a Catholic Mass). Such special ritual words may also be employed by the shaman or other types of supernatural practitioner and is often simply an archaic speech form. Unlike speaking in tongues, however, sacred languages are generally considered intelligible. How is glosso- lalia interpreted by the observer in shamanic societies? Gen- erally it is considered either as the voices of the helping spirits speaking through the shaman or as the shaman's own voicing of the spirit talk he himself hears. Generally no at- tempt is made to understand such speech by other partici- pants. Meaning, if any, usually is supplied later on by the shaman. Because of its common occurrence in many societies outside the traditional shamanic setting, glossolalia has re- cently received considerable attention (see, for example, Goodman, 1972).

In sum, we have drawn too general a picture of the shaman and his activities; we have examined an "ideal" type of su- pernatural practitioner. We have discussed the basis of his power, its acquisition, the activities of such persons and their social contexts, and the special character both behaviorally and spiritually that they assume. Before drawing the contrast between this general type of practitioner and the priest, an- other ideal type commonly identified by anthropologists, we may examine some descriptive accounts of shamanism to il- lustrate the characters drawn above and then add a brief note on some of the problems involved with such a concep- tualization.

EXAMPLES OF SHAMANISM

The Buryat

As a first example of shamanism we may discuss the Buryat who live near Lake Baikal in North Asia. They are essentially a pastoral nomadic society, and their shamans fall into the classic formula for such practitioners. In Buryat society there are various types of shamans. White shamans (good) are associated with a westerly direction and with good gods and spirits. Black shamans (evil) are connected to the east and to bad gods and spirits. Functionally, white shamans have better control over their supernatural helpers and deal with a variety of events. Black shamans have less control (are more controlled?) with reference to their spirits and are generally

called on only when disaster threatens, on occasions when
no stone can be left unturned. Both types of shamans are the
objects of some degree of fear.

The shaman, because of his nervous and psychic aberrancies, is a
difficult person in social life; the Buryats regard the shaman as the
worst kind of man . . . They are so regarded for several reasons.
First of all, they are individualists, odd, abnormal, queer, in a
society noted for its communal living; second, because they live in
a hectic, excited manner, and in a dangerous world which is not the
world of everyday life. Because of their life in the mid-world they
perform services special to themselves, and are respected, honored,
feared for these services (Krader, 1967: 119).

Shamanism among the Buryat is usually a case of heredity
with white shamans inheriting on the male side and black shamans via female descent reckoning. Only occasionally will the
gods strike someone fortuitously and call them to the position.
Usually the souls of ancestral shamans choose a descendant.
He becomes absent-minded, given to solitude, has unusual
dreams, and the like (typically an index of the call in many
societies). Generally the chosen person eventually lapses into
unconsciousness, during which time his soul is supposed to
have been taken away by the spirits. He is thus received
into the abode of the gods. Here it is tortured, his body is cut,
and his flesh is cooked. On a more "positive" note he also
has sexual relations with various female deities. After these
ordeals he is then instructed in the secrets of the trade by
the ancestral shamans. He has now received his power and
his spiritual initiations. "For many years after his first ecstatic experiences (dreams, visions, dialogues with the spirits,
and so forth) the apprentice shaman prepares himself in solitude, taught by old masters and especially by the one who
will be his initiator and who is called the father shaman"
(Eliade, 1972: 115). After a few years of engaging in such
activities there occurs a formal initiation into the profession.
This is in effect a ritual of consecration. The procedures are
too complex to describe in detail, but they consist essentially
of the following events. A tree is set up in the shaman's hut
with roots in the hearth and the top projecting through the
smoke hole of the roof. This opens up the sky for the shaman
as well as indicating his abode as that of a shaman. Other
trees (poles) are placed in the ground—nine for the nine
heavens of Buryat cosmology. After many sacrifices and offer-

ings to the gods and ancestral spirits and prayers, the candidate climbs the tree in his hut to invoke the aid of the gods. Then he, his teacher, and assistants go to the other nine trees. A goat is sacrificed and the candidate smeared with its blood. After more preparations and more sacrifices:

Then nine or more animals are sacrificed, and while the meat is being prepared, the ritual ascent into the sky takes place. The father shaman climbs a birch and makes nine notches at the top of it. . . . The candidate ascends in his turn, followed by the other shamans. As they climb, they all fall into ecstasy. (Eliade, 1972: 119).

After more climbing (symbolic of shamanic journeys), the meat from the sacrifices is consumed and the Buryat shaman duly consecrated in his professional position in this society.

The Netsilik

Another example of shamanism, also from the area of classic distribution, is found among the Netsilik Eskimo of Arctic North America. The Netsilik data not only confirm most of the basic characters of the shaman but also indicate the problem of what to call closely related types of practitioners. Among these people, Asen Balikci (1967) recognizes the existence of four types of supernatural practitioners, only one of which truly qualifies without reservation as a shaman. This is the Angatkok. This practitioner type is characterized by a spirit possession trance and has protective spirits. Generally speaking, one gains the office by receiving a call—objectified by one's unusual behavior that is noticed by practicing shamans. A period of formal training and apprenticeship is required along with the observation of numerous taboos.

The novice, assisted by a spirit, slept intermittently and began having visions. Then he moved to a separate igloo where, during a period of several weeks, he was taught the secret vocabulary together with the shamanistic techniques and obtained his paraphernalia . . . from his parents. Finally his teacher presented him with a protective spirit (tunraq), and they officiated together. Initially the tunraq was the master of the novice, and only gradually did the young angatkok learn to control it. Eventually, the novice became a full-fledged shaman, possessing a competence and a strength apparently equal to that of his master (Balikci, 1967: 194).

In practice the shaman could send his protective spirit to perform many tasks, divining information and especially aiding in curing the sick. When curing, the shaman called a protective spirit into his body and went into trance; the spirits spoke, and the evil spirits in the patient's body left it and hid outside the dwelling. The shaman then directed his helpers to chase the evil spirits back into the igloo where he would kill them. As indicated earlier, such acts were usually accomplished while the shaman himself remained in a special state of being.

A second "shamanistic" type of practitioner was the Krila-soktoq. This leader appears to lack the trance state practices of the first type and requires no special apprenticeship or training. There are helping spirits whose powers are an aid in practice, but they are weaker sorts of deities than those of the Angatkok and do not bind themselves to single practitioners. These supernatural practitioners also involve themselves in curing the sick. The basic technique involved "head-lifting." This consists of tying a thong around the leg of the shaman or around his wife's head. He then calls the spirits to pull on the thong, an easy pull meaning a no answer in response to questions and a heavy pull indicating a positive reply from the spirits. After questioning the spirits as to the actual cause of illness, the evil spirits were supposed to depart from the body of the patient.

Still another class of "shaman" practitioner among the Netsilik was the Angatkungaruk. Such people were also helped in their endeavors by some rather weak spirit beings, but like the second type they were not apparently possessed by them. No formal training was required, nor did their powers have long-range applications (i.e., divining the future). Their main technique seems to have been to simply sit near a patient and ". . . in perceiving the evil spirit and localizing it in the patient's body" (Balikci, 1967: 197). One then declared that the spirit was leaving and encouraged the patient so informed to recover. A last category and one considered far apart from those discussed above is a form of supernatural activity called *ilisiniq*. Apparently various persons could engage in this activity, which consisted primarily of what might be called black magic. Manipulation of objects was the main technique—menstrual blood or things associated with the victim. Mental wishes or spells were also necessary to bring about the desired result. Spirits and special training seem to not have been involved, and the aims were anti-social.

The Angatkok or "shaman proper" among the Netsilik functioned along lines drawn for true shamans in most societies. They dealt with or attempted to prevent disastrous situations, divining the whereabouts of game or calling them to hunters, discovering the cause of famine or other difficulty (brought on by breach of taboo), controlling weather, and curing sick persons. Shamans were also thought to harm other people either due to jealousy and desires for revenge as well as to use their powers for obtaining wives for themselves. Shamans also engaged in competition among themselves, as tests of supernatural strength intended to increase their prestige. "Finally, there is the large class of shamanistic achievements, such as journeys to the underworld, travels to the moon, or meetings with strange monsters . . ." (Balikci, 1967: 204).

The Penobscot

Still another example of shamanism is drawn from the Penobscot, an American Indian group of the Northeast. Here the shaman was called the *Mudeolinu* or "drum sound person" from the use of a drum by such individuals in their practices. Such a practitioner may well have had some special in-born power (or merely a predisposition?), but his main means of power was acquired from the world of the supernatural.

Every magician had his helper which seems to have been an animal's body into which he could transfer his state of being at will. The helper was virtually a disguise, though we do not know whether the animal was believed to exist separately from the shaman when not in the shaman's service or whether it was simply a material form assumed by the shaman when engaged in the practice of magic. The helper then is known by the term baohigan, a very interesting term which may be explained as meaning "instrument of mystery" (Speck, 1919: 249).

If data from surrounding groups better known to anthropologists are any indication, this spirit may have been both a disguise and at least originally a separate being. In fact the baohigan is itself basically acquired by the would-be shaman by going into the woods, singing to it, and then stroking it to make it into one's servant. Baohigan were generally conceptualized in animal forms. As among the Netsilik and elsewhere, this spirit could be sent on errands by its master while he was in the trance state. So close, however, was the connection between the two that if the spirit (disguise) was harmed, a similar fate would befall the shaman.

The chief activities of the shaman were closely connected to the needs of his own kin group. "Different family groups, we are told, had their own shamans whose talents were employed in the protection of their family hunting territories against trespassers. A shaman could detect when other hunters were intruding upon his family tract. He could then take measures to thwart and punish the infringement" (Speck, 1919: 244). Other common activities were the foretelling of events, curing illnesses, and dealing with other misfortunes, helping in hunting, aiding in warfare, and competing with rivals in displays of power.

Because of their special powers, persons designated as Mudeolinu were both respected and feared. Another type of supernatural practitioner was not feared. This was the Kiugwasowino, the "man who searches about in dreams." This person, who apparently had no spirit helper, had a special ability to discover the future or hidden knowledge in his dreams. Such dreams had no revelatory nature for ordinary people. This type of supernatural practitioner mostly functioned in war and hunting activities.

The Nuba

A fourth example of shamanism comes from the work of S. F. Nadel (1946) on a series of African tribes collectively called the Nuba. Here the shaman occurs in classic form as well as in another variety and in addition coexists with still other specialists in the supernatural. The Nuba shaman is possessed by several spirit beings. These manifest themselves to the would-be shaman via unusual or prophetic dreams as a sign of their intentions. Such a person soon exhibits hysterical symptoms. Selection of candidates is mostly of the spontaneous variety; the spirit chooses freely its human receptacle. When seizures (possessions) occur repeatedly, this indicates the permanency of the bond between human and spirit. This bond must then be reinforced. About three years after the first call a ritual occurs during which the new shaman performs while in the trance state to demonstrate that the spirit is indeed present. In fact at this time it reveals the full extent of its powers. A shaman may begin to practice after this ritual, but he is not considered fully consecrated in his position until after a second ritual, one occurring about ten years later. This is a longer and more elaborate rite with many guests and sacrifices. At its conclusion the shaman is felt to have reached the full capacity of his powers.

Since the processing spirits differ widely in their powers, the shamans they aid likewise engage in specialized practice. They work in particular spheres of life. In general, however:

The aid offered by the spirit vessels . . . falls under the two headings of divination and guidance. In trance, the shaman divines auspicious times and conditions for various tasks such as war, farm work, or rituals; he warns the people of impending events and prescribes the procedure, ritual or otherwise, to avoid or ensure particular happenings . . . The healing powers of the shaman correspond to the same conceptions. Consulted by the patient or his family, the shaman goes into trance and discovers the cause and cure of the disease. . . . In no case does the shaman perform anything in the nature of a therapeutic manipulation . . . Spirit possession is a means of discovering the right treatment, and not a part of it (Nadel, 1946: 26).

The only time shamans engage in actual cures is when the ailments are unknown or mysterious. The medicine men who do most of the curing engage in their activities without the aid of spirits.

There is a second general type of supernatural leader among these people. This is the Hill-Priest, so called due to his presiding over the symbolic hill on which the community lives. This office is hereditary, passing along male descent lines from father to son. This hereditary bias goes back far enough in time to include the mythical founder of the community whose reincarnation into the officeholder is also a qualification for this position; so they are like shamans in the respect of spirit possession. Functionally, the Hill-Priest is in charge of the most important group rituals of the community —those concerned with land use, the passing of seasons, and with the initiation of youths. All of these are considered essential for community survival and continuity. A last super-natural leader, one wholly free from spirit possession, is that of the Rain-Priest. Unlike the shamans who are local in function and the Hill-Priest who functions only on behalf of his own community, the Rain-Priest exists for the benefit of a series of villages (on a tribal level). His gifts include the securing of rain, health, and fertility for all. This position is also hereditary along male lines. There are still spirit connections, however, since the sanction for the position is bestowed by the supreme deity whose interests the Rain-Priest serves and whose ear he has. At least in the past this official had powerful political functions as well, ". . . he had the most powerful sanction at his command—the threat to stop the rain. He would use it, too, in the sphere of law, to break a blood feud . . . or to enforce the punishment of a criminal by a reluctant clan or local community" (Nadel, 1946: 33). The example of the Nuba, then, clearly shows that the relationship of practitioner to spirits need not always be couched in the terms of classic possession.

The above notion, in fact, leads us to a very vital although unresolved question in the anthropology of religion. We can grant that there is a type of supernatural practitioner who functions with the direct aid of spirits or is in some way intimately connected with them. If we call such an individual a shaman, we should develop some further terminological distinctions to deal with the varieties of shamans, with those of a nonclassic type. It has become abundantly clear that one cover term is not sufficient. To declare that two societies both have shamans is misleading (as it is to say they occur in one society without qualification). We also have to deal with the possibility of other kinds of leaders who have special abilities but who do not employ and are not backed by spirits in their endeavors. What are the types of these practitioners?

One very illuminating attempt along the above lines is that of Metzger and Williams (1963). In their study of a Tzeltal-speaking community in Mexico, they have systematically analyzed the position of curer, using native categories and distinctions. In this society the ability of curing is widely distributed with a high proportion of people being so designated. This skill is considered a gift from God, and no formal training is required. The primary attribute of a curer is the "ability to pulse"—to feel in the movement of blood what the illness must be and its appropriate cure. Curers also have the ability of "true prayers." This act they share with others, but their diagnostic attributes render such prayers more effective when used by curers. Likewise the use of medicinal plants by curers is not a trait restricted to themselves alone, but since they pray over these and know their best application, plants are rendered more effective when used by curers.

The people themselves recognize differences between curers, whom they divide into master and junior categories based upon two criteria. Curers differ in terms of the knowledge they possess. Master curers know better how to treat a variety of illnesses, especially witchcraft-induced problems, and can pray and prepare medicine on a high level. Junior curers are generally less potent in these matters and cannot deal with witches. Curers are also said to differ in terms of their actual performance. The master curer extracts more information from the preliminary pulsing session and shows great confidence; his junior colleague is hesitant in diagnosis and often tries to gain information from the patient or his family, rather then relying upon the pulsing activity alone. Though the distinction is more complicated than this, the study does provide us with a fairly clear-cut description of a category of supernatural practitioner and its internal distinctions. Clearly, much more work along similar lines is necessary before a reliable taxonomy of these sorts of leaders can be created.

Before we pass on to another general category of supernatural leadership, we can very briefly indicate another unresolved but highly interesting problem relative to the understanding of shamans. This concerns the mental stability or personality types of such persons. It is common in the literature to discover the view that shamanism is a sort of culturally defined outlet for those who are abnormal, that by becoming shamans they are given a legitimate social role to play. Hence, in this view, the abnormal character of the position basically stems from those who come to occupy it. This problem was indicated earlier in this chapter, and it was suggested that such was probably not the usual case. Shamanism may well exploit any potential abnormality and channel it along defined and productive lines, but it does seem fairly clear that to function as they do—in a regular and valuable fashion—shamans indeed must be normal at least most of the time.

This does not mean, on the other hand, that those people who become shamans do not differ mentally in some ways from other individuals in their societies. In a most provocative study, Richard Shweder (1972) has indicated some interesting data for Zinacanteco shamans in Mexico. Very briefly, he devised a test employing a series of photographs varying in clarity from a blur to clear focus to show to shamans and other people to elicit their perceptions of the subject matter being viewed. Of considerable interest was the result that the shamans (as opposed to others) seemed more productive in their responses, with richer interpretations, and that they avoided bafflement by imposing more form on the blurred photographs. They also gave more responses outside the range of those suggested by the experimenters. Clearly the shamans demonstrated a degree of cognition beyond that of the ordinary person. Again, however, was this a result of experience in the role, or was it due to the gravitation of special personalities in the position? This remains unclear! We are left with a number of interesting research possibilities on this type of practitioner.

THE PRIEST

The second general type of supernatural practitioner usually recognized by anthropologists is the priest. Along the dichotomous lines of magic and religion, this position is defined ideally as the opposite of that of the shaman with regard to the behaviors exhibited by its occupants. As before, we can list some of the general characteristics of this leadership type.

1. First of all, in contrast to the special selection of shamans by gods and spirits and the powers bestowed upon them, the priest—though a servant of the gods—does not gain extraordinary abilities as a result. Priests, at least ideally, lack the supernatural "gift." Some may occasionally serve as mouthpieces for the gods, but usually it is an interpretation of their will rather than in a medium fashion. Priests mostly involve themselves in performing rites in honor of the gods, in ad-

ministering affairs relating to the cult of those gods, and in giving advice to lay persons. They fall, then, into the shepherd–flock category of supernatural practice rather than into the professionalism of the shaman.

2. Because priests do not ordinarily have any direct contact with the supernatural, the techniques and knowledge they come to acquire are generally the result of apprenticeship to other human beings; it is gained by going to "priest school." This does not mean that the candidate aspiring to such a position may not feel a sense of being called to the position (as the will of the gods or whatever), since one may even undergo a revelational experience in this regard; but one does not receive instruction in the tasks of the office by the gods themselves. E. O. James has summed up the role of the priest very nicely along the above lines. In his estimation, the priest:

. . . supplicates and conciliates forces superior to himself, guards the sacred tradition in his care, and acts as the master of its sacrificial technique strictly within the limits of his office. . . . serves at the altar and in the temple or shrine as the representative of the community in its relations with the gods and the unseen world. . . . they are masters of a technique or holders of an office, conferred upon them by consecration. . . . the priest must have an expert knowledge of sacred learning and of all that pertains to the sacerdotal office, its ritual, mythology, law, doctrine, and organization. . . . since the priest is responsible for maintaining a right relationship between the community and its gods he exercises his functions in a corporate capacity. . . . the altar is his cult centre as against the shamanistic seance . . . (James, 1955: 33, 34).

3. A third generally cited characteristic of the priest is that such an individual tends strongly to be a full-time specialist. He devotes all of his time to a concern with the higher reality of the sacred and in participation in activities predicated upon it. In many societies priests combine to form societies or priesthoods, often enormous in size and most often structured internally in a hierarchical fashion with high priests and lesser types of functionaries. Some may even be lay priests and only be involved in a part-time way. Even where aggregations of priests do not occur, there is a decided tendency for priests to evoke a greater sense of cooperation among themselves than seems to be the case in most shamanism.

4. Priests in their classic sense also correlate with more complexly developed societies, for example those with advanced agriculture as the technological base. In such societies control over the food supply has progressed to such a level that they can afford the luxury of supporting nonproductive specialists, including those of a nonsupernatural nature. Hence the person called to a supernatural life has the opportunity for extra benefit in such societies. In fact, they may even have political influence or actually rule along theocratic lines. Of course shamans may still exist as alternative leaders in developed societies as has been previously mentioned.

5. Priests, because they center their behaviors around the cult of the gods, are generally seen to function in ritual endeavors best categorized as *calendrical*. This is partly due to the fact that the gods whose worship they supervise usually require regular attention and are also generally associated with cyclical benefits—ripening of the crops, passage of seasons, and the like. Might it also stem in part from the fact that priests—if supported full-time—ought to prove themselves busy and worthy of such support? Many priestly activities, however, may be less cult-oriented and of a more private nature. Such acts range from praying in times of crisis for a sick person to the essentially withdrawn experience of the contemplative monks in many Eastern religions. Moreover, many priestly cult activities may be performed essentially without contact with lay persons—washing statues of deities, making offerings to them, and the like.

6. Finally, it may be remarked that by and large, priests appear to be "normal" individuals within the context of their societies. They are not, at least in the ideal sense, given to unusual psychological or physiological behaviors. In fact being supernormal may even be a precondition for holding office. It should be pointed out, however, that various types of priests (prophets, seers, and the like) may at least occasionally behave in ways that pass beyond the accomplishments of others in their societies, for example, in performance of mechanical divination to ascertain the will of the gods. So here again the subtypes of a supernatural position have yet to be even generally drawn. The fascination of anthropologists with shamans has surely retarded our full examination of the priest type of supernatural practitioner. We have also not really concerned ourselves with evolutionary speculation

relative to shamans and priests. Does one position develop out of the other as the basic structure of society changes—shifting the psychological qualifications involved—or do they evolve essentially as more-or-less independent alternatives? Research is urgently required on this topic. We can now briefly examine some cases of priesthood to give some descriptive flavor to the above discussion and to reveal the problems involved in its application.

The Egyptian Priesthood

The priests of ancient Egypt furnish an excellent example of the variety and hierarchy of such practitioners as found in complex societies. A priest there was a person set aside from others in the community so that he might perform services for a god. Special purity was the key to this position, since it was expected in all people and things in any way associated with a deity. Originally there was a tendency for almost anyone to aspire to this position and be consecrated in it. As time passed, however, the position came to be more and more hereditary, and by the twentieth dynasty families of priests were common. Great numbers of priests occurred in connection with the temples to the various gods.

By priest we must indeed understand every man who, through bodily purification, puts himself in the state of physical purity necessary to approach the holy place, or to touch any objects or dishes of food consecrated to the god. The process was brief and the installation, at least in the lower orders of the priesthood, encountered hardly any delays, but it is certain that if the number of the purified was considerable, there remained an abyss between the ordinary chaplain and the priest permitted to see the god (Sauneron, 1960: 56).

Our understanding of the types of priests and their actual activities is not entirely clear.

In theory, during historic times the king himself was the high priest of all the various deities. Since he was believed to be the son of the Sun God, he was the natural person for such a position, being both man and god. In practice he could only rarely exercise such prerogatives, delegating great authority to the chief priests on a local level who had actual charge of the various temples. These temple complexes were the "houses of the god," and the attendant priests functioned chiefly in a caretaker capacity, serving the main deity involved plus a few minor types. Each temple complex had a high priest who was ultimately responsible for the administration of it; care of buildings, control of wealth, supervision of rituals, and so on. Such a priest reflected the political power of the god he served and its current popularity so that not all of these persons were equal throughout the kingdom. Such a high priest might have risen from the priestly ranks but more commonly was appointed by the king. There seems also to have been an assistant high priest who assisted the high priest and who could exercise the functions of that person in the event of his absence from the temple.

Beneath these officials the clergy appears to have been divided up into those of higher and lower degrees. The higher clergy existed to perform a variety of rather specialized functions and were often divided into shifts that had active responsibilities over certain periods of time. One such type of priest cared for the god's statues in the inner sanctuaries of the temples, being in charge of clothes, ornaments, and other cult objects. As such they could enter the most sacred areas and undergo elaborate purifications. Another type consisted of scholar-scribes who were responsible for keeping up the liturgical books necessary to the cult and who also functioned as theologians, working out the details of the sacred knowledge. Those lower on the scale of importance in this class may not have been fully consecrated priests but simply kept temple accounts. Members of this general type were often chosen to go on special missions for the king.

Another class of higher clergy were timekeepers and astrologers. The first of these served to establish the specific days and hours for rites; the latter took a more overall time responsibility, setting feast days and reckoning calendrically to see if days would be good, bad, or neutral for sacred and other endeavors. A most numerous class of Egyptian priests consisted of various sorts of singers and musicians, both male and female, who performed in a variety of sacred and other contexts. Lower clergy, many of whom were also purified, were involved in the cults of the particular gods only in a secondary fashion. The classes here are numerous and overlapping and include the bearers of sacred objects, supervisors of crafts, sacrificers of animals, interpreters of dreams (when visitors spent the night in the temple to receive the advice of the gods), and many more types including auxiliaries (not purified?) whose activities were necessary for the day-to-day temple functions. These last included bakers, painters, door-keepers, and so forth. There also appears to have been a class of voluntary recluses, either pious persons or those seeking asylum for some reason from the outside world. All these priests derived their subsistence from two major sources. Revenue and material items were derived from estates belonging to the temple and were allocated by priestly rank (as well as providing for the upkeep of the temple itself). A second source was derived from offerings made to the temple, also divided by the priests along rank lines. In addition, high priests apparently had special privileges and stipends and, of course, all priests were exempted from labor drafts, taxation, and other impositions placed on ordinary people. Quite clearly the rewards of priesthood were considerably above those a shaman could expect!

We can very briefly indicate some of the range of priestly functions. Basically these revolved around a series of daily rites performed in the inner rooms of the temple where the statues of the gods resided. Each morning an offering procession went into the temple, which had previously been purified. Bearers brought food and other offerings and then withdrew. A member of the higher clergy then opened the door to the inner sanctuary as the sun rose. Prayer and chanting took place. The priest then approached the god's statue and prayed before the image four times to reach all the corners of the world. Once the offerings were placed, the priest withdrew so that the god could feast. The spirit of the food was consumed by the god and his statue was then washed, the clothes from the previous day removed and replaced, and the statue painted and then annointed with special oil. The god was now equipped to carry on its heavenly activities for another day, and the doors to the inner sanctum were again closed after incense was burned for purification.

A midday service also occurred in abbreviated fashion for the lesser gods, deified kings, and the like, who were also in the temple—plus more general purifications for the temple itself. An evening ritual also occurred consisting of offerings, libations, and many other replications of the morning service. This, however, was performed outside of the inner sanctum.

Every week or so another ritual would take place in which priests would carry the statue of the god (placed on a ship) on their backs outside of the temple in a procession so that the common people might be afforded a glimpse of the divinity. At this time questions might be put to the god, the answers in a yes–no fashion being indicated by the ship's movements. As the bearers felt the will of the god seize them they would move forward, meaning a positive answer, or backwards, indicating a negative response. So divinatory potential seems to have been a prerogative of at least some kind of priests.

In all, however, the priests remained essentially the servants of the divinity, assuring his service in the temple and outside the temple: at these outings, the participation of the crowd was purely formal: they acclaimed the god and rejoiced in his passing, but did not contribute, to speak of, in the ceremonies required. It is only on very particular occasions . . . that we see the priests serve as intermediaries between the god and the human beings who worshiped him (Sauneron, 1960: 94).

In such outdoor activities the priestly and the practical aspirations of supernaturalism appear to have found common expression. Most of the time, however, the priests functioned as caretakers of the god, and ordinary people simply relied upon their activities to keep their deities strengthened and satisfied and thus maintain the order of the universe.

Sherpa Monks

A second example of the priestly position and one demonstrating somewhat different behaviors and context is the situation among the Sherpa of Nepal as described by Furer–Haimendorf (1964). The Sherpa, famed as guides for mountain-climbing expeditions, are agriculturalists and herders of yak, sheep, and goats. Basically, their religion is a variant on the North Indian–Tibetan pattern, consisting of an aboriginal tribal faith overlain by Tibetan Buddhist institutions (lamaism). Shamans exist who function in a trance state with reference to illness, as do "soothsayers" who—without the aid of spirits—can determine which evil spirits have caused misfortune. The priest position in this society is represented by Buddhist monks (for the most part), many of whom reside in monasteries. This is due to the notion of salvation by works espoused in Buddhism and the emphasis upon private salvation (see Trevor Ling, 1973).

The monasteries are collections of monks organized in a hierarchical fashion. In a typical monastery there is a *Chief Priest* or *Abbot*, generally a person thought to be reincarnated from a previous priestly existence. His chief duties, in addition to seeking further enlightenment on a personal basis, are to supervise the functioning of the institution, engage in study and some teaching, preside at major rituals, and to receive pilgrims. A second rank is that of the *Loben*, whose duties include advising the other monks and officiating in the absence of the Abbot. A third type of priest is the *Umse*, who conducts all the services in the temple at the monastery. Beneath this level is the *Gerbu*, who functions to keep the accounts of the monastery funds and properties and to maintain discipline among the monks themselves. Still another group are the *Nierwa*, who are in charge of trading and other economic activities. Beneath these monks are a series of many lower ranks who serve in more menial capacities: serving tea (an accompaniment of rituals), reciting prayers, and making music.

Among the Sherpa, persons become monks for a variety of reasons in addition to the formal quest for individual salvation. They might be placed in a monastery by parents, so that they might gain the knowledge to become a village priest (lama) or because their family has no place for them. They might go there to acquire merit for higher reincarnation in the next life, and it might even be—if one could inherit a house from a previous monk—simply to pursue an easier life. In fact in this society, monks are required to provide for their own maintenance, so that many are drawn from wealthier families or have a relative who is a monk already with whom to share expenses. There are requirements of chastity, a host of regulations based on Buddhist morality, and a renunciation of many worldly occupations. To fail these requirements leads to expulsion from the monastic institution.

Village priests take no such vows. They have received some monastery training equipping them to officiate at certain rites, but they have left the monastery and may marry and reside in the surrounding villages. Such persons may still strive for higher spiritual levels and might fast in isolation and

receive further instruction from higher-ranking clergy. Many
of their activities take place in the village temple. Supernatural activities performed by monastery monks fall into two
classes—those of a private nature (prayer and meditation)
and public rituals of wider benefit. One of the most outstanding of these is the monastery feast, which attracts great
crowds and consists of the monks performing elaborate dances
costumed as gods and spirits. Its aim is to symbolize the victory of humans and gods over the forces of evil, and attendance is considered a meritorious act for lay persons.
Monks also officiate in conjunction with shamans in death
rites, an example of the overlap between Buddhism and
aboriginal practices. At any rate, we see in the Sherpa monk/
priest an alternative in supernatural leadership to that of the
general sort discussed previously. We can now turn to a
consideration of participation on a somewhat more general
level.

OTHER CONSIDERATIONS ON PARTICIPATION

As previously mentioned, anthropologists have concentrated most of their attention on the role of leaders in supernaturalism and on the functions associated with such types.
These have been shown to resolve themselves into shamanistic and priestly roles of behavior. What about the participation of the rest of the members of a society in their supernatural activities? Unfortunately for comparative purposes,
though some descriptive data does exist, no other categories
of participation have been drawn in general theoretical terms
—save those of client and congregation. Such a state of affairs points up an urgent need for the anthropological student
of supernaturalism. We may on logical grounds of course divide such possible participation into *active* and *passive* roles,
depending upon whether the nonspecialist assists leaders in
some fashion or carries out some appreciable integral portion of the ritual or if they are merely onlookers on the
ritual scene, expecting benefit but not being overtly active.
Such distinctions quite certainly exist within a society with
respect to particular rituals and may be expected to vary
cross-culturally as well; that is, the degree of nonspecialist
activity may be defined as necessary or desired in some

societies but not in others. A correlation between this and leadership types would be most interesting!

San Juan Pueblo

As one last example of participation, one only partly responsive to what has been said above, are some distinctions in participation recognized by the people of San Juan Pueblo in New Mexico. In this American Indian Society the natural and supernatural worlds are each divided into three hierarchically ranked categories. In the natural world are the Dry Food People, the common person who is rather passive with respect to supernaturalism; a group of special "political" officers; and the Made People, who are the members of supernatural societies. Their counterparts in the world of the supernatural are the souls of ordinary people, spirits of mythic significance, and a group of deities who are joined by the souls of society members after they die. The common people undergo a number of passage rituals to become certified members of their societies. At birth a mother and child are secluded, and the child is named. During the first year a rite is held to install the child in its proper social division. Some time later (between six and ten) children are instructed in traditions and are bathed with medicine water. When a sufficient number of children over the age of ten exist, a "finishing rite" is held. Rain Spirits are impersonated, and the children are whipped. The boys later have the secret of impersonation revealed to them.

The "political" officers are persons selected from among the commoners to fill one-year terms and ". . . are those known to have a firm commitment to and knowledge of native ritual" (Ortiz, 1969: 69). They function to protect society members during their rites and serve also as protectors of customs. "However, their primary and most time-consuming duty throughout the year is to coordinate . . . all rituals planned and directed by the Made People and participated in by the Dry Food People" (Ortiz, 1961: 72). They also serve as a check on the power of other persons, since (while impersonating certain gods) they may whip with impunity any person who has deviated from the norms. The Made People, or society members, comprise a large proportion of the entire village population. Each society has a leader and two assistants—his right and left "arms." Society membership is comprised of persons who have joined voluntarily, have been dedicated in by parents, or who have had to join for some other reason. The societies themselves vary as to function and include the following: medicine or curing societies, ritual clown groups, a hunters' society with powers to aid in securing game, a warriors' society (perhaps in the past consisting of scalp-takers) and a women's group.

In essence, then, the involvement in supernaturalism in this society—beyond that of leaders—is recognized to fall into three general classes and is provided with supernatural equivalents to reinforce the distinctions. There are also levels within the societies themselves. Surely comparable data of this general sort can be secured from other societies and general ideal types derived to stimulate further research and refinement. We can turn now to the other major related issue in supernaturalism, that of the gods themselves and the lesser supernatural beings who often accompany them.

REFERENCES

Balikci, Asen.
    1967. Shamanistic Behavior Among the Netsilik Eskimo. In *Magic, Witchcraft, and Curing,* ed. John Middleton, pp. 191–209.
    Garden City: The Natural History Press.

Eliade, Mircea.
    1972. *Shamanism: Archaic Techniques of Ecstasy.*
    Princeton: Princeton University Press.

Furer–Haimendorf, C. Von.
    1964. *The Sherpas of Nepal.*
    Berkeley: University of California Press.

Goodman, Felicitas D.
    1972. *Speaking in Tongues: A Cross Cultural Study of Glossolalia.*
    Chicago: University of Chicago Press.

Harner, Michael J., ed.
    1973. *Hallucinogens and Shamanism.*
    New York: Oxford University Press.

James, E. O.
    1955. *The Nature and Function of Priesthood.*
    New York: The Vanguard Press.

Krader, Lawrence.
  1967. Buryat Religion and Society. In *Gods and Rituals*,
      ed. John Middleton, pp. 103–132.
      Garden City: The Natural History Press.
Lewis, I. M.
  1971. *Ecstatic Religion*.
      Harmondsworth, England: Penguin Books.
Ling, Trevor.
  1973. *The Buddha*.
      New York: Scribners Sons.
MacCulloch, J. A.
  1924. Shamanism. In *Hastings Encyclopedia of Religion
      and Ethics*, pp. 441–446.
Metzger, Duane, and Williams, Gerald.
  1963. Tenejapa Medicine I: The Curer.
      Southwestern Journal of Anthropology 29:216–234.
Nadel, S. F.
  1946. A Study of Shamanism in the Nuba Mountains.
      Journal of the Royal Anthropological Institute 76:
      25–37.
Ortiz, Alfonso.
  1969. *The Tewa World*.
      Chicago: University of Chicago Press.
Radin, Paul.
  1957. *Primitive Religion*.
      New York: Dover Publications.
Sauneron, Serge.
  1960. *The Priests of Ancient Egypt*.
      New York: Grove Press.
Shweder, Richard.
  1972. Aspects of Cognition of Zinacanteco Shamans: Ex-
      perimental Results. In *Reader in Comparative Re-
      ligion*, eds. William A. Lessa and Evon Z. Vogt, pp.
      407–412.
      New York: Harper and Row.
Speck, Frank.
  1919. *Penobscot Shamanism*.
      American Anthropological Association Memoir Vol.
      6 #4.
Wach, Joachim.
  1962. *Sociology of Religion*.
      Chicago: University of Chicago Press.

CHAPTER 8

Supernatural Beings and Myths

Basic to the conceptualization of the supernatural is the notion of the existence of various types of supernatural beings. In fact, these are a part of the definition of religion itself. Such beings literally come in all shapes and sizes, and most societies entertain a belief in the multiplicity of such beings, a belief generally called polytheism. Some modern faiths are monotheistic, believing in the existence of but one supreme being, and a few primitive faiths are similarly oriented (although the data in such cases are problematical). Apparently the usual human condition is for supernatural beings to occur in more than single forms.

GODS

How many types of supernatural beings exist? No appreciable amount of anthropological writing appears to deal with this problem, although some ideas are discussed in Swanson, 1960. For the present purposes we can discuss three very general categories of such beings. The first is most common cross-culturally and may be designated as *gods*. Generally speaking, although significant exceptions exist, gods are high-powered supernatural beings. Not only do they possess powers much greater than human beings, but they have eternal existence as well—generally preceding humans into the world and never having to face death. Because of the great variation in gods, it is most difficult to pin them down in typological terms, although careful reading of anthropological reports leads one to see them from at least three different perspectives. First, gods may vary as to the *form* they take. Some gods are *naturalistic,* that is to say they appear as personifications of nature. Such range from rather remote sun gods, thunder gods, and wind gods down to more immediate types such as tree gods and gods of rivers. The powers of such supernatural beings generally seem to diminish along the same lines, those of more general natural phenomena being more powerful than those of specific natural locations. Another form variety is *zoomorphic.* These are gods that are conceived of as animals or in mostly an animal form. There are bear gods, snake gods, and leopard gods. Many of these gods may also take fantastic forms or shapes as well—feathered serpents, many-headed animals, animals with sharpened feet, and the like. Still another form the gods may take is *anthropomorphic.* These deities appear conceived of in human or humanlike forms; witness the gods and goddesses of the ancient Greeks. Quite clearly humans often create the gods in their own images. In fact, though we do know that human societies create their gods along the lines of their own social structures, it would be most interesting to research the form the gods take (naturalistic, zoomorphic, and so on) and the societal contexts involved. Finally, there are *philomorphic* gods. These are cases where the gods (or god) are more in the nature of philosophical speculations and are not really endowed with specific form. It should be pointed out that any form of god may upon occasion take some other form; remember the Ainu gods taking on their bear disguises.

A second general variation of gods permits us to classify them in terms of their *functions,* what they are supposed to do for their human dependents. Here again some general types emerge. Most societies (really all?) appear to believe in *creator* gods. These are beings who create the world or transform it, as well as often bringing the other gods and humans into existence. Such deities often become the "high" gods, those of greatest power and importance. Among many of the simpler primitive societies who have creator gods, these are rendered otiose; that is, once such supernatural beings have done their creation, they retire from the world, remain aloof from human affairs, and may be relegated only to myth—receiving no active prayer or other ritual attention. A second functional type is the *culture-hero* god. This being is usually an assistant to the creator god and is conceived of as personally responsible for aiding human kind. This is achieved either by specifically creating humans or at least by bestowing certain knowledge or gifts upon them; for example, agriculture, weaving, and the like. Culture-heroes are often thought in myth to have fought with monsters or in other ways to have made the world safe for human occupation. Culture-heroes are usually actively worshiped and are considered as still interested in human affairs. Another functional type of fairly widespread occurrence is the *trickster*. This is a god who is usually fairly well disposed toward humans but who seems to especially delight in playing tricks and in testing them. Such gods, in the course of their game playing, may also reveal useful information or secrets to human beings. This type is quite widespread among North American Indian societies. Finally, there are what might be called *specialist* gods. These deities have interest in and generally control over some specific things, and their variety seems to be almost endless. To name just a few, there are weather gods, fertility gods, love gods, war gods, gods who control animal species, gods who control night and day, gods of death, and gods who control illness or who may help shamans.

A third way to conceive of the gods is in terms of their *attributes*. Here two general common possibilities emerge, both rather logical axes of conceptualization. First, gods may be defined as *male, female,* or *neutral*. Generally speaking, male gods seem to outnumber those of the goddess type, and at least in most societies they seem to have more powers as well—again a direct reflection of the human societies that create them. The other conceptualization divides gods into divisions dependent upon their relation to humans. Gods may be *beneficent;* they may always be favorably disposed toward their worshipers, looking out for them, bestowing gifts, and the like. They may also be *evil;* they may be out to harm humans, and their worship may include entreaties for such gods to focus their attention elsewhere. Such bad gods may well become the special patrons of sorcerers, highwaymen, and other evildoers. Finally, along these lines, gods may be *problematical;* they may be neither bad nor good. Their activities with reference to humans may be entirely a case of how much or little ritual attention is paid them or be a result of which other gods are influencing them at the time. While there are undoubtedly other ways to classify the god type of supernatural being, enough possibilities have been suggested here to outline some of the bewildering variety they may take. Specific examples are supplied later in this chapter and have been mentioned in earlier chapters.

ANCESTRAL SPIRITS

A second general class of supernatural beings is that of *ancestral spirits*. These types of deities also generally have powers superior to human beings but do not have eternal existence, if only because they represent the continued soul life of humans themselves. As such, ancestral spirits are re-lated to conceptions of the soul and notions of some kind of an afterlife, even though societies do differ markedly on the emphasis placed on such future existences. Such beliefs in some form or another may well be a universal element of humanity.

All cultures have techniques and methods which serve, if not to eliminate, at least to reduce problems arising out of the fact of human mortality. This they do both by reducing the individual's anxiety stemming from the contemplation of his own demise and by facilitating the orderly resumption of interpersonal relations fol-lowing the death of a member of the group. . . . Without attempt-ing to suggest causality or primacy to either the spirit concept or that of life after death, it may be said that virtually all cultures provide both the concept of some non-material aspect of life which will survive death and some beliefs regarding where and how this spirit would exist. . . . Belief in an afterworld may assuage an in-dividual's fears but, at the same time, it places him in more or less intimate contact with a host of non-mortal beings, either the de-parted members of his own group . . . or with the spirits of all departed human beings . . . (Lessa and Vogt, 1965: 419, 420).

Many possibilities exist here. The soul may have to undergo various trials on its way to continued existence—for example, passing through hells, fighting monsters, and so forth. It may in fact be destroyed there. It may survive but may require its living descendants to worship it or still face extinction, as is the case in ancient China. It may even eventually fade away as part of the general nature of things. In such contexts, however, two possibilities exist. Such a soul spirit may either hang around for a time, or it may go on to a deified kind of existence. In the first case, it is generally called a *ghost,* and it is either avoided or actively beseeched to go elsewhere. Ghosts are almost always believed to be at least temporarily harmful to their own descendants and often to other persons as well. In the second case, if the soul lives on and if it is believed to be able to influence or help the living, it becomes an *ancestral spirit;* and much ritual attention may be engendered in the attempt to secure the aid or favor of such beings (or at the very least to avoid giving them offense).

Quite often, complex beliefs develop in relation to ancestral spirits. We may briefly indicate an example of these as reported upon by Elizabeth Colson (1965) from the Plateau Tonga of Africa. When a person dies in this society two spirit beings remain in existence. The first is the Ghost. This is newly created at death (perhaps from the dying breath). These ghosts apparently are immortal from this point on, have harmful aspects, and may be controlled by sorcerers and applied to evil purposes. The other spirit entity is the Mizimu. "Mizimu as a general term includes all the spirits of former members of the lines of the father and mother, and may even be used still more generally for all the spirits of former members of any group with which a person feels a kinship relationship" (Colson, 1965: 439). The Mizimu is not automatically immortal but depends upon the rituals of the living for its continued existence. In fact, they may visit sickness or other misfortune on their descendants to remind them of their obligations. In return, they offer the living general assistance in obtaining the good things of life and may also help protect them against harmful spirits. The individual himself comes in contact with many Mizimu. Some, the Guardian Mizimu, are those associated with names a person receives soon after birth.

The names, which thus recognize the existence of the child and give it its initial place in the society, are bestowed some months after birth. The first name is given by the father or his relatives, and it is a name belonging to a former member of this line. The second is given by the mother's relatives and is the name of a former member of her line. Each name is associated with a Mizimu. The Tonga say that the Mizimu themselves may decide which of their living kin shall receive their names, and thus become their special charges (Colson, 1965: 439).

These Guardian Mizimu are protectors of the individuals throughout their lives. Still other Mizimu may be installed as special guardians of a household, generally those of the husband's side. When a person dies, if he or she has formed a household, they will also become a Mizimu in their own right—one that will eventually be inherited by their matrilineal kin. So the number of ancestral spirits is constantly being increased.

DEMONS

The third major type of supernatural being may generally be called a *demon*. The conceptions relating to these suggest that they have powers and abilities greater than those of human beings but that they fall below gods and ancestral spirits in this regard. They are sort of "junior grade" supernaturals. Further, they are usually not made the objects of formal attention in ritual activities, at least not to the extent of the other types we have discussed. Demons may well be disposed to aid human beings in some way, like the Irish leprechauns, but most often they appear as pranksters or demonstrate completely evil natures. We can give one example of demons here before turning to more overall descriptions.

Among the Tuareg of the Sahara Desert in North Africa we find a belief in a type of being of this sort called a jinn.

Jinns were created before men and are a different kind of being, having nothing to do with ghosts . . . They die, or can be killed, but they live for centuries. They outnumber mankind because the females give birth to many young at once, and procreation takes place through the male of the species simply rubbing his thigh against that of the female. What they look like is not known, because they are invisible, but of course they can take whatever shape they wish, often disguising themselves as men and women to have dealings with humanity proper: they may even marry or seduce mortal people . . . (Howells, 1948: 206).

On some occasions jinns may aid human beings in some manner. Most of the time, however, they harm humans in many ways, mostly due to their propensity for being easily angered. When so offended, they may send disease objects into a person's body, possess them, or visit a wide variety of other afflictions. In a less dramatic fashion they may simply harass humans with minor misfortunes. A great number of rigid taboos are placed on those behaviors that particularly offend jinns, and beyond these there are other things that a "careful" person seeks to avoid. On a more positive note, not only do behavioral avoidances protect the person from the wrath of the jinns, but one can fire off gunpowder to scare them off (as in ancient China); and since the Tuaregs are Muslims, they also feel that recitations from the Koran may aid in keeping the jinns at a distance.

SUPERNATURALS AMONG THE IFUGAO

As a first detailed example of types of supernatural beings we may examine the forms they take among the Ifugao of Northern Luzon in the Philippine Islands (as of 1914). Among these people, the gods were thought to inhabit all areas surrounding human beings—in the earth itself, in the sky world, in the underworld, and in the adjacent regions up- and downstream from the Ifugao villages. There were countless deities, but they were divided into classes. These were generally named after the principal gods or spirits in each. Such beings were invoked in rituals, although depending upon the number of priests involved, not all the countless constituents of a class would be invoked; in simpler rites, only a few classes would receive attention. All of these deities shared general superhuman powers. Beyond this they had specialized powers in keeping with their class, and beyond even this, within a class they might display particularities of attribute and function. To give the student some appreciation of the vast range of potential in these supernatural beings we can paraphrase the account of R. F. Barton (1946) of the main classes of Ifugao deities.

1. *The Paybackables.* These deities are gods who in myth used to trade with human beings and who had given the Ifugao their domestic animals, knowledge of rites, and other

valuable things. Such culture-hero types were thus owed an enormous debt and were those to whom the principal offerings were given in general feasts. Perhaps due to the variety of favors given in the past, this class comprised the most varied type of gods in terms of location, function, and form. This class also contained the greatest number of deities.

2. *Clustered Village Deities.* These gods are considered to be important in agriculture and other food-related concerns. They are believed to live in villages in uninhabited areas. "Not only do they own the locusts which they turn loose in great numbers about one year in six, but they are also connected . . . with the return of the souls of consumed pigs, chickens, and rice to be reborn" (Barton, 1946: 35, 36). So they are specialist gods of a problematical nature.

3. *The Deceivers.* This class includes three main gods plus a host of more minor beings. Manahaut, the chief deity, betrays humans into all kinds of danger and coaxes away their souls. Death in childbirth is also ascribed to the evildoings of this being. The Sun and Moon are the other principal gods of this class and are also rather hostile toward humans, fulfilling functions as war gods, occasionally as sorcerers, and as gods of justice and divination (as such invoked in oaths). All of the deities in this class live in the sky world and are many in number.

4. *The Omen Deities.* These gods are "believed to guide and warn men through the medium of snakes, birds, insects, and the like" (Barton, 1946: 42). As such they function in divination and take the form of the animals involved. Many of these deities are limited to myth and so are not actively invoked for aid.

5. *Gods of Reproduction.* This class of gods controls the general processes of human reproduction, although they can also cause sickness and death. Female deities are most numerous in this class, and all members live in the up- and downstream regions.

6. *The Convincers.* These rather numerous deities have the ability to bind the will of a person to that of the invoker. Thus they are invoked to gain control over persons from whom one wishes to collect debts or to kill or injure in warfare. Apparently they may also be invoked to make other people forget vengeance or that a debt is owed. Many

of these deities are deified states of mind (for example, "gasp of fear") and hence qualify as philomorphic gods. They are located in many areas.

7. *Regulators of Relations Between Enemies.* These gods are felt to punish individuals who have eaten with an enemy, a taboo of great importance, the enforcement of which was a stimulus for continued warfare among the Ifugao. The punishment consisted of special diseases not remediable by normal curing rituals but only by a sacrifice to these gods. Some of these gods were also invoked in peace-making rites to overlook their customary punishments.

8. *Guardians of Property.* These deities, when invoked properly, guard property against trespass or pilferage—for example, against strangers entering a village or a house and protecting fruit trees. Shrines are often built near the object to be protected for gods to reside there. Members of the upper ranks might also have personal protectors to give them power over commoners. Such deities visit the trespasser of their property with all manner of illness.

9. *The Messengers.* These gods intercede with other deities on behalf of humans and commonly were invoked first in rites to summon the other gods to human feasts. Such gods also were responsible for drawing men into shamanism by visiting them with diseases whose cure required entering into that profession.

10. *Gods of the Winds.* These deities, who are generally conceived of in anthropomorphic form, control the winds by raising their arms and having the wind come from their armpits. Some of these gods originally are thought to have human ancestry. Such beings are generally considered negatively, since strong winds are inimical to fruit trees and growing crops.

11. through 19. These nine classes are all exclusively *pathogenic.* "All deities are believed to be capable of afflicting men with disease . . . [but] . . . they have abilities or powers that lie outside a solely pathogenic function. [These] . . . never do anything else than cause sickness" (Barton, 1946: 62). The sicknesses such evil beings cause vary widely from dysentery to boils and abscesses to headaches and arthritis. They are invoked to obtain relief from the specific diseases they are believed to cause.

20. *Minor Deities of War.* These gods are invoked to seek

help against enemies as well as in any hostilities arising between kinship groups. They may also be invoked to help interpret certain types of disease.

21. *Talisman Activators.* These gods are thought to be responsible for the powers embodied in talismans—objects (usually stones) possessing supernatural powers that can be employed by humans. When such an object is found, the discoverer must sacrifice to these gods so that the object's powers can be employed properly. Such objects are used primarily to protect the individual from accident and enemies.

22. *Deities of the Chase.* The gods of this class have ownership of the game animals. Sacrifice was made to them in general as well as to specifically seek their aid in nullifying the dangers of the hunt.

23. *Granary Deities.* These supernatural beings were invoked to invest idols (carved wooden statues of humans or animals) that were placed in the rice granaries. They were thought to have the powers to increase the quantity of the rice after it had been stored, possibly by leaving a supernatural "essence" in the idols. The Ifugao also considered the help of these deities necessary to obtain a successful rice crop in the first place.

24. *Mountainers.* These deities reside only in the downstream region, are anthropomorphic, and are thought to cause sickness by spearing those persons they encounter as they wander about at night. A closely related class is that of *hunting spirits,* who are like the Mountainers but apparently more numerous and invoked in a wider variety of rites.

25. *Flying Monsters.* These are the most feared of evil spirits due to their ability to prey upon human souls. They were conceived of in birdlike form (zoomorphic) and lived in rocks, trees, and other natural locations.

26. *Ending Deities.* These deities were invoked in funeral rites, and their function was to end life or death.

27. *Place Spirits.* "These deities are believed to inhabit large rocks, springs, trees, banks, and other natural features in every locality . . . Their principal activities are theft of the souls of rice and men, . . . they are also believed to be the owners of all game living in their vicinity" (Barton, 1946: 85). A large proportion of all sickness experienced by the Ifugao was attributed to these gods.

28. *Conductors of Souls.* These deities were used by other

gods when they wished to summon the soul of a man (causing his death) or by the living to call back an ancestor's soul to the funeral rites.

29. *Ghoul and Cannibal Deities.* These are all deities who are invoked in sorcery activities in the effort to harm other human beings.

30. This class consists of the souls of recently deceased individuals that wander about for a period of time after death. Those resulting from violent death were greatly feared. Ghosts of animals were also included in this class.

31. *Obstetric Deities.* These deities specialize in causing difficult birth for human beings, each class member causing a different complication.

32. *Wrapping and Tying Deities.*

The special power and function of these deities is to tie up men's stomachs so that they will eat and drink but little, and men's passions so that they will not fight, especially when they are guests at a drinkfest. With . . . possible exception . . . they are about as nearly beneficent as any deities the Ifugao has. But no more than any other deities do they confer benefit unless paid by sacrifice. Nor are they by any means always beneficent (Barton, 1946: 88).

33. *Divination Deities.* These are the major gods invoked in divination, chiefly in the diagnosis of disease (is it any wonder?), detecting thieves, and finding lost property.

This has been a lengthy catalogue of deities, with the classes numbering over twelve hundred separate supernatural beings; and one can see in them a rather clear reflection of the major concerns of the Ifugao. Health, childbirth, agriculture, hunting, divination, sorcery, war, protection, and other aspects of life are all represented in terms susceptible of supernatural manipulation or at least explanation. We can turn now to the examination of several briefer examples.

SUPERNATURALS AMONG THE BURMESE

As our second example of supernatural beings we can turn to contemporary belief among the people of Burma in South Asia. In terms of world religious affiliation most of the people of Burma are classified as followers of Theravada Buddhism. This faith, as in so many Asian cases, has been superimposed upon more aboriginal systems to create a working synthesis in which first one and then another element is emphasized. The data presented below follow the excellent account of Melford Spiro (1967). For the details of Buddhist thought and organization see Spiro, 1970.

Among the Burmese, supernatural beings are divided into a number of categories. One major category includes *Ghosts*, the disembodied spirits of the dead. These appear to comprise two major types. *Leikpya* represent the souls of deceased individuals who remain around to bother the living because they were not accorded the proper funeral rites. This type is considered as less harmful than a second type, the *Tasei-thayr*. These beings represent the souls of persons who have been reborn as ghosts as a consequence of having been evil persons during life. They must remain as ghosts until they have worked out their destiny (defined in Buddhist karma terms) and are reborn into another plane of existence. Such ghosts are generally invisible, and they ". . . generally live on the outskirts of villages, especially near cemeteries, where they feed on corpses. They also enjoy the flesh of living people, however, and at times . . . they enter a village in order to attack and eat one of its inhabitants" (Spiro, 1967: 34). The evil ghosts do appear to be greater if they are also under the control of a witch.

Ghosts are warded off by the use of amulets, magical symbols, and other protective devices. More actively, rituals may be performed to frighten them off or proper performances of funeral rites in the case of the first type of ghost. A supernatural species closely related to ghosts are *Demons*. These, for the Burmese, are also considered evil beings. Like the ghosts, they feed on human flesh or in some other way harm people. Most demons are *Bilus*—ogrelike beings—although children born deformed are also believed to be (incarnated) demons. Such children are generally killed.

The major class of supernatural beings among the Burmese are the *Nats*. Unlike ghosts and demons, the Nats are involved in a system of complex worship involving highly detailed beliefs and ritual endeavors. "Generically, 'nat' refers to a class of supernatural beings who are more powerful than man and who, therefore, can affect him either for good or for evil" (Spiro, 1967: 41). There are three recognized types of nats. The first may be designated *Devas* after the Sanskrit word for deity. These spirit beings are derived from Buddhist cosmology and occupy places in a series of heavens. Their function is to protect human beings in general and also to respond to specific requests, although some are in such a high heaven as to be beyond taking such notice. Those that are given offerings of food and prayers are really Hindu-derived gods taken over in Buddhism. Besides being a part of ritual, such devas are represented by images placed in religious buildings. Of considerable importance is the notion that to receive their protection or assistance, the worshiper must live in accordance with the ethics of Buddhism; their aid is only for the righteous and faithful person.

A second major variety of nat is comprised of *Nature Spirits*, which differ greatly in power and other characteristics. They are associated with various natural phenomena; trees, rice fields, and the like. These nature spirits appear to be essentially evil and represent the source of those misfortunes that strike people though not as a result of their own bad actions—for example, drowning due to floods. It is because of their propensity to cause misfortune that these beings receive ritual propitiation. Some of these spirits receive annual ritual attention in public rites; others are invoked only when possible contact with them occurs. Many taboos also exist to protect the unwary from receiving harm at their hands.

The most conspicuous category of nat for the Burmese, however, is that called the *Thirty-Seven Nats*. These supernatural beings ". . . are conceived to be the spirits of deceased human beings who, because of their violent deaths, become nats" (Spiro, 1967: 51). Each of these beings is named (although few people are familiar with all of them), and the number of specific deities exceeds the number suggested by their title. There is an "inside" group whose worship in the past was officially ordained by Burmese kings and inscribed on royal lists and an "outside" group whose number is indeterminate. All, however, were originally human beings, if only mythically so described. These beings represent a type of deity that is problematical. They are potentially evil, but they can also use their powers to protect those who propitiate them. Failure to do so, however, leads to harm. We may discuss a couple of these nats to indicate their functional positions and natures in the pantheon of Burmese deities.

Perhaps the most common of the Thirty-Seven Nats is *Min-Mahagiri,* the *House Nat.* This being is thought to reside in the coconut that hangs from the southeast pillar of the Burmese house. It is also considered as an offering to him, and whenever the coconut stem falls off it is replaced and offerings are given. This is done roughly three times a year. Min-Mahagiri is generally supposed to protect the house and its occupants from harm, and specific requests may be made to him in event of difficulty. However,

Since he lives inside the house, there are specific activities related to the house which are offensive to him. Thus, the coconut must be removed during childbirth because the house is polluted at this time. Similarly it must be removed when someone dies . . . Not to do that would result in harm. It is especially offensive to have sexual intercourse on the Southeastern side of the house . . . because the brother and sister nats are offended by the sight of sexual activity. It is for this reason that spouses never sleep on this side of the house (Spiro, 1967: 94).

One is hard put to discover if the fear engendered by belief in nats of this sort outweighs the positive aspects of their cult!

Another variety of this type of nat is the *Miazin-Hpazain,* which Spiro translates as "mother's side–father's side nat." The basis of the worship of these nats is difficult to understand. Apparently such a nat was originally worshiped as residing in some particular locality. As persons left such localities they continued to worship the associated deity, and their descendants—mainly via the father's side—continued the worship even though they resided in different locations. They simply based their worship on the fact that their relatives had done so. "The same . . . nat may be shared by persons living in widely scattered parts of the country and . . . different miazin-hpazain nats may co-exist even within one village" (Spiro, 1967: 99). Some individuals may derive an obligation for worshiping two such nats, one from each side of the family. At any rate, such worship entails the necessity to offer food at festivals to the nats and often to do so on Buddhist holy days as well. Again this is primarily in the effort to ward off any danger from them. Positively such nats may protect their followers from danger and are often requested to aid humans in their financial affairs. Others of the Thirty-Seven Nats are conceived of along similar lines.

SUPERNATURALS AMONG THE NORSE

As another partial example of supernatural beings we can present some of the better known Norse (Viking) deities as worshiped in the first millennium A.D. The beliefs of these hardy seafarers were close to those of other Northern European peoples and have been written about extensively by many scholars. The present brief account follows those of Branston (1961) and Davidson (1964, 1969). Norse conceptions of the supernatural involve numerous accounts of the origin of the gods as well as definitions of cosmological regions. The oldest of the gods is a shadowy being called the *Allfather* (a term attached as well to later beings) who had absolute powers over all things. He was the original author of creation. The first living being (in one myth) was a giant called *Ymir*. In the beginning there was a yawning gulf with two regions—Niflheim in the north, an area of fog and ice, and Muspelheim, an area of heat and fire, in the south. Between was the source of all waters. When ice and fire were brought into contact the ice melted, and Ymir took shape. Not only did other giant beings descend from him, but in many tales he also figures in later creations.

One tradition is that the first man and woman grew out of the left armpit of the giant Ymir, while from his two feet the race of frost giants was engendered. But the giant was slain by three gods . . . and these three set to work to form the world from Ymir's body. They used his flesh for the soil, his bones for mountains and stones, his hair for vegetation, and his blood for the sea. From the dome of his skull they formed the sky, giving it to four dwarfs to raise high above the earth, while his brains formed the clouds (Davidson, 1969: 114).

One of these three gods was Odin.

Odin is one of the major Norse deities and represents some of the most profound concerns of these people. He probably was considered their supreme deity and is often identified as the oldest of the gods. He is the war god par excellence, being represented as wearing a golden helmet and carrying a spear as a symbol of his power. Of his many names those of "father of victory" and "lord of hosts" are prominent in many myths. This god was also associated with a special afterworld called *Valhalla*. To this heaven went the souls of those who fell in battle, and here apparently they fought again each day and feasted, only to die and repeat the process endlessly. Possibly only upper-class warriors were accorded this fate! Special goddesses lived in Valhalla and assisted Odin. These were the *Valkyries;* ". . . there are certain beings who form a link between Odin and the slain, and between the worlds of the living and the dead. These are the female spirits called Valkyries, who wait on the warriors in Valhalla . . ." (Davidson, 1964: 61). They themselves are like warriors, riding horses and carrying spears, and are dispatched to battles by Odin to choose those who shall die and those who will live and have victory. They also apparently aided the gods in general against their enemies.

Beyond presiding over Valhalla, Odin could also aid humans in victory by sapping the will of the enemy, or he could give humans special protection against wounds and the dangers of battle. In fact there was a class of special fighters, the Berserks, who had received such a gift from him. He himself was manifested in a noisy, billowing movement across the sky, although he could assume a variety of shapes or disguises—especially that of an old man with a staff. One of the most characteristic sacrifices to Odin involved the killing of the first person captured in a battle, usually by stabbing or hanging. Burning of the dead was also customary along with their possessions. As an anthropomorphic god, Odin was married to the goddess *Frigg.* She herself was a deity connected to love and fertility and no doubt represents an older earth-goddess type of being. In her role of wife she is also a kind of mother to many of the rest of the gods. In her specific fertility functions she had great influence over childbirth. She also apparently had the power to know the future but, alas, had no powers to direct it.

A second god of major importance was *Thor.* Although he ranks second to Odin he often appears to be the strongest deity.

In the myths Thor appears as a burly, red-headed man, immensely strong, with a huge appetite, blazing eyes and a beard, full of enormous vitality and power. He could increase his strength by wearing a special belt of might. Other prized possessions of his were his great gloves, enabling him to grasp and shatter rocks, the chariot drawn by goats which took him across the sky, and his hammer . . . This last was regarded as the greatest of all the treasures . . . (Davidson, 1969: 57).

The hammer of Thor is probably the best known of Norse mythic motifs. In some accounts Thor is represented as the son of Odin and Frigg. He is definitely a sky god and is associated with the thunder and storms. As such his worshipers prayed to him for good weather and favorable winds, especially important for a seafaring people. His image stood in many temples, and periodic offerings of bread and meat were made to him. His followers also looked to him when faced with difficult decisions. This god especially was the chief defender of Asgard (the abode of the gods) against the supernatural enemies who were attempting to destroy the established order of things. Many of his mythic adventures are encounters with such enemies, especially a serpent.

Still another prominent deity was the god *Njorthr* (Njord). This god also held powers over the wind and could smooth the sea. As such, he was the special patron of voyagers and fishermen. He was especially worshiped by coastal peoples. He also appears to have had functions as a fertility god and seems to have ruled over the seasons. He had two children who were also of importance. *Freyr* was a god with fertility functions and power over rain, sunshine, and the natural increase and prosperity of earth. He was often called the god of plenty and helped human worshipers acquire good fortune. As such sometimes his image in temples was one of a phallic nature. Regular sacrifices were offered to him, horses as well as human beings. His sister, *Freyja*, was a love goddess and was considered as the most beautiful of female deities. She often assumed birdlike form and was connected with divination. "Freyja is concerned only with human love. She seems to have some authority in the world of death. [And her] . . . name is specifically linked . . . with a special kind of witchcraft . . ." (Davidson, 1964: 115, 117). So she apparently had her evil side as well.

Beyond these deities a host of other gods existed whose functions sometimes are specific and sometimes overlap with those discussed above. In addition there were a host of lesser supernatural beings. For example, there were the *Norns* or mistresses of fate. These goddesses were thought of as spinners who held the threads of destiny in their hands and who judged the fate that was merited by each person. In myth they even pronounced the fate of the gods. Another class was the *Elves*, various demon types associated with particular aspects of nature. As typical demons they might be helpful to humans, but more often they were spiteful toward them. Elves were organized in groups and spent much of their time in games and dancing. One variety of elf—dwarfs—was a deformed group who lived in secret places and owned gold and other precious things buried in the earth. In sum, then, we can once again ascertain from this extremely incomplete account of Norse supernaturals the values, desires, and aspects of a group of people immortalized into their conceptions of their gods and other supernatural beings. We can turn now to a last brief example, that of the Aztec of ancient Mexico.

SUPERNATURALS AMONG THE AZTEC

At the time of contact with the Spanish in the sixteenth century the Aztec of Mexico expressed belief in a great number of supernatural beings and engaged in considerable expressions of ritual (often including human sacrifice) with respect to them. Not unlike the case in ancient Egypt much of the worship and interaction relative to these deities was confined to the priests, although numerous public rites also occurred. There were ultimate creator gods, many other beings (each with their own specific attributes and functions), and a complex mythological system. Apparently much of the theological sophistication of the priests was lost on the practical level of the common people; what to the priests might have been one god with multiple attributes to the commoner may have been many different gods. And of course there were many different strands in their sacred conceptions, anyway, since they inherited the beliefs and practices of earlier peoples in their region and grafted their own customs onto them. The following account largely follows Caso (1958), Leon–Portilla (1963), and Sejourne (1960).

Essentially there were two rather shadowy creator deities—*Two Lord* and *Two Lady*—and they were the ultimate generative force behind all things, being called "our lord and lady of flesh and sustenance." In the dim past it was these beings who were responsible for life in general. They had four sons who accomplished the actual creation of the other gods, the world itself, and human beings. The four sons lived in (were associated with) the four directions as were Two Lord and Two Lady in the center direction (up and down), which was called the Place Two. In the specific creation myth of the Aztec,

The world and man have been created several times . . . and each creation has been followed by a cataclysm that has destroyed mankind. The last time man was created . . . Quetzalcoatl, . . . the beneficent god of all mankind, descended to the world of the dead to gather up the bones of past generations, and sprinkling them with his own blood, created a new humanity. Since man was created by the sacrifice of the gods, he must reciprocate by offering them his own blood in sacrifice. . . . Man must nourish the gods with the magic sustenance of life itself, found in human blood and in the human heart (Caso, 1958: 12).

It was believed that another cataclysm would occur every fifty-two years (when the ritual calendar expired), and much world-renewing ritual took place at this time.

One of the most important gods was *Huitzilopochtli*, represented by the sun. In myth this deity had been born to the earth goddess and had defended her against her other children—the moon and the stars. In visible reality, the journey of the sun seemed to spring from the earth and of course brought the day, which overcame the moon and the stars of night. Huitzilopochtli was quite specifically a special deity for the Aztec, who believed themselves to be his chosen people. Since he went into combat each day, he required human aid ". . . for he has to fight against the unnumbered stars of the North and South and frighten them all off with his arrows of light" (Caso, 1958: 13). This required sacrificing captives gained in war, since he required their blood. Because of the need for such victims, this deity became also a god of war.

A second notable Aztec deity is *Quetzalcoatl*. As we have seen, it was this god who resurrected the bones of the dead to create the Aztec, so he stands out pre-eminently as a god of life. His activities, however, did not end at this point, since as a culture-hero type of supernatural being he was believed to have continually worked for human benefit. He gave humans many gifts including the knowledge of corn, cotton, and precious stones. "But above all he taught man science . . . he taught him how to arrange the calendar and devised ceremonies and fixed certain days for prayer and sacrifices" (Caso, 1958: 25). This god is also represented in a number of more specific guises, i.e., as the god of wind. His nature seems to have been such that he was constantly being tempted into sin by gods less favorably disposed toward humans, and his ensuing struggles against them is cosmologically the explanation for the destructions and creations in the history of the world.

A third major deity was *Tezcatlipocha*, who symbolized the night sky and darkness. He is a sort of mirror image of Huitzilopochtli, sort of an earth man. It is this god who works against the god of life and who brings cataclysms. "He is Quetzalcoatl's brother and also his enemy, the creator and destroyer of the earliest mythical eras; he is god of . . . failure and ruin, . . . he protects sin and foments quarrels . . ." (Sejourne, 1960: 166–168). Because of his association with night and his basic negative nature, he is especially the patron deity for sorcerers and highwaymen. This god also was associated with war, and a special sacrifice of a young man captured in battle and specially trained to symbolize him was a highlight of the Aztec ritual year.

Still another major Aztec supernatural was the god *Tlaloc* who was responsible for rain and associated phenomena and who represented one of the oldest attempts at deification in the Central American area. Like many of the more minor gods he had been created by the main gods and seems to have fallen into the problematical category of deities. He sent the rain that aided crop growth but ". . . he had the power to unleash floods and send droughts . . . Consequently he was a god to be feared when angry . . ." (Caso, 1928: 42). He, too, required human sacrifices, especially children. There were also many other deities that have association with the earth or with growing things. *Coatlicue* was the earth goddess who had given birth to Huitzilopochtli and other gods. Many living things were therefore considered her children, since they are sprung from and nourished by the earth itself. She was also called the "devourer of filth" since she was believed to feed upon the corpses of humans. She was worshiped in many of these aspects and as the special patron of women who died in childbirth. No doubt, as a single deity she represents a synthesis of somewhat different beings.

Another important Aztec goddess was *Chicomecoatl*, who was especially involved in sustenance. She controlled the fertility of the earth—all necessary for growing things—and by extension became a goddess of human fertility as well. Beyond her, many specific plants or aspects of fertility each had controlling deities; for example, corn gods, cactus gods, gods of spring, and the like. So no aspect of any importance seems to have been overlooked. Finally, among countless other beings, there were the gods of death, especially *Mictlantecuhtli*. This deity, along with his wife, ruled over one of the abodes of the dead—that one to which most deceased persons were thought to go, journeying for four years through nine hells filled with all manner of privations. There were also three other possibilities. Warriors who had been sacrificed or who had fallen in battle went to the "house of the sun," women who died in childbirth went to the "house of corn," and those who died from water-related causes went to the "house of rain." Other gods ruled over these afterlife worlds, and each along with the main "heaven" was assigned a direction. Having briefly indicated the nature of supernaturals among the Aztec for comparison to the Ifugao, Burmese, and Norse conceptions, we can turn now to a closely related topic.

MYTHOLOGY

As has been seen in the major portion of this chapter, the various types of supernatural beings, especially gods, are often mentioned in mythology. In fact, as observed, some have their only real significance in such a context. It is evident then that if one wishes to understand the nature and function of such beings, one must seek also to understand the related mythology. This is equally clear in the case of rituals, since supernatural practices also are supported by beliefs, and mythology is a major dimension of these; recall the discussion of the ritual specific called *mythological paraphernalia* in Chapter 2. In fact, many early students of myth felt that such beliefs and ideas were prior to ritual and that supernatural practices were simply enactments of such myths, in Eliade's terms the expression of the archetype! Later on, the notion was reversed; the ritual was believed to serve as a stimulus for myth reflecting the practice that they justified. As Clyde Kluckhohn (1942) pointed out some time ago, this controversy as to the priority of myth or ritual is not completely amenable to solution. Rather the important thing is their interdependence; they often do go together, reinforcing each other and catering to those needs of humans that supernaturalism in general seeks to serve. More current scholars on myth also take such an evenhanded approach.

To the observer who does not enter the dispute, the question of Myth-From-Ritual is akin to "Which came first, the chicken or the egg?" The answer to the alternative propositions is that neither did, since chickens and eggs have a complex evolutionary history tracing back to simpler forms. So it is with myth and ritual. It seems inconceivable that any well-developed ritual could exist prior to some mythological ratification. It might be more reasonable to postulate that myth and ritual grew together, making reciprocal contributions one to the other (Clarke and Clarke, 1963: 35).

Most general collections of readings on mythology contain articles supporting more biased views (see the bibliography at the end of this book).

FORMS OF MYTHOLOGY

What is the nature of mythology and what are its varieties? There is no clear consensus here, much less official definitions. Mythology is usually considered as part of the oral literature of a society; part of its folklore that of course may contain much of little relevance to the understanding of supernaturalism (jokes, hunting lore, and the like). Mythology, in a more restrictive sense, would include those stories (prose narratives) that do have some kind of supernatural content. This content, however, may vary enormously. In the effort to order some of this content numerous scholars have devised classification schemes. None of these attempts has met with universal acceptance, but one effort does seem fairly useful and has the added virtue of brevity. Since this section on myth is included only to remind the student of its importance in supernaturalism and to exhibit a few examples, we can employ this scheme, that of William Bascom, in this chapter. Bascom distinguishes three major forms of such prose narratives (mythology), which he calls *myths, legends,* and *folktales.*

Myths

"Myths are prose narratives which, in the society in which they are told, are considered to be truthful accounts of what happened in the remote past" (Bascom, 1965: 4). So we are dealing here with stories relating to the long, long ago situation. Such a world/time is generally conceived of as being different from the present world or perhaps as being a different kind of world altogether; for example, underground or in the sky or prior to creation of the earth. Along the lines suggested by Eliade, such a world no doubt was more real than that lived in by humans today. Perhaps for this reason and because the major protagonists and the actors in myths are usually the gods themselves (or special animals and such), such stories have the ring of truth. Since the gods are sacred and sacredness is truth and reality, such stories are endowed with the same sacredness and truth. In fact, myths are usually the sacred literature of the believing society or part of its theological system and as such constitute a most important prop to the ritual system. So, myths are sacred and true, refer to remote times and places, and detail the doings of gods, although humans may play a supporting role.

Legends

"Legends are prose narratives which, like myths, are regarded as true by the narrator and his audience, but they are set in a period considered less remote, when the world was much as it is today" (Bascom, 1965: 4). Generally speaking, human beings are the principal actors in legends, although their activities may take on a superhuman element, and they may be aided or hindered in their adventures by gods or other supernatural beings. Perhaps because humans are so centrally involved, the past cannot be of times too different or remote from the present. Likewise, the truth is less rigorous than that of myths. They are not accepted with the same degree of faith, because legends seldom develop sacred overtones or the same close ritual connections. They are more secular in nature and often comprise the folk history of some past events. A well-known example here would be the *Odyssey* of Homer. Legends can, however, refer to less substantial subject matter and may merely serve to explain some cultural condition or facet of the natural environment. So, legends are true but not sacred, deal with a less remote past, and relate the doings of human beings as their primary concern.

Folktales

Finally, Bascom defines folktales as ". . . prose narratives which are regarded as fiction" (Bascom, 1965: 4). Even to the people who tell and listen to them, they are not considered as true but rather are held in the sense of being amusing stories ("Once upon a time, . . ."). Because of this, their format is less rigidly defined than those for either myth or legend. Their heroes can be god or human (or animal), and their settings can occur in almost any time or place. Because of their pure story nature, they do not have sacred or ritualistic connections. A typical well-known example of folktales would be *Aesop's Fables*. G. S. Kirk (1970) has suggested that in folktales the supernatural elements have become subsidiary to the pure appeal of the narratives themselves; they are not primarily concerned with the more serious subjects, nor are the stories themselves as complicated. So, folktales are neither sacred or true, they take place any time, anywhere, lack a serious character, and involve almost any manner of actor. Of these three forms of mythology, myths— with their sacred and ritual connections—are of most interest to students of religion.

OTHER ASPECTS OF MYTHOLOGY

There have been many approaches taken with respect to the study of mythology. This is especially true, since folklorists and others who are interested in such stories are not always anthropologists. In fact the latter are probably in the minority. As a result, the treatment given mythology and the aspects of it selected for analysis differ. Certainly most approaches agree that such stories must be studied cross-culturally to gain data on all the versions of a particular narrative and to discover its history and diffusion. Beyond this, however, a dichotomy exists (less so today than in the past) between treating mythology as comparative literature, which of course it is, and taking a more social science-oriented approach. In this second case the researcher is perhaps more interested in the role of such stories in human life. Anthropologists generally feel that knowledge of the social and cultural contexts of mythology is necessary if we are to fully understand it. Since mythology may mirror the other beliefs and behaviors of a people, it is important to understand this connection and to examine the functional role of myths, legends, and folktales. As one writer has put it:

Although the . . . comparative method is probably the most traditional way of studying folklore, it has several serious weaknessess. For one thing, it tends to concentrate on "lore" while ignoring "folk". Folktales . . . are often tracked down around the world with little or no attention paid to the people who tell and listen to these marvelous forms of oral art. . . .
In this newer, anthropologically oriented method, the folk as well as the lore are treated. . . . The abiding concern with origins has been largely replaced by a concern for function—that is, what does the folktale mean and do for the members of the society among whom the tale is found, and when is it told (Dundes, 1968: 42)?

So the student reading an account of the mythology of some society must remain aware of the theoretical background of the writer. An excellent example of the anthropological approach is that of Thomas O. Beidelman (1961) who discussed a folktale from an African society that seems understandable only with reference to full knowledge of the kinship relations/obligations whose dynamics it appears to mirror. The functions of mythology are briefly indicated in the following chapter. We can now give a few examples of mythology to present the flavor of such narratives.

EXAMPLES OF MYTH

Since myths are of the most interest to anthropologists, we reprint two rather brief examples of suggestive cases of such materials. As a first example we offer a cosmological or origin myth. Such myths are universal in human societies and deal with why the world is the way it is, with how it came into being, and with the position of humanity. The Judaeo–

Christian accounts of Genesis can be recalled by the student as a case in point. Our specific example is taken from myths common in the past among American Indians living along the North Pacific coast.

Example 1

Before people were on the earth, the Chief of the Sky Spirits grew tired of his home in the Above World, because it was always cold up there. So he made a hole in the sky by turning a stone round and round. Through this hole he pushed snow and ice until he made a great mound that reached from the earth almost to the sky. Later, people named it Mount Shasta.

Then the Sky Spirit stepped from a cloud to the peak and walked down the mountain. When he was about halfway down to the valley below, he thought, "On this mountain there should be trees." He put his finger to the ground here and there, here and there. Wherever his finger touched the ground, a tree began to grow. In his footsteps the snow melted and the water ran down in rivers.

The Sky Spirit broke off the small end of the giant stick he carried from the sky and threw the pieces into the rivers. The long pieces became beaver and otter; the small pieces became fish. From the big end of the stick he made the animals.

Biggest of them all were the grizzly bears. They were covered with hair and they had sharp claws, just as they have today, but they walked on two feet and could talk. They looked so fierce that the Sky Spirit sent them away from him, to live in the forest at the base of the mountain.

When the leaves dropped from the trees, he picked them up, blew upon them, and so made the birds.

Then the Chief of the Sky Spirits decided to stay on the earth, and to bring his family down from the sky. The mountain became their lodge. He made a big fire in the center of the mountain and a hole in the top so that the smoke and sparks could fly out. When he put a big log on the fire, sparks would fly up and the earth would tremble.

Late one spring, while the Sky Spirit and his family were sitting around the fire, the Wind Spirit sent a big storm that shook the top of the mountain. It blew and blew, and roared and roared. Smoke blown back into the lodge hurt their eyes. At last the Sky Spirit said to his youngest daughter, "Go up to the smoke hole and ask the Wind Spirit to blow more gently. Tell him I am afraid he will blow the mountain over."

His little daughter was glad to go. As she started, her father spoke again, "Be careful when you get to the top. Don't put your head out. If you do put it out, the wind may catch you by your hair and blow you away. Just thrust out your arm, make a sign and then speak to the Wind Spirit."

The little girl hurried to the top of the mountain and spoke to the Wind Spirit. As she was about to start back, she remembered that her father had said the ocean could be seen from the top of their lodge. He had made the ocean since the family moved from the sky, and his daughter had never seen it.

She put her head out of the hole and looked toward the west. The Wind Spirit caught her long hair, pulled her out of the mountain and blew her down over the snow and ice. She landed among the scrubby fir trees at the edge of the timber and snow line, her long red hair trailing over the snow.

There Grizzly Bear found her when he was out hunting food for his family. He carried the little girl home with him, wondering who and what she was. Mother Bear took good care of her and brought her up with their family of cubs. The little red-haired girl and the cubs ate together, played together and grew up together.

When she became a young woman, she and the eldest son of the grizzly bears were married. In the years that followed they had many children. The children did not look like their father or like their mother. They were not so hairy as the grizzlies and yet they did not look like spirits either.

All the grizzly bears throughout the forest were proud of these new creatures. They were so pleased and were so kindhearted that they made a lodge for the red-haired mother and her strange looking children. They built the lodge near Mount Shasta—Little Mount Shasta it is called today.

After many years had passed, Mother Grizzly Bear knew that she would soon die. Fearing that she had done wrong in keeping the daughter of the Chief of the Sky Spirits away from her father, she felt that she should send him word and ask his forgiveness. So she asked all the grizzlies to join her at the new lodge they had built. Then she sent her oldest grandson to the top of Mount Shasta, in a cloud, to tell the Spirit Chief where he could find his long-lost daughter.

The father was so glad that he came down the mountainside in giant strides. He hurried so fast that the snow melted off in places under his feet. Even today his tracks can be seen in the rocky path on the south side of Mount Shasta.

As he neared the lodge, he called out, "Is this where my little daughter lives?"

He expected to see a little girl exactly as she had looked when he saw her last. When he saw the strange creatures his daughter was taking care of and learned that they were his grandchildren, he was very angry. A new race had been created, and he had not

known about it. He frowned on the old grandmother so sternly that she died at once. Then he cursed all the grizzlies.
"Get down on your hands and knees. From this moment all of you grizzlies shall walk on four feet. And you shall never talk again. You have wronged me."
He drove his grandchildren out of the lodge, put his daughter over his shoulder, and climbed back up the mountain. Never again did he come to the forest. Some say that he put out the fire in the center of his lodge and took his daughter back up to the sky to live. Those strange creatures, his grandchildren, scattered and wandered all over the earth. They were the first Indians, the ancestors of all the Indian tribes.
That is why the Indians living around Mount Shasta would never kill a grizzly bear. Whenever one of them was killed by a grizzly, his body was burned on the spot. And for many years all who passed that way cast a stone there until a great pile of stones marked the place of his death." (*Indian Legends of the Pacific Northwest,* ed. Ella E. Clark, University of California Press, 1958: 9–11).*

As the second example of myth we can offer one of the type generally known as a *myth of the hero.* In these accounts a heroic figure—either a god or a human with special attributes —engages in quests, accomplishes extraordinary things, fights monsters, and so forth. Such myths often explain why aspects of human life are the way they are or give humans an understanding of themselves. Our specific example comes from the ancient Near Eastern civilization of the Sumerians and is the epic of Gilgamesh and his quest for immortality.

Example 2

"Hear me, ye elders of Uruk" cried Gilgamesh, from where he sat by the body of his friend. "I weep for my brother Enkidu, my friend, my companion. All the beasts that ran with you, Enkidu, mourn you as I do: let the elders of Uruk weep for you also. You were the axe at my side, my brother: my hand's strength, my sword and my shield. Listen! The beasts that we hunted, panther and tiger, weep for you; Listen! The mountain we climbed to slay the watchman Humbaba mourns for you. Listen! The rivers of Kullab, Ula of Elam and the blessed Euphrates, weep for you. Listen! The warriors of Uruk, where we slew the Bull of Heaven, mourn for you. Listen! The harvesters weep for you now, and the servants, the women, and the temple harlot who brought you to me. Can you hear them? What is this sleep which lies over you now? What is this darkness which cloaks you so that you cannot hear the words of my mourning?"

For a long time Gilgamesh stayed by the body of his friend: seven days and nights he sat, numbed and silent, until at last the worms, who serve the Annunaki, the judges of the dead, fastened on Enkidu to take him below. Then did Gilgamesh bury his friend and make an offering to Shamash. Then he covered himself with the pelts of wild beasts, and streaking his face with ashes, he set forth to find Utnapishtim.

"At the end of the world lives Utnapishtim, who is called the Faraway," said Gilgamesh to his heart. "Him will I seek whom the gods spared from the Flood. They set him in a land far away, at the mouth of the rivers of the earth, in the garden of the gods. To him they gave eternal life. Him will I seek because I am afraid of death. I will seek him and learn from him the secret of eternal life."

A long path through the wilderness Gilgamesh walked, and when he came at last to the mountain passes, he made his camp. For a time he watched the embers of his fire, and then he slept. But in the night he awoke from a dream and beheld a strange sight. There in the moonlight were lions, and they leapt and played and gloried in their life. Then Gilgamesh took his sword and fell on them like an arrow from a taut bowstring and he vanquished them, he destroyed and scattered them.

In the morning he rose and went his way, coming at length to the great mountain Mashu, which guards the rising and setting of the sun. At its gate stand the Men-Scorpions, the dragons, who guard the passes and whose glance is death. For a moment only did Gilgamesh shield his eyes; then he went forward.

"Who are you who come to us without fear, without trembling? Your courage is that of the gods, but you are dressed as a wild man, in pelts. Stand and tell us the reason you come," said the Man-Scorpion, the captain of dragons.

"Gilgamesh is my name," answered that one. "I come for Enkidu, my friend. Him I loved dearly; together we suffered and together we gloried. Now he is dead, and surely that is my lot also. I seek Utnapishtim, the Faraway. To him the gods gave life everlasting. I need to question him about the living and the dead. Open the gate of the mountain and let me pass!"

"No man has done what you have done," replied the Man-Scorpion. "None, not one has made the journey through the mountain. Twelve leagues does the way run under the mountain, all in darkness. Three leagues are in darkness, and three more. Yet three more leagues are in darkness, and yet three more. Would you go that way? There is no light there, the presence of Shamash does not find a way in. Yet if you would go that way, Gilgamesh, I will open the gate to you. Go with the blessing of the gods, may you find what you seek. Go, the Gate of Mashu is open."

Now three leagues under the mountain went Gilgamesh, and darkness cloaked every step. Nothing could he see before him, nothing behind. Three leagues more he went, and yet three leagues. Nine leagues thus he went in darkness, the darkness was thick about him, it enveloped him like a cloak. Nothing could he see before him, and nothing behind. After nine leagues, the end was near, a cool wind blew upon his face, yet he could see nothing. So yet three more leagues he went, and at last he came out from under the mountain and beheld the sun, the light of Shamash, streaming down upon him.

So it was that Gilgamesh came, weary and worn, to the garden of the gods. Golden trees were there, and fruit of gems. Lapis lazuli were the leaves, and grapes of carnelian hung upon the vine. There Gilgamesh sat down by the shores of the ocean, and there Shamash saw him, saw his weariness, saw the labors of this man dressed in pelts of wild beasts. And Shamash spoke to him.

"Gilgamesh, listen to me! To me you dedicated yourself and slew Humbaba, the watchman of the forest; and it was I whose supplications spared your life when you slew the Bull of Heaven. Listen then to me, Gilgamesh! Never will you find the life you are seeking. Better it were that you never came this way, a way no man has gone before."

And to Shamash Gilgamesh replied, "Long have I toiled in darkness, through the wilderness and over the mountain passes. In darkness I came here, to seek Utnapishtim the Faraway. And I to cover my head with earth now? Though I may be no better than a dead man, let me at least look upon the glory of the sun."

With her golden bowl she sits by that sea: Siduri, the maker of wine. With a veil she is covered, none can see her face. To her gate came Gilgamesh, and from afar she saw him approach. She saw a man dressed in the pelts of wild beasts, a man with the marks of a long journey on his face, with despair in his heart. To him she barred the way, she drew the bolt across the gate, saying to herself, "Surely this is a thief who comes this way."

But even as the bolt shot home, Gilgamesh lodged his foot in the gate and called in anger, "Woman, wine-maker, who are you to bar the gate to me? I will smash your gate, I will tear down your door. I am Gilgamesh, who slew the Watchman of the Forest, who slew the Bull of Heaven, who vanquished the lions in the mountain passes. You may not bar the way to me!"

Then Siduri said to him, "This is not Gilgamesh, lord of Kullab, slayer of Humbaba and the Bull of Heaven, vanquisher of lions.

This is one who is dressed in pelts of wild beasts, whose face is weary, whose heart is full of despair. Why do you come this way? Are you looking for the wind?"

"And why should I not be weary and full of despair?" Gilgamesh replied. "My friend Enkidu is dead, whom I loved as a brother. Now I seek Utnapishtim, who lives at the mouth of the rivers, and to whom the gods granted eternal life. I would ask him about life and death. Woman, I have looked upon your face: let me not look upon the face of death, that face I fear so much."

"Gilgamesh," Siduri said to him softly, drawing him inside her hut, "you will never find that life for which you are seeking. The gods have not given that to man. To man they gave the fruit called Death; the fruit called Life they kept for thsemselves. As for man—as for you—fill your belly with good food and wine. Day and night, feast on the things of life, dance, rejoice in what is your lot. Soon enough all will be taken from you: food and wine, the love of family and friends. Make your garments fresh, Gilgamesh, anoint your hair. Cherish the hand of the child, make you wife happy in your embrace: this is the lot of man."

Now Gilgamesh sat by the fire in Siduri's hut and stared a long while into the embers and was silent. At last he spoke.

"Woman, wine-maker: how can I be silent, how can I rest, how can I be merry, dance, enjoy the things of life, when my brother whom I loved, is dead? Seven days and seven nights I sat by him and wept, and then the worms, the servants of the Annunaki, fastened on him and carried him below. This too is my fate, and I fear it. No, I cannot rest. I will go over this Ocean, to find Utnapishtim. What directions can you give me?—this, not soft words and wine, is the boon I ask of you. How will I cross the Ocean?"

Siduri said to him, "There is no crossing of that sea, Gilgamesh; except for Shamash, who can cross it? Deep are the waters of death that lie between this place and that which you seek. How can you cross? When you come to the waters of death, what will you do? Nevertheless, Gilgamesh, I will tell you this. In the woods, seek out Urshanabi, the ferryman of Utnapishtim. With him are the Sacred Ones, the Ones of Stone. With his help you might cross. But if it is not possible, you must turn back."

Then Gilgamesh leapt up, in a rage. He seized his axe in his hand, and he sped to the woods by the shore like an arrow from a taut bowstring. Swinging his axe wildly, shattering the Ones of Stone in his wrath, he sought Urshanabi the Ferryman. He found him as he sat by his boat, carving the prow in the shape of a bird.

"Who is this who comes wildly, shattering the Ones of Stone, the Sacred Ones who protected the crossing and the landing of the ferryboat?" said Urshanabi as he sat by the beak of his ship. "Surely this is a thief, a brigand who comes thus wildly. Would you shatter me too? I have nothing to give you."

"I am Gilgamesh, lord of Kullab, slayer of Humbaba and the Bull of Heaven. For Enkidu I come, for Enkidu my brother, who is dead. I would speak with Utnapishtim of the secret of eternal life. Take me to him! Take me now in your boat across the Ocean, across the' waters of death!"

Urshanabi stood up then and for a long time looked at Gilgamesh in silence. He looked at the clothing of Gilgamesh, the pelts he wore. He looked at the marks of mourning and weariness on his face. Urshanabi looked at the despair in the heart of the lord of Kullab. Then he spoke.

"The crossing is deadly, Gilgamesh. It is doubly deadly now that you have destroyed the Ones of Stone: they protected this harbor, they protected the crossing and the landing. How will we cross now?"

"Go into the woods and do this. Go, and cut six score staves, each sixty cubits long. Caulk them with bitumen and cap them with ferrules and bring them here."

At once Gilgamesh turned and went into the woods. There with his axe he cut six score staves of straight wood, caulked them with bitumen and capped them with ferrules. He brought them to Urshanabi and placed them in the boat.

"Now listen to me again, Gilgamesh. When we come to the waters of death, you must do this. Thrust in a pole, down to very bottom of the sea. When the pole runs out, thrust in another, and another after that, and another. Make sure your hand never touches the water, for that is certain death."

For three days they sailed, they sped across the Ocean in three days, the journey of a month and a half. Then they reached the waters of death and the boat would not move. Then it was that Gilgamesh took up the first staff and thrust it down deep into the water, taking care that his hand did not touch the water of death. When the first pole ran out, he took another, and after that another. So they crossed, pole by pole, until all six score staves had thus been used. Then Gilgamesh raised his arms like a mast and fastened his garments to them like a sail, and so they crossed the waters of death and came to the other side.

From where he sat by the water's edge he saw them coming: Utnapishtim, the Faraway, he to whom the gods gave eternal life. And Utnapishtim wondered to himself, "Who is this who sails with Urshanabi, dressed in the pelts of beasts? This is none of mine, and yet he is. By his clothes and wild appearance he is none of mine. But by his face and heart he might be myself, though not for many, many years."

Then Gilgamesh approached and bowed down before Utnapishtim and prayed to him:

"Utnapishtim, the Eternal, you whom men call the Faraway, you who dwell at the mouth of the rivers, hear me! I am Gilgamesh, lord of Kullab, from the house of Anu, king of Uruk. You wonder at my appearance, but why should I not look thus? My face is of one who has made a long journey in heat and cold, in light and darkness, over the mountain passes and across the waters of death. As for my clothing, it is the raiment of mourning, and I wear it for my friend Enkidu, who is dead. For seven days and nights I watched by his side when he died, and I saw the servants of the Annunaki take him below. I watched his death, and now I fear my own. As for my heart, it is the heart of a man who has seen death a thousand times and never feared it, yet saw death but once and now cowers in despair. O you whom the gods spared, you to whom they gave eternal life, my father Utnapishtim, you who have entered the assembly of the gods, I beg you: how shall I find the life for which I am searching?"

By the sea they sit, Gilgamesh and Utnapishtim, the young king and the old man, the mortal and the deathless. Utnapishtim looks at Gilgamesh and speaks.

"Tell me, what is permanent? Tell me of the works of men, are they permanent? Do houses stand forever? Do brothers divide an inheritance to keep forever? What endures? Does the floodtime of the rivers endure? Does the dragon-fly endure forever? From the days of old there is no permanence. To all creation the gods gave death. The sleeping and the dead, how alike they are, like brothers! Yes, sleep is like a painted death. What happens when the Annunaki assemble together, when Mammetun, the mother of destinies, decrees the fates of men? This one shall live, that one shall die. But the day of death they never tell."

To Utnapishtim the Faraway, Gilgamesh now speaks.

"I came here expecting a hero, a warrior like myself, but what do I find? An old man taking his ease in the sun by the water's edge. If nothing is permanent, if nothing endures, if nothing lives forever and all shall die, how do you come to be here, how came you to enter the assembly of the gods, how did you merit everlasting life?"

"Listen to me now," says Utnapishtim. "Listen to me now, Gilgamesh: I will tell you a secret of the gods."

Then Utnapishtim spoke and told Shurrupak, where it stands by the Euphrates, a city old when the earth was young. The world was filled with people in those days, and their noise went up as a great clamor and offended the gods. They came together in council then, and resolved to destroy the earth by deluge. But Ea, whom Utnapishtim honored, warned him of the flood, and guided the

building of a boat. Onto that boat went Utnapishtim and his wife
and his servants. Onto that boat went gold and living things, the
beasts of the fields, and the craftsmen who made the boat. When
the time came, the ship was battened down, and the destroying
rains came and flooded the earth. The boat of Utnapishtim rode out
the storm. It rode out the rains and the rising waters. It rode out
the darkness and the thunder. When Enlil, the god of storm, broke
the land like a cup, the boat rode out the storm. Great was that
flood: even the gods fled before it to the highest reaches of the
heavens. And when it was over, nothing was left: over the earth
was water only, there was no land to be seen. Then on the mountain
of Nisir, the boat of Utnapishtim touched land and held fast. The
first day it held fast, and the waters receded. The second day it
held fast and the waters receded. The third day it held fast, and
the waters receded. For seven days the waters receded and the
boat held fast. On the seventh day, Utnapishtim let loose a dove, but
it found no resting place, and so returned. Utnapishtim let loose a
swallow, and it also returned. Then he let loose a raven, and the
raven did not return. Then Utnapishtim threw open everything,
and made a sacrifice to the gods and gave thanks. And the gods,
smelling the sacrifice, swarmed like flies over it. Ishtar was there,
and she saw the earth, smashed and broken and the bodies of men
and beasts strewn everywhere. Then she took her necklace, made
of the jewels of heaven, and set it above the earth. She forbade
Enlil to come to the sacrifice, for without reflection he had destroyed her people. Then came Enlil and said in anger, "Has any
mortal survived the flood? For none was to survive." Then Ea spoke
and told him of Utnapishtim, she told him that it had been she who
had warned the man. Then Enlil repented, and took Utnapishtim
and his wife, and the god touched his forehead to theirs, and so
they became immortal. Then he set them down by the mouth of
the rivers, far away at the end of the world, in the garden of the
gods, to live forever.

"How then will you find the life for which you seek, Gilgamesh?"
said Utnapishtim as he finished. "Who will call the gods to assembly for your sake? But if you are intent, put it to the test: only
prevail against sleep for seven days and seven nights. . . ." Yet
even as he spoke, a mist of sleep stole over Gilgamesh, and his head
nodded upon his breast.

"Look at this strong man now," said Utnapishtim to his wife. "Over
the wide world he travels, in search of eternal life. High over the
mountain passes he came, and over the sea, to escape from death:
yet he cannot even hear out my story, but sleep steals over him like
a cloak."

"Touch him, then, and awaken him," said the wife to Utnapishtim.

"No, let him sleep. And let him know how long he sleeps. Men are great dissemblers: even you he will try to deceive. Therefore bake bread while he sleeps, one loaf for each day he sleeps so."

So Utnapishtim's wife took flour and water and made dough and baked bread, one loaf each day as Gilgamesh slept. And when the hero awoke, he said, "I had hardly slept when you awoke me." Then Utnapishtim pointed to the loaves, seven of them, and said, "One loaf was baked for each day of your sleep, O mighty king, and look: The first loaf is hard, the second like leather, and the third is soggy. The fourth is mouldy, the fifth is mildewed, the sixth is fresh, and the seventh lies still upon the embers of the oven."

"What then shall I do, O Utnapishtim my father, where shall I go? Already sleep, that painted death, lies hold of my limbs, it crouches in the corner of my chamber. Wherever I put my foot, there I find death."

Then Utnapishtim spoke to Gilgamesh and said, "Go now, and freshen yourself. Cast your pelts aside and bathe. Anoint your hair, renew the fillet upon your forehead, put on fresh clothes. Renew yourself, Gilgamesh, and return to Uruk. The clothes I will give you will show no wear of age while you journey, always they will be fresh upon you."

Down to the water's edge went Gilgamesh and removed his clothes, which Utnapishtim burned upon the shore. And while he bathed, the wife of Utnapishtim said to her husband, "What will you give to Gilgamesh that he can take back with him? For he came here on a long journey. He must not return empty-handed." And Utnapishtim called out to Gilgamesh where he bathed, "Gilgamesh, you have come here on a long journey; you shall not return empty-handed. I will reveal a secret thing, a secret of the gods will I tell you."

"There is a plant that grows deep in the ocean, at the very bottom of the sea. Thorns it has which will wound your hands, but if you pluck it and carry it back, your hands will hold that charm which will return to a man his lost youth."

Then Gilgamesh swam to the deepest part of the ocean. He tied stones to his feet and went to the bottom of the sea. There on the bottom he saw the plant, and the thorns wounded his hand. But he prevailed and cutting loose the stones tied to his feet returned triumphant to the boat of Urshanabi.

"Look, ferryman! Behold this marvelous plant, the means for a man to win back his youth, and strength. I will carry it back to Uruk. I will give it to old men to eat, I will call it, 'The Old are Young Again', and I will eat it myself and have back my lost youth," said Gilgamesh to Urshanabi. Then he put on the clothes which Utnapishtim gave him and set sail for Uruk.

Over the seas they went, the journey of six weeks in three days time. Over the land they went after that, and when they were weary, they made their camp. Then Gilgamesh saw a well of cool water, and he bathed in it and lay down beside it.
But in the pool was a serpent, and the serpent smelled the sweetness of the herb. He came out of the well, he came to the plant even as Gilgamesh slept, and ate it. Immediately, he sloughed his skin and returned to the well.
When Gilgamesh awoke, he looked, and the herb was gone. Then he raised his voice in a loud wail and cried, "O Urshanabi, for this I toiled long and hard. For this I came over the mountain passes and over the sea. For this I was wounded in the hand—that the beasts might benefit from my heart's blood, but not myself. For myself I have nothing."
They returned to Uruk, and Gilgamesh showed Urshanabi the walls of burnt brick, the work of his building. Great is the name of Gilgamesh, lord of Kullab, king of Uruk. He knew secret things, he was wise, he brought us a tale of the days before the flood. A long journey he went, he was weary and worn out with labor. He returned and he engraved on a stone the whole story. (Reprinted from PARABOLA MAGAZINE, Volume I, Issue One, Winter 1976.)

Though there is much greater variety to mythology than these two myths suggest, some idea of the supernatural content and nature of such stories has been made apparent. We can turn now to our last topic, a consideration of the meaning and function of supernaturalism.

REFERENCES

Barton, R. F.
  1946. *The Religion of the Ifugaos.*
     American Anthropological Association Memoir #65.
Bascom, William.
  1965. The Forms of Folklore: Prose Narratives.
     Journal of American Folklore 78: 3–20.
Beidelman, Thomas O.
  1961. Hyena and Rabbit: A Kaguru Representation of Matrilineal Relations.
     Africa 31:61–74.
Branston, Brian.
  1961. *Gods of the North.*
     New York: Vanguard Press.

Caso, Alfonso.
        1958. *The Aztecs: People of the Sun.*
               Norman: University of Oklahoma Press.
Clark, Ella E.
        1958. *Indian Legends of the Pacific Northwest,* pp. 9–11.
               California: University of California Press.
Clarke, Kenneth, and Clarke, Mary W.
        1963. *Introducing Folklore.*
               New York: Holt, Rinehart, and Winston.
Colson, Elizabeth.
        1965. Ancestral Spirits and Social Structure Among the
               Plateau Tonga.
               In *Reader in Comparative Religion,* eds. William A.
               Lessa and Evon Z. Vogt, pp. 437–441.
               New York: Harper and Row.
Davidson, H. R. E.
        1969. *Scandinavian Mythology.*
               London: Paul Hamlyn.
————. 1964. *Gods and Myths of Northern Europe.*
               Harmondsworth, England: Penguin Books.
Dundes, Alan.
        1968. Ways of Studying Folklore.
               In *Our Living Traditions,* ed. Tristram Coffin, pp.
               37–46.
               New York: Basic Books.
Howells, William W.
        1948. *The Heathens.*
               Garden City: Doubleday and Company.
Kirk, G. S.
        1970. *Myth: Its Meaning and Function in Other Cultures.*
               Cambridge: Cambridge University Press.
Kluckhohn, Clyde.
        1942. Myths and Rituals: A General Theory.
               Harvard Theological Review 35:45–79.
Leon–Portilla, Miguel.
        1963. *Aztec Thought and Culture.*
               Norman: University of Oklahoma Press.
Lessa, William A., and Vogt, Evon Z.
        1965. *Reader in Comparative Religion.*
               New York: Harper and Row.
Sejourne, Laurette.
        1960. *Burning Water: Thought and Religion in Ancient
               Mexico.*
               New York: Grove Press.
Spiro, Melford.
        1970. *Buddhism and Society.*

New York: Harper and Row.
———. 1967. *Burmese Supernaturalism.*
Englewood Cliffs, N.J.: Prentice–Hall.
Swanson, Guy E.
1960. *The Birth of the Gods.*
Ann Arbor: University of Michigan Press.

CHAPTER 9

Explanations of Supernaturalism

We have briefly surveyed a number of topics central to a beginning understanding of primitive supernaturalism. We have examined the various component parts of rituals—specifics and structure—and have attempted to define our basic subject matter. We have examined four basic types of such supernatural activities, those of a technological, social, health, and of a revitalization nature. We have isolated supernatural practitioners—primarily at the leadership level—as well as supernatural beings and the myths and other stories that highlight their activities. We can finish off such an introductory presentation with a discussion of the value of such beliefs and practices and with a concluding comment on the future of such behavior.

THE VALUE OF SUPERNATURALISM

What is it that human beings derive from supernatural experiences, from their beliefs and rituals? Anthropologists and other scholars interested in this general topic have often cited similar specific conclusions, but they have come to no overall general agreements. The theory of Mircea Eliade (cited in Chapter 1) that the world of the sacred exists to give power, reality, and a sense of timelessness to humans is a general theory of considerable persuasiveness, but it is not always accepted. Likewise, the similar notions of Peter Berger, that supernaturalism is the attempt to see the Cosmos as sacred so that human culture (the Nomos) can be legitimized on the highest order or reality, is also provocative but is implicit in few writings by anthropologists or other students of supernaturalism. For the most part, the attempts at defining meaning and function for such uniquely human behavioral aspects have been couched in more specific and limited formats. We may cite two of the most general of these and then illustrate more restricted possibilities.

Parsons Approach

The sociologist Talcott Parsons (originally in 1952) has written on the motivation for religious belief and behavior. Basically his notion is that human beings are constantly brought into contact with conditions of unpredictability and uncertainty. Apparently unlike other animals our big brain and potential for thought makes us aware of the less than perfect fit between our expectations and the reality we encounter, and as a result we often are beset with frustrations. As he so neatly puts it:

In whatever kind of society some human expectations, in the fulfillment of which people have acquired a deep emotional investment, are doomed to frustration. These frustrations are of two main types. One of them consists in the fact that men are hit by events which they either cannot foresee and prepare for, or control, or both; to which, however, they must make major adjustments, sometimes practical but always emotional. . . .
A second type of frustrating experience is connected with what has come to be called in a special sense uncertainty. By this is meant the very common type of situation where there is a strong emotional investment in the success of certain human endeavors, where energy and skill undoubtedly count for much, but where unknown and/or uncontrollable factors may and often do intervene to upset any reasonable balance between action and success (Parsons, 1965: 131, 132).

In either of these cases of both specific and general uncertainty, supernatural beliefs obviously can be a useful mechanism of adjustment. The approach of naturalism is not always capable of providing the explanations, control, or whatever is needed to handle these things. How does one adjust to the death of a family member or close friend, even if it can explain the reason for that death? Death rituals, beliefs in the soul and its continued existence in a future condition, and even disease-object intrusion as the cause, can help the survivors to handle such situations. How does a skilled hunter handle the more general uncertainty of the probability of his success? Where are the game animals most likely to be found; will the arrow fly true? Hunting magic, divination, and prayers to the gods who control the animals can be most helpful in this matter, as they may also supply a satisfactory rationale for failure. It is certainly easy to see many different aspects of supernatural belief and practice as providing a kind of "insurance" against the unpredictability and uncertainty that human beings discover in their lives.

Spiro Approach

On a somewhat more comprehensive level, Melford Spiro (1966) has suggested a fairly general approach to supernaturalism based on some basic needs or desires of human beings. First, there are what he calls *cognitive* desires. Human beings wish to know and understand and discover meaning in the world that surrounds them. Why does such and such an event happen—sickness, day and night, rain, good crop growth, or poor hunting? Why are there two sexes, how can I succeed in warfare, what is it all about? Certainly there are needs recognized by many students of the human species. Many psychologists have listed the "need for an integrated frame of reference," the need for meaning and explanation in life, as one of the most powerful and fundamental needs necessary for human life. Such are only a bit less basic to human existence than those for biological functioning itself. If the natural view of science cannot explain, or fully explain or provide meaning, then supernatural beliefs and practices may step in and satisfy such desires. Spiro states that the solution to cognitive desires results in the *adjustive* function of supernaturalism.

Second is what Spiro terms the *substantive* desires and needs of human beings. These are desires along the lines of actually gaining aid in the activities of life itself and being better able to deal with life, no matter how it may be explained or how it is provided with meaning. Humans want to feel that they are able to deal with and solve the problems of living. They have, as many psychologists have pointed out, a

need for feelings of adequacy and security, and such substantive desires obviously plug into supernatural beliefs and
practices.

The most obvious basis for religious behavior is the one which
any religious actor tells us about when we ask him . . . He believes
in superhuman beings and he performs religious ritual in order that
he may satisfy, what I am calling, substantive desires: desires for
rain, nirvana, crops, heaven, victory in war, recovery from illness,
and countless others. Everywhere man's mammalian desires . . .
must be satisfied and in the absence of competing technologies
which confer reasonable confidence, religious techniques are believed to satisfy these desires (Spiro, 1966: 112).

It will be recalled, reflecting on the technological, social,
and health rituals, how many specific rites and beliefs seem
to operate to relieve the anxieties that humans may have
regarding the substantive dimensions of life. Spiro sees the
use of supernaturalism here as meeting an *adaptive* function.

Finally, according to Spiro, there are what he calls *expressive* desires and needs. Not only do humans wish to understand and control those things with which they come into
contact; they also wish to reduce or perhaps eliminate altogether those other fears and anxieties (i.e., of self-destruc-
tion) that develop as well as somehow handling those motives
(i.e., aggression) that may be culturally prohibited but that
still must be satisfied. "In the absence of other, or more
efficient means, religion is the vehicle . . . by which, symbolically, they can be handled and expressed. Since religious
belief and ritual provide the content for culturally constituted projective, displacement, and sublimative mechanisms
by means of which unconscious fears and anxieties may be
reduced and repressed motives may be satisfied . . ." (Spiro,
1966: 115). The satisfaction of these needs Spiro terms the
integrative function of supernaturalism, and psychologists constantly deal with the necessity of such satisfactions short of
maladaptive behaviors. We can summarize this fairly general
approach as follows:

Need	*Content*	*Function*
Cognitive	Explain and provide meaning	Adjustive
Substantive	Meet desires for control	Adaptive
Expressive	Reduce and express drives and motivations	Integrative

Each of these need categories of Spiro embraces a host of more specific possibilities, but many writers on supernaturalism and psychologists listing basic human needs make possible the presentation of one further, major category to investigate with equal relevance to the understanding of "Homo religious." These needs have to do with the desire of human beings to join together in groups and to seek self-esteem in such contexts. Not only are we social animals, but we are social animals par excellence. We respond to other people and pleasure in the way in which these responses meet our desires for affiliation. Think of the number of gratifications we humans derive from our group life and the many ways in which supernaturalism can function for us in this responsive manner. Along these lines we can add to Spiro's categories the following:

Need	Content	Function
Affiliative	Group memberships and sense of social worth	Responsive

Though even these general categories remain incomplete, we can now briefly examine in a more specific fashion some cases of supernatural beliefs and practices. In doing so we can relate back to examples discussed in the previous chapters.

EXAMPLES OF SUPERNATURAL FUNCTIONS

In supplying possible functions for supernaturalism, we can take specific cases of supernatural belief and behavior and see which of the functions discussed above may be being served. As we discuss them we can also make short comments on any other functions that may be involved that do not fit such categories. No attempt is made to cover all possibilities, merely to indicate some representative cases. Our first example is some possible functions of witchcraft. This is an excellent place to start, since as indicated previously, witchcraft appears to be relegated to the realm of beliefs only. Function here thus stands out quite clearly from intention and indicates the wide realm of supernatural possibility.

Witchcraft Functions

Clyde Kluckhohn (1944), in addition to discovering the categories of witchcraft among the Navaho (as indicated in Chapter 5), also suggested a great number of possible functions for such beliefs. These have now become classic quotations, and we may discuss them in the light of the four major categories of supernatural function. First of all, Kluckhohn tells us that the beliefs in witchcraft among the Navaho give at least a partial answer to problems that require explanation. Why did so-and-so die, why does an illness refuse to respond to proper treatment, why do sheep unaccountably stray, why does one have bad luck in gambling? The answer to all of these questions is—witchcraft, resulting from the machinations of evil persons. So the cognitive need, the desire for explanation, is met by resorting to witches. Along the same lines, curing rituals can likewise be substantiated through the medium of beliefs in witches. If a curing rite fails, it is not due to its lack of efficacy but to interference by witches. This is a vital explanation that helps to maintain positive belief in such supernatural practices, hence going beyond the positiveness of mere explanation itself.

Affiliative desires and needs for self-worth are similarly met. Witch beliefs function in a responsible manner. Individuals can capitalize on the belief in witches to focus attention on themselves. Kluckhohn observed that most of the people who exhibited the symptoms of witch attacks in public were individuals of decidedly lower status in their communities. He surmised (probably correctly) that since by so doing they assured that other people would immediately come to their aid—giving them the attention that normally they did not receive—they probably used such symptoms (perhaps unconsciously) to make this happen. So at least temporarily they achieved wider recognition, affiliation, and feelings of self-worth. In the absence of witchcraft beliefs, how would they have focused such attention on themselves?

Perhaps of most importance are the expressive needs and desires that are met: the integrative functions of Navaho witchcraft beliefs. Here several possibilities are suggested by Kluckhohn. First, he feels that such beliefs permit the verbalization of anxiety. In our society if one develops anxieties, we often interpret them as neurotic behavior and feel that we are less than mentally healthy. For the Navaho, witches can be held responsible for it, and people can discuss this matter-of-factly and be assured of receiving social support rather than criticism. Secondly and along similar lines, Kluckhohn suggests that witch beliefs permit individuals to express the "culturally disallowed." Incest fantasies, dreams of killing a close relative, and the like do not carry with them the guilt that they would for themselves; they are interpreted as the result of some witch attempting to do one harm. And a witch-curing rite is the appropriate remedy. Again a channel for expressiveness has been supplied (as well as secondarily, self-worth). Finally, witchcraft among the Navaho permits the expression of antagonisms, both indirectly and directly. In the first case the antagonisms that build up in a person toward kin and other community members can be vented harmlessly on some distant and unnamed witch. One can vent one's hostilities and antagonisms toward such a scapegoat in a displacement fashion and be assured of social approval for doing so. In the latter situation one may more directly express hostility toward the actual cause—someone with whom one has a strained relationship—by suggesting along lines of gossip that "his activities might not bear too careful a scrutiny." Innuendo is not direct accusation but accomplishes the same thing and allows direct expression of antagonism. So, among the Navaho, cognitive, expressive, and affiliative needs are met through a belief in the existence and functioning of witches. Add to this many more minor functions such as the entertainment value that the often dramatic stories of witchcraft can convey, and we find that witchcraft as an expression of supernatural belief makes a powerful contribution to the functioning of Navaho society.

Discussion of a second example of witchcraft will permit us to elaborate on the aggression–antagonism-handling, integrative functions of such beliefs. In another classic account, S. F. Nadel (1952) has suggested why the specific content of witch beliefs will vary from society to society. Specifically he finds that among the Nupe of Africa witches are always women, whereas among the Gwari (a neighboring group) they are both males and females. In trying to ascertain why such a specific content difference occurs, Nadel ascribes it to the fact that women occupy a rather unique role among the Nupe.

Women in this society occupy a substantial economic position, since they are often itinerant traders. Their husbands who engage in stay-at-home farming activities are often in debt to them for expenses for feasts, bride prices for their sons, and other things—a role reversal from male conditions in other societies. Moreover, many married women traders engage in moral laxness as part of trading and so become unfaithful to their husbands. These men also have to take care of the children in their absence, or—adding insult to insult—the women may refuse to have children, thus shaming their husbands.

All of these difficulties are seen as leading to the build-up of male resentment and antagonisms toward women; yet during the course of ordinary events there is a certain powerlessness to do anything about it. Such problems can, however, be dealt with somewhat by translating male–female relations symbolically onto the level of witchcraft beliefs.

In practice, then, the men must submit to the domineering and independent leanings of the women; they resent their own helplessness, and defiantly blame the immorality of the womenfolk. The wish to see the situation reversed is expressed in nostalgic talk about the "good old days" when all this was between men and women plus this wish-fulfillment are projected into the witchcraft beliefs with their . . . expression of sex-antagonism, in which men are the "real" victims but the . . . masters of the evil women. A final item of evidence, . . . lies in the identification of the head of the witches with the official head of the women traders. It relates the projection in a direct and overt manner to the conscious hostility and the concrete situations evoking it (Nadel, 1952: 21, 22).

And, importantly, since there does exist a male antiwitchcraft society, men can also control women in the real world. (See the Nupe example in Chapter 5.) Of course, the idiom of witch beliefs in this society can also explain misfortune as well as provide other need satisfactions.

Paul Radin has also suggested (1957) that there is even an economic function to be discovered for witch beliefs in Nupe society. In his estimation the beliefs permit the king of Nupe and the antiwitch group to "squeeze" wealth from the women. The witch hunts occur in the villages, and the women—fearful that they may indeed be witches and may be harmed—are allowed to get together and make a payment to the society members to stop their dances. Village chiefs may also pay the king to stop the witch hunt because of its disruptiveness. All this collected wealth is then divided between the king and the antiwitch society. Thus the beliefs may be manipulated to secure substantive advantages, reminding us that functions may occur on various levels!

We can cite one final example before turning to a different facet of supernaturalism. Robert A. LeVine (1962) has suggested some interesting aspects between witchcraft and social features in some other African societies. Here again expressive need satisfaction seems paramount. "Witches in East Africa are usually thought to be jealous individuals who direct their . . . power against rivals or persons more fortunate than themselves. In many of the same societies the relationship between co-wives is considered to be more fraught with jealousy than any other social bond" (LeVine, 1962: 39). In such societies each of a man's wives will occupy a separate house. Since each wishes her son(s) to inherit the bulk of their father's property, there is indeed a natural competition among them. The women themselves can use witch beliefs to accuse their co-wife rivals of witchcraft; if they do, it should follow that the more occasions for jealousy, the greater the number of accusations. This appears to be born out in this study. Among the Luo people, wives live close together and share a single yard between their huts. Jealousy is highly reinforced in such a situation, and these people do reveal the highest frequency of accusations. Among the Gusii, houses of cowives are spread further apart by gardens and spaces for cattle. With greater privacy there is less stimulus for jealousy. Among the Gusii, witchcraft accusations decline in frequency. Finally, among the Kipsigis, the huts of the co-wives are so widely separated as to preclude daily contact —twenty or thirty miles distant. Here ". . . the wives have practically no contact with one another; there is thus no opportunity for the occurrence of the domestic incidents on which jealous rivalry feeds" (LeVine, 1962: 41). Here there are few accusations and little concern with witches in general. Hence it would appear that (again) witch beliefs provide an outlet for aggression and reflect in their content social friction as well. In sum, then, we see witchcraft catering to cognitive, substantive, expressive and affiliative needs and desires; and if we were to add sorcery—the other brand of evil-doing—we could define even more examples, particularly of substantive natures.

Divination Functions

As a second set of general functional possibilities we can once again briefly examine divination (first discussed in Chapter 3). Here it immediately appears that it is substantive needs and cognitive desires that are foremost. Divination techniques of all kinds give human beings a measure of control over the environment by providing answers concerning elements in that environment: where game animals are to be found, what the weather will be like, the identity of witches, the probability of success in war, and the like. And, of course, in the general sense, divination does serve to supply knowledge. In its own way it functions as a science, catering to the human desire to know and be provided with meaning; it thus stimulates activity when inaction would be a difficult situation to tolerate. When one must make a choice among alternatives—do I do this, that, or something else—divination does allow one to by-pass indecision and proceed with confidence upon some course of action. Such faith is derived from the general faith in the supernatural and makes the position of diviner one of great importance.

Almost all divining methods are open to manipulation on the part of the diviner. Yet, whether he truly believes in his own powers, whether consciously or unconsciously he influences the replies of his device, is, in a sense, immaterial. The main thing is that he has the confidence of his audience and that they have faith in his abilities. This is where he is of value to his society (Reynolds, 1963: 126).

So divination provides answers to questions perplexing and otherwise, and it permits actions and pursuit of substantive needs. What kinds of answers are these? George K. Park (1963) has suggested that divination not only gives answers but that these may be socially useful answers as well. He discusses (among other groups) the Yoruba of Africa. Here, upon marriage a young man must choose a site on which to build a house and take up residence. Divination supplies an answer, thus eliminating indecision and channeling the energy into the erection of the house itself. However, the diviner's answers are of deeper value than this, since where one locates has repercussions. With which group of one's kin does one reside? Whomever is chosen, the others will be angry at being rejected. Yet if the answer is obtained supernaturally, being based on divination techniques, the person himself is not really making the decision and choosing between kin. Therefore, he is not held responsible, thus removing possible social friction.

If divination not only gives answers but useful answers, its cognitive and substantive basis become clearer. Another intriguing example of this has been suggested by O. K. Moore (1957). Speaking of the Naskapi, a former Amerindian society living in Labrador, this writer discusses the role of divination in hunting. The main technique here was *scapulimancy*. In it a shoulder blade from a large animal was held over a fire and oriented to correspond in a maplike fashion to the local countryside. As burnt spots and cracks appeared, they were interpreted to indicate the direction in which to go in seeking out game. Since these cracks were rather random in occurrence and differed somewhat each time scapulimancy was performed, this divination device also forced the Naskapi to hunt in a random pattern—sometimes to the north, sometimes south, and so on. Thus it operated as a "chancelike instrument" and as such kept the Naskapi from over-hunting the game animals in a particular area based upon past successes there. So if, as Moore suggests, humans are creatures of habit, scapulimancy kept that habit from being counterproductive—supplying not only an answer but really having a value in meeting substantive needs. It improved the chances of hunting success!

Finally, it may be mentioned that the functions of divination may also meet other needs. Certainly such supernatural practices provide answers as indicated above, but expressive needs and desires may also gain satisfaction. As John Beattie (1964) has pointed out, when someone gets involved in divination:

. . . through the ritual performance which divination entails, he is also giving overt expression to his doubts, suspicions and fears. And this, at least in some measure, is an end in itself. . . . Often . . . divination involves a vivid dramatic performance, in which, usually, all present can participate. Like other magico-religious rituals, divinatory rites have a cathartic quality. . . . Like other forms . . . divination is a rite, and so is essentially dramatic and expressive (Beattie, 1964: 59, 60).

So, no less than in other rituals, an integrative function may be discerned in divination.

Mythic Functions

We can now examine mythology as an example of the possible functions of yet another realm of supernaturalism. Perhaps the most succinct summary statement here is that of William R. Bascom (1965), who recognizes four major functions along these lines when speaking of folklore in general. We can examine each of these briefly, reorganized and expanded to fit the functional categories suggested in this chapter. A first function for mythology, one recognized by most scholars and confirmed indirectly by Eliade, is that myths play a significant role in validating cultural behavior. They serve to justify not only rituals practiced by the members of a given society but other institutions as well—kinship obligations, use of game animals, or even the existence of evil. Because myths can justify the existence of things, they certainly are responsive to cognitive needs and desires and so function adjustively for human beings. This has sometimes been called the "warrant or charter" function for mythology. By explaining and hence justifying why rites are held and why things are the way they are, they serve as a support for those things. And, of course, myths often play such a role by tracing such rites or institutions (or facets of life in general) back to the greater supernatural reality of primordial times! It is also possible, as G. S. Kirk (1970) has suggested, that in such explanations and justifications the more complex the mythic narrative the more fundamental the institution it tends to explain or reflect. So myth may be seen to function, as do so many aspects of supernaturalism, on the cognitive-intellectual level.

It is widely recognized that such stories function adaptively to meet many substantive needs and desires.

A function of folklore is that which it plays in education, particularly, but not exclusively, in non-literate societies. The importance of the many forms of folklore as pedagogic devices has been documented in many parts of the world . . . Myths and legends may contain detailed descriptions of sacred ritual, the codified belief or dogma of the religious system, accounts of tribal or clan origins, movements and conflicts. Proverbs have often been characterized as the distilled wisdom of past generations and are unmistakably so regarded by many African peoples (Bascom, 1965: 293, 294).

Myths and other aspects of folklore do this in a variety of ways. These stories may point out the results of right or wrong behavior as object lessons in correct behavior, they may point out the ideal behaviors to be striven for in a society, or they may simply sum up the general wisdom on some topic. They may even contain detailed information regarding purely technological activities and be a means of passing that on in abstract form from generation to generation. Surely in the absence of complex educational institutions in most primitive societies, such stories inculcate at least general knowledge and morality, thus contributing to the general adaptive success of such peoples.

Along similar substantive lines relating to the control of things, Bascom also points out that myths can concretely aid in the maintenance of conformity, the efforts at social control in a society. "More than simply serving to validate or justify institutions, beliefs and attitudes, some forms of folklore are important as means of applying social pressure and exercising social control" (Bascom, 1965: 294). If an individual deviates from the norms of his or her society and these norms have supernatural identifications, then such a person is doubly in the wrong; the deviate has transgressed against both the natural and the supernatural dimensions of life. Hence not only may humans apply sanctions against the wrongdoer with more justification, but quite often the gods may be believed to apply sanctions of their own—no doubt a key inhibitor of deviant behavior. Who can escape the wrath of the supernatural! So education and social control in a more active sense must be observed as going together in mythic functions.

A third major mythic function relates to the expressive needs and desires of human beings, the integrative function of supernaturalism. This function is also generally mentioned by many scholars who deal with mythology, although their interpretations often differ considerably. In a broad sense, such stories may function as a way to project human frustrations, desires, hostilities, and the like. One can certainly escape from the realities of everyday life into the fantasies provided in myths and other supernatural stories. This is sometimes called the "Cinderella function" of myth. In such accounts things happen that are not possible in real life or at least things that are not permitted. Perhaps we moderns, living in our demythologized world, have taken to television and science fiction for such psychological aids! But as Bascom carefully points out, "Both the cultural context and the environmental setting must be known before the causes of repression or frustration can be identified, and their responses can be interpreted" (Bascom, 1965: 291). Many writers have gone beyond the obvious in interpreting such expressive possibilities. G. S. Kirk (1970) has suggested that human problems can be resolved in many ways via mythic settings, among others by use of allegory to help make problems more understandable and by removing problems to the story level to make them appear less severe.

The most exciting approach along these lines has been pursued by the French structuralist, Claude Levi–Strauss, who in a number of publications (for example, 1963) has looked for even deeper meaning and problem-solving levels in myths. We cannot take up even the most meager complexities of his views here, but basically his view runs as follows. The meaning of myth is best derived from the way in which the elements of a narrative are combined into major constituent units. As we examine the relations between these, the myth can be reorganized to reveal fundamental oppositions—for example: life and death, good and bad, or moral and immoral. As a myth delves into such contradictions and problems, it ultimately becomes a way whereby the human mind can project such "unwelcome contradictions" into a different and more detached level—that of the myth—and make them appear less final than they really are. Such notions are currently eliciting very suggestive results in mythological research.

A number of very useful functions have been suggested for mythology. It appears to meet profound human needs along cognitive, substantive, and expressive lines. Certainly other needs of a more affiliative nature can also be discerned. Since some myths are repeated on ritual occasions, they help form a basis for human interaction, and certainly at some level they are entertaining in and of themselves. We have, however, suggested some definite functional possibilities, and we can now again shift our attention to a few other supernatural possibilities.

Initiation Rite Functions

We have examined a case of health ritual functions (for witchcraft) and speculated as to the needs served by a technological rite (divination) and by myth. We turn now to the possibilities offered by a social ritual—rites of passage and more specifically, that of initiation. Based on the general purpose of social rituals to control behavior, we can assume that most of the presumed functions of initiation rites will be responsive to affiliative needs and desires. A. P. Elkin (1964) has suggested three major social functions of such rituals for males among Australian Aborigines. First, the rites are a medium through which the importance of males in such societies can be reflected. This is especially so since the boys are being given special sacred knowledge. "From the point of view of the tribe, the novice is being made . . . a worthy member of society and a future custodian of its sacred mythology and ritual" (Elkin, 1964: 176). So such rituals are symbolic of a special kind of status among these peoples; as such rites no doubt are elsewhere as well! Second, more from the view of the individual, such rites do provide a valuable transition from youthful to adult status. In fact this is their avowed function—to make boys into men. The discipline and guidance that the novices receive during the initiatory period certainly helps to prepare them for their new positions of adult responsibility. They insure that the social worth of such individuals will be up to the demands soon to be placed upon them. Finally, initiation rites have positive social value for all the participants and the group as a whole. This they do by enhancing feelings of social unity and togetherness as well as overall respect for tradition. As Elkin has put it:

It is almost impossible for those who have not witnessed such ceremonies to realize the important part they play in enhancing the individual and in strengthening the unity and sense of common purpose in the tribe as a whole. Indeed, the very possession of great secrets, won as the result of a difficult journey through initiation on the part of all men of the tribe, helps to bind the tribe together and to counteract any disruptive tendencies which may arise from the localized character of much of Aboriginal social and spiritual life (Elkin, 1964: 176, 177).

So, quite definitely, social needs are met by initiation rites.

Some writers have gone beyond such easily recognizable social functions to inspect initiation rites more deeply for affiliative functions and other possibilities and have extended their hypothesis in a more cross-cultural manner. As examples of such more intricate attempts, we can briefly survey two accounts. Roger Burton and John Whiting (1961) have advanced what can be called the *status envy hypothesis* relative to male initiation rituals. Briefly summarized, their arguments run as follows. A young boy, while still a child, learns to identify with people who have control over resources—i.e., occupy an envied status. One can inspect a number of societies to ascertain whether such primary identification is biased toward males or females. In societies where both parents are at home both are seen as important, and a boy will simply envy the adult status. However, in societies where there is exclusive mother care in infancy—because the boy sleeps with his mother due to the absence of the father and through restrictions on male–female relations for some time after childbirth—then the mother's status will be the one envied, and a boy will develop a primary identification with her. Later on, of course, secondary identifications will occur. This identification will be in terms of certain rules of residence after marriage. If men remain at home (patrilocal), men will appear important; if women remain at home (matrilocal), it will be they who are identified with. As Burton and Whiting see it, there is a heavy correlation between the presence of elaborate male initiation rites, patrilocal residence, and primary identification of boys with their mothers as one inspects a sample of world societies. Hence they interpret the function of such rites as attempts at "brainwashing" young boys of their primary feminine identifications, thus resolving the crisis of sex identity that comes from a lack of similarity between their primary and secondary identifications. This is a most suggestive function for such rites.

Using much of the same data, Frank Young (1962) has arrived at a somewhat different view. He accepts the notion that such rites help to strengthen male sex role identity. He sees, however, this to be a real problem only where boys do not have the usual access to learning such roles adequately. This problem, Young concludes, occurs when males have a high degree of male solidarity and spend much time together as adults (in a men's house or whatever), hence keeping much of adult male behavior masked from young boys as they are growing up. Since when they become adults young boys must learn their male role quickly, initiation rites, by forcing adulthood and learning upon boys in a quick and dramatic fashion, are a most apt mechanism by which to accomplish this task. Hence it is male solidarity and initiation rites that are best correlated together—another interesting hypothesis.

Now it must be realized that these authors (and others) have carried such arguments on further and have since refined their positions. The reason for including the above is only to make a dual point—not to summarize all the thinking on this topic. First, they suggest potentially deeper levels of function for initiation rites. Functions may certainly be conceived of as operating on a number of levels. We have perhaps only begun to scratch the surface of our inspection of supernatural behaviors. Second, however, we must be careful in our derivations of such functions. If two different possibilities are gleaned from the same data we must determine that our postulated functions are indeed real; that our manipulation of statistics, correlations, and anthroplogical imagination does not create realities but merely confirms them. With this caveat in mind we can pass on to one last example of functional considerations, one drawn once again from the realm of health rituals.

A Health Ritual Function

We have already pointed out (in Chapter 5) that positive health rituals exist to restore an afflicted individual to normal functioning. This is their basic purpose. Along the previously suggested lines of deeper functioning, however, curing activities may cater to deeper needs and desires, especially those of an expressive nature. An example of such a case is provided by I. M. Lewis (1971) from the pastoral Somali of Northeast Africa. "In this Muslim society public supernaturalism . . . is almost exclusively dominated by men, who hold all the major positions of religious authority and prestige. Women are in fact excluded from the mosques in which men worship and their role in religion is little more than that of passive spectators. More generally, in the Somali scheme of things, women are regarded as weak, submissive creatures" (Lewis, 1971: 73). Yet women have to work extremely hard in this male-dominated society. As a result of such circumstances women desire liberation, yet no natural way exists for them to achieve it. They can, however, manipulate part of the illness process towards this desired end. Among the Somali, much illness is interpreted as the result of the intrusion into the body of jinnlike demons called *sars*. The prime targets of such evil spirits are the married women. A woman so possessed will only recover when certain demands of the sar spirit in her body are met. Such requests by these demons seem to coincide with needs and desires of the women themselves.

In these circumstances, it is hardly surprising that many women's ailments, whether accompanied by definable physical symptoms or not, should so readily be interpreted by them as possession by sar spirits which demand luxurious clothes, perfume, and exotic dainties from their menfolk. These requests are voiced in no uncertain fashion by the spirits speaking through the lips of the afflicted women . . . The spirits . . . have their own language, but this is readily interpreted . . . by female shamans who know how to handle them. It is only when such costly demands have been met, as well as all the expense involved in the mounting of a cathartic dance . . . attended by other women and directed by the shaman, that the patient can be expected to recover (Lewis, 1971: 75, 76).

So at least on a temporary basis women can gain a bit of domination over their husbands and some relief from the strenuous nature of their daily lives. Lewis goes on to demonstrate comparable use of possession activities in many societies as a way for those persons of low status to temporarily reverse their situations, hence utilizing supernaturalism in its capacity for integrative functions.

We have now rather randomly examined a series of cases that illustrate the adaptive, adjustive, integrative, and responsive functions of supernatural belief and behavior. Such examples are only a meager sample of the data that exist to substantiate the reality of such benefits to be derived from this area of human behavior. Of course, such functions are not the only value to be derived from such experiences; other more specific functions surely exist. Prior to drawing out these examples we have presented an overview of the supernatural itself, examining its theoretical aspects, ritual dimensions, participants (human and supernatural), and mythological supports. We can end this brief excursion with a concluding comment on the future of supernaturalism.

THE FUTURE OF SUPERNATURALISM

What is the future of supernatural beliefs and behaviors for the human species? What position will they come to occupy in the repertoire of human behavior? Part of the answer to these questions depends upon the different position supernaturalism has already come to occupy in our society, as opposed to its role in the societies discussed earlier in this text. In the so-called primitive societies the worlds of the sacred and the profane, the supernatural and the natural, appear to be heavily interconnected. Few behaviors fail to suggest some supernatural aspect; magic and religion find a place in almost all activities, which are seen as incomplete without them. The ultimate meaning and goals of life are derived from the realm of supernaturalism in such societies, and rituals are "the" activities. In the social and cultural evolution of the human species, however, the profane world—supported by science and naturalism—has separated at many points from that of the sacred. Many human endeavors, especially those related to technology, have become totally divorced from supernatural aids and referents. Thus the supernatural aspects of life, instead of being parallel to and a part of all or most of human behavior, become separated from it and come to occupy their own compartment, applying to only some of the concerns of life and having little overlap. In the modern era this process has clearly accelerated. Supernatural beliefs and behaviors and their appropriate applications to everyday life have continued to shrink as not only their relevancy but their ultimate truths have been called into question. At least the advanced industrial societies of today's world are heavily composed of very secular people, many of whose concern with the sacred is limited to one hour a week. Homo religious becomes Homo secularis, and such a trend clearly indicates not only a shift in the priorities of world view but suggests—if the trend continues—a deeply troubled future for supernaturalism. This shift can be represented as follows:

| Primitive | Sacred |
| | Profane |

| Transitional | Sacred / Profane |

| Modern | S | Profane |

Against the picture suggested by such an evolution what speculations as to the future of the supernatural experience can be made? Surprisingly, although perhaps not so if the functional potentials of supernaturalism are considered along with life today, one may even suggest that the supernatural view will make a more than modest comeback, at least until we solve some of our current difficulties. The modern situation has been described for the United States as follows:

In the late 1960s, a small group of theologians said God was dead. Throughout America, there was religious unrest. The churches were facing a crisis. Attendance was down. The age of technology and urbanization was causing more and more people to question ancient doctrines. There were efforts to "modernize" faith and to seek more church involvement in great social issues. . . .
Today, who would deny that God is alive? The churches are still facing a crisis . . . But there is today a growing awareness of God. We no longer hear that "God is dead". Instead we hear the 1970s described as the decade of evangelical revival (Newman, 1972: 15).

And indeed such a reawakening has taken place. The Jesus people, Pentecostalism, a fascination with Eastern religions, and a general turn toward the occult are current phenomena under investigation by students of supernaturalism (see Zaretsky and Leone, 1974). Though there are many specific reasons for the rise of such phenomena, at the risk of oversimplification it can be suggested (and has been by many) that the natural world view itself has come to be questioned and has proven unsatisfactory for many people. Many of today's major problems—pollution, the terrors of a nuclear holocaust, and a variety of difficulties stemming from urbanism—are all directly traceable to the advancement of science and technology. In light of this, it is not surprising that naturalism has been scrutinized afresh and found wanting and that at least some of the more dissatisfied people should turn again to the supernatural world as a source of comfort and security as well as a source of ultimate meaning for their lives.

Such a casting about for new directions and escape from the preoccupations of science and technology has been not only a temporary resurgence of supernatural beliefs and practices but has led to a great proliferation of primarily psychologically based human potential movements. Most of these have individual salvation as their goal. Are these secular revitalization rites? At any rate, it certainly appears that secular man is beginning to question the natural world he has created and that he may well be seeking more sacred grounds for his existence. In many ways it is more easy to be created than to create! One can safely, I believe, predict no immediate demise for the supernatural element in human existence. Our most human of behaviors lives on!

REFERENCES

Bascom, William R.
　　　　　1965.　Four Functions of Folklore.
　　　　　　　　 In *The Study of Folklore,* ed. Alan Dundes, pp. 279–298.
　　　　　　　　 Englewood Cliffs, N.J.: Prentice–Hall.
Beattie, John.
　　　　　1964.　Divination in Bunyoro, Uganda.
　　　　　　　　 Sociologus 14:44–61.

Burton, Roger V., and Whiting, John W. M.
    1961. The Absent Father and Cross Sex Identity.
        Merrill–Palmer Quarterly of Behavior and Development, 7:85–95.
Elkin, A. P.
    1964. *The Australian Aborigines.*
        Garden City: Doubleday and Co.
Kirk, G. S.
    1970. *Myth: Its Meaning and Function in Other Cultures.*
        Cambridge: Cambridge University Press.
Kluckhohn, Clyde.
    1944. Navaho Witchcraft.
        Peabody Museum Papers 22:1–149.
LeVine, Robert A.
    1962. Witchcraft and Co-Wife Proximity in Southwestern Kenya.
        Ethnology 1:39–45.
Levi–Strauss, Claude.
    1963. The Structural Study of Myth.
        In *Structural Anthropology,* pp. 206–231.
        New York: Basic Books.
Lewis, I. M.
    1971. *Ecstatic Religion.*
        Harmondsworth, Penguin Books.
Moore, Omar Khayyam.
    1957. Divination: A New Perspective.
        American Anthropologist 59:69–74.
Nadel, S. F.
    1952. Witchcraft in Four African Societies: An Essay in Comparison.
        American Anthropologist 54:18–29.
Newman, Joseph, directing editor.
    1972. The Religious Reawakening in America.
        Washington, D.C.: *U.S. News and World Report Inc.*
Park, George K.
    1963. Divination and Its Social Contexts.
        Journal of the Royal Anthropological Institute 93: 95–209.
Parsons, Talcott.
    1965. Religious Perspectives in Sociology and Social Psychology.
        In *Reader in Comparative Religion,* eds. William A. Lessa and Evon Z. Vogt, pp. 128–133.
        New York: Harper and Row.

Radín, Paul.
    1958. *Primitive Religion.*
    New York: Dover Books.

Reynolds, Barrie.
    1963. *Magic, Divination and Witchcraft Among the Barotse of Northern Rhodesia.*
    Berkeley: University of California Press.

Spiro, Melford.
    1966. Religion: Problems of Definition and Explanation. In *Anthropological Approaches to the Study of Religion,* ed. Michael Banton, pp. 85–126.
    New York: Frederick A. Praeger.

Young, Frank W.
    1962. The Function of Male Initiation Ceremonies: A Cross-Cultural Test of an Alternative Hypothesis. *American Journal of Sociology* 67:379–396.

Zaretsky, Irving I., and Leone, Mark P., eds.
    1974. *Religious Movements in Contemporary America.*
    Princeton: Princeton University Press.

Selected List
of Readings on
Supernaturalism

In addition to reading several general texts on supernaturalism, a student can profit greatly from browsing through the more technical articles in readings collections. The following list is given with this notion in mind and is by no means intended to represent a complete listing, merely a citation of some works that contain provocative reading materials on supernaturalism from a predominantly anthropological point of view. All are listed by editor, or first author et al.

Banton, Michael.
    1966. *Anthropological Approaches to the Study of Religion.*
    New York: Frederick A. Praeger.
Brothers, Joan.
    1967. *Readings in the Sociology of Religion.*
    Oxford: Pergamon Press.
Dundes, Alan.
    1965. *The Study of Folklore.*
    Englewood Cliffs, N.J.: Prentice–Hall.
Eister, Allan W.
    1974. *Changing Perspectives in the Scientific Study of Religion.*
    New York: John Wiley and Sons.
Georges, Robert A.
    1968. *Studies in Mythology.*
    Homewood, Ill.: The Dorsey Press.
Goodman, Felecitas D. et al.
    1974. *Trance, Healing, and Hallucination.*
    New York: John Wiley and Sons.

Kiev, Ari.
    1964. *Magic, Faith and Healing.*
        Glencoe: The Free Press.
Leach, Edmund.
    1967. *The Structural Study of Myth and Totemism.*
        New York: Barnes and Noble.
Leslie, Charles.
    1960. *Anthropology of Folk Religion.*
        New York: Random House.
Lessa, William A., and Vogt, Evon Z.
    1972. *Reader in Comparative Religion.* 3rd ed.
        New York: Harper and Row.
Maranda, Pierre.
    1972. *Mythology.*
        Harmondsworth, England: Penguin Books.
Marwick, Max.
    1970. *Witchcraft and Sorcery.*
        Harmondsworth, England: Penguin Books.
Middleton, John.
    1967. *Gods and Rituals.*
        Magic, Witchcraft and Curing.
        Myth and Cosmos.
        Garden City: The Natural History Press.
Robertson, Roland.
    1969. *Sociology of Religion.*
        Harmondsworth, England: Penguin Books.
Shaughnessy, James D.
    1973. *The Roots of Ritual.*
        Grand Rapids: Eerdmans Publishing Co.
Streng, Frederick J. et al.
    1973. *Ways of Being Religious.*
        Englewood Cliffs, N.J.: Prentice–Hall.

Index